INTERROGATING
ETHNOGRAPHY

INTERROGATING ETHNOGRAPHY

WHY EVIDENCE MATTERS

STEVEN LUBET

OXFORD
UNIVERSITY PRESS

OXFORD
UNIVERSITY PRESS

Oxford University Press is a department of the University of Oxford. It furthers
the University's objective of excellence in research, scholarship, and education
by publishing worldwide. Oxford is a registered trade mark of Oxford University
Press in the UK and certain other countries.

Published in the United States of America by Oxford University Press
198 Madison Avenue, New York, NY 10016, United States of America.

CIP data is on file at the Library of Congress
ISBN 978–0–19–065568–6 (pbk.); 978–0–19–065567–9 (hbk.)

1 3 5 7 9 8 6 4 2

Paperback printed by Webcom, Inc., Canada
Hardback printed by Bridgeport National Bindery, Inc., United States of America

To Doris Lubet

CONTENTS

Preface   ix

Introduction: The Ethnographic Trial   1

1. Testimony   9

2. Opinion and Documentation   15

3. Unreliability   29

4. Credulity   43

5. Selectivity   61

6. Rumors and Folklore   75

7. Anonymity   91

8. Criminality   109

Conclusion: Toward Evidence-Based Ethnography   127

Acknowledgments   139
Notes   141
Bibliography   171
Index   187

PREFACE

Why would a law professor write a book about ethnography? Like so many questions, this one calls for both an extended explanation and a more immediate answer. The lengthier backstory is that I have devoted much of my scholarly life—as a trial advocacy specialist, legal ethicist, and historian—to the study of proof. Although my academic fields may at first seem somewhat unrelated, each one ultimately involves the evaluation of witness accounts and documentation for the purpose of determining the reliability (and utility) of the available evidence. In other words, the critical assessment of facts has been my overriding concern for many years, informing nearly all of my previous works. I have written books on the presentation of witnesses at a modern trial and the discovery and evaluation (to the extent possible) of historical events. So the long answer is that my attention to evidence and ethnography is a natural extension of a decades-long exploration of the quality of facts and assertions in diverse settings. The short answer is that I read a fascinating book.

It is easy to become fascinated by ethnography. In a time when the social sciences, and even the humanities, have turned increasingly to various "metrics," ethnography stands out as a discipline that remains devoted to the actual stories of real people. Rather than overwhelm the reader with dense tables and graphs, ethnographers concentrate on the lived experiences of individual subjects, which can be used to illustrate the nature and consequences of social structures in ways that cannot fully be captured through quantitative modeling. As a lawyer and historian, I am naturally attracted more to personal narratives than to multiple regressions; as an ethicist, I prefer to see the way problems are addressed in real life, rather than as abstractions; as an author, I am never surprised when ethnographies are perennially among the best-read works of social science; as a reader, I don't have to be told twice when a friend or colleague recommends an ethnography for my reading list. In short, I am a fan.

Thus, this project began when I received an email from a friend, urging me to read Alice Goffman's *On the Run: Fugitive Life in an American City*. I picked up the book on his advice—he'd also sent me Christopher Jencks's glowing review in the *New York Review of Books*—expecting to be duly impressed, and in many ways I was. *On the Run* is an account of the six years Goffman spent conducting an ethnographic study in a poor black community in West Philadelphia. Beginning in her sophomore year at the University of Pennsylvania and continuing through her graduate work at Princeton, she observed a group of young men in a neighborhood she called 6th Street. Goffman eventually moved into an apartment near the neighborhood, sometimes taking in two of her informants as roommates, while she chronicled their lives, challenges, and, most notably, their almost endless interactions with the law on matters ranging from trivial to felonious.

It is a gripping story and well told, bringing to light the lives of young men who have been forced into daily "dipping and dodging" because of their nearly unavoidable encounters with the legal system. Goffman's research subjects, whom she calls the 6th Street Boys, were almost constantly subject to arrest on outstanding warrants—for missing court dates or failing to pay fines and fees, for parole or probation violations, or because they were wanted for serious violent crimes. Lacking official identification or burdened by past convictions, Goffman's subjects could not obtain or hold steady jobs. They were therefore forced into an underground economy of loans, barter, theft, and drug dealing, simply as a matter of survival. Ever fearing arrest, they avoided such ordinary places as hospital emergency rooms, driver's license facilities, and even their children's schools.

Even other highly regarded urban ethnographies had never managed to report on subjects as elusive as the 6th Street Boys, and the story of their underground lives contributed greatly to our understanding of big-city police policies. Goffman's obvious concern and affection for her subjects added another dimension to the book, which made it far more than a dispassionate or descriptive study of "the other." She took us deeply into the world of the 6th Street Boys and allowed her readers to see a set of predicaments that most had never known to exist. It is an understatement to say that *On the Run* was reviewed very favorably in prestigious journals such as the *New Yorker* and the *New York Times*. Alex Kotlowitz called *On the Run* "a remarkable feat of reporting" and Tim Newburn, of the London School of Economics, hailed it as "sociology at its best."[1]

That was not my reaction. While I shared the general appreciation for Goffman's empathetic treatment of her subjects, I was dismayed by many of her factual claims. Almost from the opening pages, there were vignettes that struck me as implausible at best. I began writing "unlikely" in the margin next to particularly questionable passages, and I eventually had a list of more than a dozen claims of police and law enforcement activity that were inconsistent, to say the least, with my own experience as a defense lawyer in Chicago's criminal justice system. I wondered whether the situation could be so radically different in Philadelphia. Goffman repeatedly depicted events that ranged from improbable to virtually impossible to have happened as she related them—which I later confirmed by reviewing Philadelphia newspapers and public records, as well as from interviews with knowledgeable public defenders and defense lawyers, police officers, prosecutors, hospital staff, university employees, city officials, and neighborhood residents.

Then I reached the end of the book, where Goffman describes her own involvement in what reads like a conspiracy to commit murder. Following the murder of one of her subjects, whom she calls "Chuck," Goffman volunteered to act as the driver on a manhunt for the killer. On a "few nights," she drove through the streets and alleys of Philadelphia, looking for the presumed killer, while her friend "Mike" kept his handgun at the ready in case they saw their target or one of his pals. This was not an exercise in sociological investigation, says Goffman. Rather, she took the wheel of the getaway car because "I wanted Chuck's killer to die." That was a remarkable admission—worthy of an Oprah-esque memoir or an episode of *The Wire*—but how could it possibly be responsible behavior for an academic sociologist?

I returned to Jencks's *NYRB* review, in which he predicted that *On the Run* would become an "ethnographic classic."[2] He said nothing about unreliability or potential criminality. Exploring further, I saw that Goffman's dissertation, also titled *On the Run*, had been honored by the American Sociological Association with its annual prize for 2012, and a spinoff had been published as a lead article in the flagship journal *American Sociological Review*. The *New York Times* declared *On the Run* one of the fifty most important nonfiction books of 2014, and Goffman had been invited to give talks at numerous sociology departments and academic conferences. Her TED talk had been viewed over six hundred thousand times when I first saw it, and the number is now nearly 1.5 million. What could explain the dissonance? Social scientists and mainstream critics were praising the book to the skies, while I found it deeply flawed and ethically questionable. Were they missing something, or was I?

It was a comment of Jencks's, however, that led me to begin thinking in general terms about the ethos of academic sociology. Deeply impressed by Goffman's six years of study in the 6th Street neighborhood, Jencks said, "This is a world with which few readers of this journal are likely to have had much contact. I certainly haven't despite having spent a lifetime writing about social policy."

And that indeed was the explanation. Jencks, and others like him, began from a position of apparent unfamiliarity with crime and the courts, which evidently led them to accept Goffman's descriptions as accurate. But those who knew more about the criminal justice system—as did Dwayne Betts and James Foreman, who wrote two of the few negative reviews of *On the Run*—realized that she had at the very least embellished her stories in aid of her larger social and political conclusions.[3] In vignette after *On the Run* vignette, the cops are up to no good, defendants have been at least partially framed, drug dealers have been caught with only a "small amount," warrants have been issued over trivialities, and fugitives are the victims of police persecution. It seemed that Goffman's account of social reality had been influenced by her identification with her subjects, while her progressive agenda (which I happen to share) had compromised her objectivity. It made a riveting read, but was it valid social science? And perhaps even more to the point, did it embody ethnography "at its best"?[4]

In other words, the problem is not so much the unreliability of *On the Run*. Rather, the problem is that the work had been read in various stages of preparation—dissertation, journal article, book manuscript— by over a dozen highly credentialed academics, none of whom seem to have noticed the manifest factual discrepancies. Was this an aberration in ethnography, or the norm?

To answer that question, I embarked on an extended exploration of ethnography, looking primarily, but not exclusively, at sociologists' studies of U.S. cities. My general focus on urban sociology was pragmatic. There was no way to survey the entire field of ethnography, which is vast and spans several scholarly disciplines, and it would have been unworkable to fact-check books on communities or institutions about which I had little or no background knowledge. I also decided to concentrate on sociology, rather than anthropology, in view of the latter's turn toward postmodernism. As one text explains, "Few critical ethnographers . . . think in a language of evidence; they think instead about experience, emotions, events, processes, performances, narratives, poetics, and the politics of possibility."[5] Those are all worthwhile inquiries, but they are well outside my empirical wheelhouse.

With that in mind, I read classics such as W.E.B. Du Bois's *The Philadelphia Negro* (1899), William Whyte's *Street Corner Society* (1943), and St. Clair Drake and Horace Cayton's *Black Metropolis* (1945). I worked my way through the postwar era and the second half of the twentieth century, with books including Elliot Liebow's *Tally's Corner* (1967), Laud Humphreys's *Tearoom Trade* (1970), Carol Stack's *All Our Kin* (1970), Elijah Anderson's *Streetwise* (1992), and Mitchell Duneier's *Slim's Table* (1994). I concluded with recent books such as *Between Good and Ghetto* (2010) by Nikki Jones, *$2 a Day* (2015) by Kathryn Edin and Luke Shaefer, *Crook County* (2016) by Nicole Gonzalez Van Cleve, and *Evicted* (2016) by Matthew Desmond. In all, I read and studied over fifty ethnography monographs and a like number of journal articles, and I consulted hundreds more essays, reviews, textbook chapters, and other sources. Ultimately, my selection was both systematic and serendipitous; wide-ranging but not all-inclusive. I followed wherever the research trail led, with occasional excursions away from U.S. cities into other materials that seemed especially interesting.

The goal of my self-guided tour was to assess the use of evidence in ethnography—in terms of sources, collection, presentation, and dependability—by comparing it to the standards that have been developed to determine the reliability of evidence in law practice. My professional life has been largely devoted to the investigation, evaluation, and presentation of facts, both in academics and in practice, which led me to ask a series of questions:

How much have ethnographers tended to rely on rumors or hearsay?
How rigorously have they fact-checked their sources?
Have they ignored or discounted contrary or inconvenient evidence?
Did they accept the word of undependable witnesses?
Have they generalized or offered opinions that go beyond their factual support?
Did they assume that the criminal law did not apply to their research?

I was pleased to see that most of the books held up relatively well under critical reading, although all had their shortcomings and some were much better than others. As it happened, one of the most recent books set an exceptionally high—perhaps the highest possible—standard for the use of evidence in ethnography. In the appendix to *Evicted: Poverty and Profit in the American City*, Matthew Desmond explained his methodology:

Writing this book, I have prioritized firsthand observation. When something important happened that I didn't see, I spoke to multiple people about the event whenever possible and checked details by drawing on other sources, such as news reports, medical or court records, and mortgage files. I have indicated in the notes all events sourced from secondhand accounts. I said that someone "thought" or "believed" something only when they said as much to me. When writing about things that happened in people's past, I said someone "remembered" or "recalled" it a certain way. To interrogate those details, I would ask the same person the same question multiple times over several years. This proved to be incredibly useful, as some things people told me at the beginning turned out to be inaccurate. Sometimes, the truth comes out slow.

As much as possible, I vetted the material in this book by reaching out to third parties. Often, this meant confirming the possibility of something happening, if not the thing itself.[6]

In addition, Desmond hired an independent fact-checker who corroborated episodes in the book by conducting additional interviews, locating public documents, and reviewing Desmond's field notes.[7]

Only a few other ethnographies appear to have come even close to Desmond's exacting protocol. I have consequently used *On the Run* and *Evicted* as endpoints for my consideration of evidence in ethnography. *On the Run* serves as a cautionary example because it recounts so many incidents that, upon fact-checking, turn out to be farfetched at best. At the other extreme, *Evicted*, which won the 2017 Pulitzer Prize for general nonfiction, stands as a scholarly paradigm because it is by far the most rigorously documented of the many ethnographies I considered. Although I do not rank order them, it is fair to say that every other book fits somewhere in between.

Three additional comments are in order before we proceed. First, I do not want my criticism of *On the Run* to be taken as wholly dismissing the book's distinct virtues. Despite its deep flaws, we may appreciate the author's admirable determination to bring attention to a deeply misunderstood aspect of urban life, while making a powerful case for reforms in the criminal justice system. Second, I feel obliged to point out that Desmond had the benefit of resources—including a faculty position at Harvard and multiple foundation grants—that are unavailable to most ethnographers, especially graduate students and others who are early in their careers. In that light, *Interrogating Ethnography* can be viewed as a guide to the middle course, highlighting major pitfalls that can be avoided with sufficient care, even by those with limited funds.

Finally, and most important, I have great respect for ethnographers, whose work is time-consuming and painstaking. It requires special dedication—and often a good amount of courage—to spend months or years in a subject community, especially one that is marginalized or poorly understood. Many ethnographies have produced crucial insights and invaluable knowledge regarding social structures, and my purpose in writing this book is to suggest ways in which the field can be strengthened and supported.

Introduction: The Ethnographic Trial

SUCCESSFUL ETHNOGRAPHY REQUIRES THE establishment of trust at multiple stages of the process. First, the researcher must obtain sufficient trust from relevant subjects to gain entry into the society or culture under study. Equally important, the researcher must determine which subjects are themselves trustworthy, and to what extent, in order to gauge the degree to which the information collected is accurate, reliable, and typical of the community. Finally, the ethnographer must earn the trust of the reader. Because ethnographic results cannot readily be replicated, we must ordinarily depend on the researcher's word that the sample is sufficiently representative to tell us something meaningful about the social context and the larger population.

Princeton's Mitchell Duneier has proposed that ethnographers test the accuracy of their own work, and the validity of their conclusions, by holding an "ethnographic trial," in which the researcher imagines that he or she has been accused of ethnographic malpractice. The plaintiffs in the hypothetical case would be the readers who are concerned that they have been given a false or misleading account of the underlying reality.

In Duneier's model, the imagined plaintiffs would produce the testimony of "inconvenient witnesses," who are likely to expose the researcher's biases, assumptions, or elisions. When ethnographers don't have to worry about hearing from inconvenient or contradictory witnesses, explains Duneier, they can too "easily sidestep alternative perspectives or deceive themselves into thinking that these alternative perspectives either don't exist or don't have implications" for the study.[1]

I

The ultimate objective of an ethnographic trial is to guarantee "the reader's right to a reasonably reliable rendering of the social world," which should not otherwise be taken for granted. An author may have emphasized some facts while omitting others, whether intentionally or inadvertently, or may have generalized too broadly on the basis of singular events. Even an exceptionally careful ethnographer may have had her impression skewed by happenstance—perhaps having encountered an unusual cluster of subjects, or having located in an unrepresentative corner of the research site. Because ethnographers almost inevitably work with relatively small samples, Duneier cautions that readers and authors alike "should be skeptical of claims that attribute great weight to what 'sometimes,' 'often,' or 'frequently' happens."[2]

Duneier calls for rigorous confirmation that observed events map reliably onto a broader social reality, and one might well expect that approach to be broadly followed among ethnographers. Others, however, evidently believe that their observations should be accepted at face value—assumed to be generally applicable—without reference to the potential disagreement of inconvenient witnesses.

In contrast to Duneier's model, Charles Bosk has argued that the ethnographer's only obligation is to describe "those identifying characteristics that lead us to believe that we can generalize from our research setting to some wider social world." He thus justifies "deliberately misleading" readers to believe that his research site—called "Pacific Hospital"—was on the west coast, when it was actually elsewhere (most likely the University of Chicago, judging from the presence of gargoyles), on the ground that the location was irrelevant to his generalized conclusions:

> I specified that the surgical training program that I was studying was in a poor urban area, was associated with an elite academic medical center and university, and was highly regarded for its past achievements and present accomplishments. I still do not see what more a reader would want to know, what anything else would add to understanding, what benefits are provided by more specificity.[3]

An ethnographic trial would provide a counterweight to arguments such as Bosk's, in which the author claims the authority to preempt any reader's interest in more precise information. It was former Vice

President Spiro Agnew who said, "If you've seen one city slum, you've seen them all," but many sociologists would maintain that "poor urban areas" differ considerably from region to region—as do patient communities, as do elite universities, as do the employee pools for non-physician hospital staffs.[4] Although they may look the same in gowns and surgical masks, even doctors are not fungible.

The surgeon and author Atul Gawande has shown that medical cultures can differ markedly within the same state, with a significant impact on both treatment modalities and cost structures. Similarly, the journalist Luke Dittrich described a rift in the 1970s between the medical schools at Yale and the University of Connecticut, which led to the abandonment of their joint residency program in neurosurgery. "The problem was that the cultures of the two hospitals were very different, a direct by-product of the huge differences between the two chiefs of neurosurgery," who disdained each other's methods.[5] At Pacific Hospital, as Bosk explains, there was even a tense cultural gap between the two surgical services—one was primarily clinical while the other emphasized research.[6] It turns out that hospitals are not happy families, and consequently, as per Tolstoy, they are not all alike.

Bosk insists that any distinctions make no difference. "To the argument, 'But Pacific might be unique,' I can only shrug in bewilderment," he says, because "that argument places the burden of proof in the wrong place." According to Bosk, "If one quite clearly sees something happen once, it is almost certain to have happened again and again. The burden of proof is on those who claim a thing once seen is an exception."[7]

An ethnographic trial would take the opposite approach to the burden of proof, placing it—as in both courtroom and scientific trials—on the party making an affirmative assertion. A thought experiment will show why that is necessary. Imagine that an ethnographer (or a witness) made the following statement: "I saw a doctor yesterday in a representative setting that allows me to make generalizations about other doctors and hospitals." The natural response would not be to nod in agreement, but rather to ask questions: What were the doctor's personal characteristics? What was representative about the setting? How do you know your experience was typical? Which other doctors and hospitals are you using for comparison? And so on. In other words, the person making the claim would ordinarily be expected to back it up with details. In legal terms, the proponent of the proposition would bear the burden of production, which is one aspect of the burden of proof.[8]

If Bosk wants us to accept the cross-site typicality of surgical training at Pacific Hospital, he must offer sufficient evidence to that effect, rather than rest on an assumption that something seen to "happen once" is representative of the entire social reality. In addition to demanding the nearly impossible task of proving a negative, Bosk's approach collapses the possible frequency of events. Because almost nothing is unique, he argues, everything must be assumed typical unless proved otherwise. He leaves no room for events that might be rare, occasional, context-dependent, unusual but not unheard of, or situational, and he provides no guide for distinguishing among the possibilities.

Bosk's example illustrates the benefit of ethnographic trials for both readers and authors. An ethnographic cross-examiner would question the typicality of Pacific Hospital, asking to hear from inconvenient witnesses while invoking Duneier's warning to beware generalities that are not supported by specific facts. If Bosk remained unwilling to consider counter-evidence—shrugging in bewilderment at the very idea—then an ethnographic trial would adduce it for him. In Duneier's language, the intentional deception concerning Pacific Hospital's locale has made it impossible to determine whether there has been a fully "reliable rendering of the social world." Or, as others have put it, Bosk has risked creating the sort of "pseudo-generalizability" that may not be "representative of other unobserved cases."[9] A rigorous ethnographic trial would allow us to test the validity of Bosk's claim to typicality. His conclusions might or might not hold up, but they would have to rest on something other than outright assumptions.

Duneier has shown great respect for counter-evidence in his own work, including his widely admired *Sidewalk*, which was published twelve years before his call for ethnographic trials. In *Sidewalk*, Duneier cautions against the "ethnographic fallacy" that "begins when observation is taken at face value." Instead, a responsible ethnographer should adopt the "stance of the skeptic," declining to "take people's accounts as history without doing some checking." Duneier provides the example of one of his subjects, a man named Mudrick who "related his inability to read and write to the fact that he saw lynchings when he was a child" in South Carolina. Upon investigation, however, Duneier learned that the story was implausible, given the actual situation in South Carolina during the years of Mudrick's youth.[10]

It may be a mistake, however, to fashion potential ethnographic trials on the model of "malpractice" (which is a legal term for conduct that falls below a generally accepted metric of professional care), as opposed to simple negligence (which is an objective failure to exercise ordinary caution). In other words, medical malpractice occurs when a doctor fails to live up to the standards of other physicians; likewise for legal, engineering, psychotherapy, and accounting malpractice, all of which are judged by the practices of others in the subject profession. According to Duneier, however, there is no general expectation of fact-checking among ethnographers, as it is a process that many have not "taken seriously in their work."[11] An ethnographer's work might be incomplete or inaccurate, but it isn't malpractice if everyone else does it, too. In contrast, the broader negligence standard will allow us to draw comparisons to additional fields that face similar challenges, including journalism and other evidence-based disciplines.

Whatever the standard, I have come across only one ethnography in which the author made an explicit point of holding an ethnographic trial by locating potentially contrary witnesses.[12] In *Crook County: Racism and Injustice in America's Largest Criminal Court*, Nicole Gonzalez Van Cleve recognized that her opinion of public defenders—whom she called "co-opted players for *racialized* justice"—might have been influenced by her own assumptions. "What would that public defender think of *my* impression of defense attorneys?" she asked. "If my ethnography were to (hypothetically) stand trial against a jury of defense attorneys, would they feel that I had painted their image in the service of my theory or their reality?" Inspired by Duneier, Van Cleve's solution was to create an "inconvenience sample" by obtaining a position in the public defender's office and observing the defense lawyers first-hand.[13]

The production of contrary or rebuttal witnesses, whether real or imaginary, can work well when it comes to correcting errors of omission. Some lapses may be more serious, however, and these situations call for sharper tools. Taking the ethnographic trial one step further, therefore, this book will apply some techniques of adversarial testing to a number of episodes in ethnographies. Rather than simply imagine the additional perspectives of missing witnesses, the following chapters will also interrogate the original stories, probing for inconsistencies, implausibilities, and contradictions. And rather than look for malpractice—in the sense of the failure to adhere to ethnography's norms—we will instead consider more objective standards such as accuracy and reliability.

The great evidence scholar John Henry Wigmore may have overclaimed when he declared that cross-examination is "beyond any doubt the greatest legal engine ever invented for the discovery of truth."[14] There is an uneasy relationship between truth and trials, as lawyers jockey for position and attempt to cast doubt on each other's witnesses, no matter how truthful or sincere they might be. Wrongful convictions and other erroneous verdicts are an enduring problem, for which the adversary system has no absolute solution. Even so, Wigmore was not far off the mark. Cross-examination may not inexorably lead to truth, but truth in many circumstances cannot be found without it.

A skilled cross-examiner can locate the fault lines in a narrative by exposing unspoken assumptions and unsupported assertions. Cross-examination can likewise show that certain facts lack documentation (in circumstances where documents are known to exist), that informants are unreliable (based on past behavior), that alleged details are mutually incompatible (when compared side by side), that important sources have been omitted (but can easily be found), or that obvious questions cannot be answered satisfactorily (and sometimes not even coherently).

Although many advocacy techniques are not applicable to evaluating ethnography—there is really no place for character evidence, for example—I will show how lawyers' methods of analysis, inquiry, and fact-testing can be used to scrutinize works of scholarship, while also addressing ethics issues and related problems raised by ethnographic studies. Are the author's observations accurate and reliable? Are the stories representative of a larger social reality? Are the author's interpretations objective rather than agenda-driven? Has conflicting or contradictory evidence been ignored or suppressed? Are there explanations for the gaps between informants' impressions and documentary evidence? And finally, has the author adhered to appropriate professional standards of conduct?

Much of the discussion involves my fact-checking of various eth-nographies, which sometimes revealed discrepancies and sometimes confirmed the author's original account. Following Desmond's lead, I aimed for transparency in my critique by providing the names of my own informants and the dates and nature of our interactions. I have also included the locations and descriptions of my secondary sources, with hyperlinks where available. A few of my informants required ano-nymity for professional or personal reasons, in which cases I have none-theless included the dates of our emails or interviews and the reasons for withholding their names. A professional fact-checker has reviewed the entire manuscript—with access to my notes, correspondence, and documentation—and has provided emendations or additions where needed.

What follows is an extended essay on the nature of proof in qualita-tive social science, and the use of trial techniques to test, and thereby strengthen, ethnographic studies. Chapters One and Two discuss aspects of American trial evidence—specifically testimony, hearsay, opinion, and documentation—that can shed light on the use of sources and informants in field work. Chapters Three through Eight apply these principles to specific problems in ethnography, namely unreliability, credulity, selectivity, rumor, anonymity, and criminality. The conclu-sion offers proposals for enhancing evidence-based ethnography.

I

Testimony

LITIGATORS AND ETHNOGRAPHERS HAVE more in common than might at first be apparent. Practitioners in both professions must immerse themselves in new or unfamiliar situations for the purpose of explaining them to others. A criminal lawyer may spend months, or years, learning about the perils of eyewitness identification or the psychology of false confessions, in order to present a case at trial. A civil lawyer might do the same, on matters ranging from hard drive patents to obstetrics. (I have been involved in all four types of cases, and more.) A lawyer does not become an actual expert, but he or she does acquire vast amounts of information that must later be winnowed and clarified if it is to make any sense to a judge or jury.

An ethnographer does much the same, typically observing a discrete milieu—perhaps a violence prevention program or the world of professional chess—and then describing it in close detail for the benefit of readers and scholars. Ethnographers face many of the same challenges as lawyers, especially the need to condense volumes of detailed research into something that is readily understandable by a lay audience.

But there is one important distinction. Everyone recognizes that a trial lawyer is an advocate, and that a case is assembled to advance a particular point of view. Because a lawyer's client is always identified, there is no pretense of anything approaching neutrality. Ethnographers typically make a different claim, maintaining that they have presented a reality as it actually exists. A responsible ethnographer will of course acknowledge her own standpoint or perspective, while still maintaining

9

a degree of objectivity. Thus, ethical ethnographers ought to assume a greater burden of disclosure when it comes to presenting evidence, because there is neither a judge nor opposing counsel present to keep them honest. A lawyer's case is immediately tested by the adversary system; in ethnography, for the most part, we have only the author's word.

In any case, both lawyers and ethnographers are in the business of adducing testimony, with the expectation, or at least the hope, that others will believe it. Trials are governed by formal rules of admissibility that do not pertain to ethnography (which generally operates on the honor system). Nonetheless, there are concepts in the law of evidence that should be very helpful even in ethnographic trials. When should we accept witnesses' stories, and when should we doubt them? When should we seek confirmation, and what counts as meaningful corroboration? The law of evidence provides a rough hierarchy that can be usefully adapted to ethnography, if only by analogy.

First, a witness is presumptively allowed to testify about his or her own actions or observations, subject only to the requirement of relevance. It is almost always permissible to ask "What did you see?" or "What did you do?" so long as the answers are likely to have sufficient bearing on the case at hand. This is called direct or percipient evidence or, more commonly, eyewitness testimony (although testimony about sounds or other sensory impressions would also qualify). It may or may not be wholly reliable, given the frailty of memory and other problems, but its admissibility is seldom in question, in large part because it is subject to immediate cross-examination or other forms of testing.

The counterpart in ethnography would be a researcher's first-hand observations. Examples include Loïc Wacquant's description of boxing in Chicago's Golden Gloves, David Grazian's account of his own saxophone playing in a Chicago blues bar, Elijah Anderson's story about retrieving his stolen car in Philadelphia, and Victor Rios's encounters in Oakland with "knives and guns, often hidden in paper bags and thrown on the curb five feet away from where the boys hung out."[1] Or consider Kimberly Hoang's narrative of her work in several nightclubs in Ho Chi Minh City, in which she describes watching as "the hostesses lined up in two rows on the dance floor" for inspection by the male patrons.[2] Mario Luis Small expressed surprise when he saw "almost no white attendees" at the Betances Festival in Villa Victoria, despite its proximity to nearby white neighborhoods, noting that while "the Villa's isolation from the surrounding South End is not unimaginably extreme, it is unmistakable."[3] In each of these cases, we have the ethnographer's personal account of a directly observed phenomenon, as opposed to a story heard secondhand from an informant or other subject.

This might be called first-order evidence, because of its nearly universal acceptability. An ethnographer's account could nonetheless prove inaccurate or unreliable upon further investigation (which I am not suggesting in these instances), just as not every trial witness turns out to be trustworthy or truthful. Still, we ought to think of first-hand observation as the gold standard in ethnography. Interviews with informants can still play a crucial role, but as Christena Nippert-Eng put it, "the temptation may be to cheat, substituting conversation for observation."[4]

HEARSAY

The other broad category of testimony consists of what the witness (or, to continue the comparison, the ethnographer) has heard from others, which raises the hearsay rule. The legal rule itself probably seems convoluted: a hearsay statement is one that was made out of court, and that is offered for its truth value. An example should make this more understandable. Consider this statement by an imaginary ethnographer: "Donald Trump told me that he saw thousands of Muslims in New Jersey dancing in the street on 9/11." That would be hearsay if offered to prove that there really were such Muslim celebrations—in other words, for its "truth value." It would not be hearsay to show Trump's attitude toward Islam, which does not depend upon the truth of the underlying statement.

Although there are many exceptions to the rule, pure hearsay is considered unreliable because it cannot be subjected to the ordinary methods of exposing inaccuracy or deceit.[5] By definition, a hearsay statement occurred in the past, out of the presence of the current audience, which means there was no contemporaneous opportunity to challenge its accuracy or observe the demeanor of the "declarant." In these circumstances, the chance for error is great, even when everyone is acting in good faith. The original observer may have misperceived the events described in the statement, or may have remembered them incorrectly. The account may have been affected by inattentiveness, self-interest, emotional involvement, preconception, wishful thinking, or prejudice. And some declarants may have been insincere or conniving. It is hard enough to uncover and cope with such factors when evaluating the dependability of the actual observer, and it is that much harder (and sometimes impossible) when the information comes second-hand.[6]

Hearsay has a bad reputation among non-lawyers, but some second-hand statements can be both admissible and persuasive in court. The most common "exception" to the hearsay rule, and the most meaningful for our purposes, applies to testimony offered to prove the declarant's "state of mind." We accept hearsay as proof of what the speaker was thinking or feeling when the statement was made. For example, FBI director James Comey once attributed a rise in the crime rate to the so-called Ferguson effect, in which increased scrutiny is said to have caused police officers to be less aggressive, and therefore less effective, in law enforcement. In support, he recounted something that he evidently heard from street cops: "Where we are stepping back a little bit is at the margins, where we might otherwise have gotten out of our cars and talked to a group. We're not doing that so much anymore because we don't feel like being that guy in the video."[7] While Comey's statement would not be good evidence of actual police behavior, much less an increase in crime, it is quite useful as a descriptor of common beliefs or attitudes among the cops themselves. Still, it would have to be taken with a grain of salt, given the obvious self-interest of the declarants (and putting anonymity aside), who might well be motivated to exaggerate the situation for reasons of resentment or defensiveness, or other presentations of self.

The ethnographic equivalent of hearsay, again by analogy, would be the statements of a researcher's informants, which can be important to show their states of mind—including beliefs, rationalizations, or intentions—but not necessarily descriptive of an underlying reality. As Colin Jerolmack and Shamus Khan put it, "life histories, stated beliefs, and folk theories of social structure" provide sociologists with "a window into the normative and cognitive frames that actors use to explain their actions and anchor their identity."[8]

An example can be found in Carol Stack's *All Our Kin*, in which the author tells of accompanying a subject to the local welfare office. "Here we are," said the woman as she entered the building, "where the devils is."[9] The point of this particular passage is obvious—it is intended as social commentary, not theology—but an informant's words in other situations can be more subtle or ambiguous.

It is essential, therefore, that ethnographers draw a sharp distinction in their writing between things they have personally seen or experienced and things they have heard or were told. The former observations are entitled to a greater assumption of real-life accuracy, not least because they may sometimes be fact-checked.

Elijah Anderson resolves the hearsay problem in *Streetwise* by including lengthy quotes from his field notes—set out in italics—that are clearly identified as the statements of informants. There is no doubt that it was the "old head" Mr. Pitts who told Anderson that "you must force the police to do their job." We can understand this passage as an expression of Mr. Pitts's frustration with the police, without necessarily accepting it as true in every circumstance. Even when not in italics, Anderson typically makes it clear when he is relying on a subject, as in his account of a young man coping with deductions from his paycheck for child support. "After the mothers of his four children got papers on him and he began to see less and less of his money, one of my informants quit his job and returned to the street corner."[10] It is obvious from the context that Anderson is not claiming first-hand knowledge of either the extent of the child support payments or his subject's employment situation, but is instead relating a story from his unnamed informant.

As we will see in later chapters, the line becomes blurred when ethnographers summarize multiple conversations or conflate several sources. To be sure, such summaries are the basic stuff of ethnography, as distinct from, say, oral history. If the point of a vignette is to convey the general attitudes or beliefs of the subject community, then hearsay is not an issue. If the purpose is to describe historic (or economic) reality, however, then it may be a problem indeed. Thus, we can benefit from an author's wrap-up, as when Mitchell Duneier tells us, in *Slim's Table*, that "participation in the collectivity at Valois fosters a consciousness of oneself as an elevated human being."[11]

On the other hand, we must question Kimberly Hoang's observation that the high-end nightclubs of Ho Chi Minh City, featuring young women available for sex with patrons, were "crucial to local Vietnamese elite men, allowing them to establish social and personal relations of trust that enabled them to broker deals worth millions of U.S. dollars." Hoang spent months observing the interactions between affluent male patrons and young hostesses in the bars, but she was not privy to the details of international financial transactions. It is therefore fair to ask whether the presence of sex workers was truly "crucial" to consummating deals, or whether Hoang's informants were simply rationalizing their carnal behavior in economic terms.

It would take more than ethnography to answer that question, but it does provide a perfect example of the hearsay problem. The nightclub habitués might have convinced themselves that the confluence of sex and alcohol was "responsible for much of the country's recent economic growth," but that does not mean they were describing a meaningful reality. Hoang herself tells us that the bursting real estate bubble eventually caused the hostess bars to shut down, which implies an entirely different relationship of cause and effect between money and commercial sex. "To encourage capital flow," she says, "banks were offering a 15 percent return on all deposits," which appears to have been a much more effective economic stimulant than supplying sex workers to potential investors.[12]

It would be unrealistic and unworkable to expect ethnographers to adopt law's strict standards of evidence. The outcome of a trial may result in the deprivation of liberty or property, while ethnography puts no one at immediate risk. Law, moreover, sometimes suppresses valuable evidence in pursuit of other goals—for example, by applying an exclusionary rule to improperly obtained confessions—while ethnography, in theory, omits nothing significant. In Laurence Ralph's perceptive observation, "the past is both 'what happened' and 'that which is said to have happened,'" which together may be used to find a "point of departure precisely in the murkiness of everyday life."[13]

Even so, law's hierarchy of evidence, ranging from direct observation to unreliable hearsay, can be instructive when evaluating the work of ethnographers.

2

Opinion and Documentation

THERE ARE TWO ADDITIONAL subjects in our overview of evidence: opinion testimony and documentation. In a sense, they are complementary. Opinions provide us with a witness's (or author's) interpretation of facts or events, typically developed specifically for the trial or book. Opinions are derived from facts, but they are not facts themselves. Documentation, on the other hand, looks at facts that have been frozen in time, usually in the form of contemporaneous writings or other records. Such documents predate the trial or study, and exist independently of the lawyer or writer.

OPINION

Television's Detective Joe Friday famously insisted on getting "just the facts," but the law of evidence actually allows a great deal of opinion testimony in trials, from both expert and lay witnesses.[1] Experts may provide opinions to the court, so long as they are qualified by "skill, experience, training, or education" to give testimony that is premised on "scientific, technical, or other specialized knowledge" that would "help the trier of fact" understand the issues in the case. Lay witnesses, in contrast, are generally expected to testify only from "first-hand knowledge or observation," without drawing conclusions or making characterizations. There is an important exception, however, which allows even lay witnesses to state opinions that are "rationally based" on their sensory perceptions. Thus, it is common for non-expert witnesses to draw conclusions about physical perceptions such as speed or distance, as well as more abstract concepts such as another person's demeanor or attitude: "He was about fifteen feet away from me, and he looked angry." A recent police brutality case provides a good example of the difference between expert and lay opinion. A non-expert witness could not opine that the officer had used "excessive, unreasonable force" when making the arrest in question, but it was permissible for him to testify that he "heard a sound like a tomato hitting a concrete wall" when the cop punched the victim in the nose.[2]

Nonetheless, there are limits. Experts are restricted to matters within their professional qualifications, which seems obvious enough. Lay witnesses are not allowed to speculate or draw unfounded conclusions—a rather imprecise standard that is mostly left to the discretion of the court. A non-expert witness might be allowed to say that a ladder looked "unsteady," but she could not add her opinion that it was improperly designed.

An ethnographic trial would have to be more open to opinions than are real trials. After all, ethnographers are trained observers who typically hold advanced degrees in sociology or anthropology. We read ethnography because we want to know what the authors have seen and experienced, and good examples of "sensory perceptions" can be found on almost every page of successful ethnographies.

In *Crackhouse*, for example, Terry Williams tells us that the police tended to "ignore" cocaine and crack dealers, even when the "selling spots" were obvious.[3] Other ethnographic observers have come to similar conclusions, going beyond a mere description of police inattention or fecklessness to draw an inference about the cops' willing toleration of drug sales in certain locations. Elijah Anderson reported it in *Streetwise* and *Code of the Street*, Victor Rios saw it in *Punished*, and Sudhir Venkatesh wrote about it in *American Project*, among others.[4] In evidentiary terms, this would be called a classic "lay opinion," meaning that the conclusion would be obvious (or at least reasonable) to an ordinary person who observed the same situations. We see similar observational opinions throughout ethnography, as when Nikki Jones notes that a subject went home from school "concerned more over how best to deal with her mother's response to the suspension than over what to do about her obviously injured hand," or when Nicole

Gonzalez Van Cleve questions whether a Spanish-speaking defendant had been provided adequate translation services in court. Kathryn Edin and H. Luke Shaefer conclude of their subjects that "it is typically the opportunity to work that is lacking, not the will."[5]

Ethnographers also arrive at expert opinions based on their training and education. We are interested in their books because they are going to interpret the data and add meaning to their observations. Consequently, we expect to see ethnographers' expert opinions in the form of conclusions about their work. These can take the form of professional critique, as in Duneier's description (circa 1992) of certain sociologists as "politically correct stereotype guardians."[6] A different example is David Grazian's *Blue Chicago*, which sets the scenes at various blues clubs while offering somewhat fewer explicit judgments than other ethnographies (apart from comments on the quality of the music). Grazian nonetheless provides his opinion—as a sociologist—of the various personae adopted by the musicians, which range from provocateur to folklorist.[7]

Another type of expert opinion is the policy recommendation, which seems almost de rigueur in urban ethnography. Edin and Shaefer's *$2 a Day* includes a concluding chapter on solutions to extreme poverty that explores "strategies that will lift up the $2-a-day poor in a radically different way than has been done before." Randol Contreras's *The Stickup Kids* likewise includes a section on "reducing drug market violence," and Laurence Ralph's *Renegade Dreams* proposes means of "unearthing alternate frames" for the entire discussion of urban life.[8]

Nonetheless, even the most highly regarded ethnographers sometimes offer opinions that extend well beyond what a court would recognize as their professional expertise. In *Street Corner Society*, William Foote Whyte ventured far afield from sociology by making observations more suited to clinical psychology (in which he had no training). Having first noted a "relationship between position in the group and performance at the bowling alleys," Whyte reported a further epiphany about "the three- way connection between group position, [athletic] performance, and mental health." This theory, Whyte believed, could explain one subject's "dizzy spells" and another's neurosis (which had evidently driven him from the ranks of the top neighborhood bowlers).

As Whyte opined, "the individual becomes accustomed to a certain pattern of interaction. If this pattern is subject to a drastic change, then the individual can be expected to experience mental health difficulties." Whyte recognized that "much further research would be needed" to confirm his theory. Remarkably, he proceeded to conduct the research himself:

> If my diagnosis was correct, then the line of treatment was clear: re-establish something like Long John's pre-existing pattern of inter-action, and the neurotic symptoms should disappear. This was the first real opportunity to test my conclusions on group structure. I embraced it with real enthusiasm.

Long John was then provided a "skillfully executed therapy program" under the care of "Doc" (who was a factory worker, not a physician). The results left Whyte "awestruck" at the accuracy of his own prediction:

> Long John not only lost his neurotic symptoms but also closed out the season by winning the prize money in the final bowling contest. Of course, this victory was not necessary to establish the soundness of the diagnosis. It would have been enough for Long John to have re-established himself *among* the top bowlers. His five-dollar prize was just a nice bonus for interaction theory.[9]

It is highly unlikely that any ethnographer today would engage in amateur psychoanalysis, much less claim to have relieved a subject of "neurotic symptoms" on the basis of success in a neighborhood bowling tournament. Even the best contemporary ethnographers, however, occasionally do venture into other disciplines, offering opinions for which sociology provides no evident "scientific, technical, or other specialized knowledge."[10]

Matthew Desmond, for example, rigorously identifies the current housing crisis for poor people, and then tells us that the remedy lies in creating a "housing voucher program so that *all* low-income families could benefit from it."[11] As attractive as the idea may be, a sociologist like Desmond lacks the expertise to support his claim that "Evictions would plummet and become rare occurrences. Homelessness would

almost disappear." Although there is obviously no rule against expressing an extracurricular opinion in an ethnography, this is precisely the
sort of overbroad statement that would be disallowed in court. And
an ethnographic cross-examiner would at least note that, according to
many economists, a flood of government money might actually result
in raising rents across the board, especially for working-class tenants,
perhaps leading to even more evictions as working families get pushed
out of previously low-cost housing.

As to funding for such an expansion of benefits, Desmond further opines that "we have the money," although it would have to be
redirected from "housing-related tax expenditures" such as the home
mortgage deduction from federal income taxes and the capital gains
exclusion for home sales.[12] He says nothing, however, about the impact
on the housing market of eliminating such tax preferences. According
to housing economists, an immediate change might well send home
values tumbling as much as 20 percent, and might also suppress new
construction, thereby throwing carpenters, bricklayers, electricians,
plasterers, and plumbers out of work. Or maybe not: economists are
uncertain about the full effect on the housing market if tax preferences
were eliminated or reduced, because there are so many moving parts to
consider.[13]

Our ethnographic cross-examiner would also point out that
vouchers—at whatever cost to the rest of the economy—might not
even help many of Desmond's own subjects. Vanetta went to prison for
armed robbery; Scott was a drug addict; and Crystal was once thrown
out because she put her roommate "through one of the apartment's
windows."[14] None of these problems would be solved with housing
vouchers. Perhaps channeling Edin and Shaefer, ethnographic counsel
could also argue that the repurposed funds would be better spent on
restoring cash assistance to needy families. My own background in law
does not qualify me to determine the economic and other consequences
of a national rent voucher program, but neither does Desmond's training in ethnography.[15]

I do know something about the delivery of legal services to low-
income clients, however, having worked in the field for twelve years.
I am therefore sympathetic to Desmond's proposal to provide free
attorneys to tenants facing eviction. He is right that "good lawyers

would raise defenses tenants often don't [and] would curb frivolous evictions and unchecked abuses." Desmond cites a pilot program in the South Bronx that provided lawyers to 1,300 families in housing court, and which "prevented eviction in 86 percent of cases."[16] The program cost about $450,000, but saved the city over $700,000 in emergency shelter costs. Notably, Desmond does not say anything about the costs imposed on landlords, which must have been considerable and in many instances passed on to tenants. Nor does he evaluate the impact of thwarted evictions on the quality of life for paying tenants. In my experience, good tenants are often quite eager to see a bad tenant depart, and there would be significant adverse consequences if 86 percent of evictions were to fail nationwide.

Desmond argues that extending the right to counsel to housing courts "would be a major step on the path to a more fair and equitable society," while observing that there is a right to counsel in civil matters "not just in France and Sweden but also in Azerbaijan, India, Zambia, and many other countries we like to think of as less progressive than our own."[17] I cannot speak to Azerbaijan or Zambia, but I did look into the situation in India, where the "right to counsel" does seem to exist on paper. According to an experienced Indian lawyer, however, "the reality on the ground is very different." As he explained, "there are no funds to turn such a right into anything meaningful and no dedicated group of lawyers who are willing to take on this kind of work for indigents in civil matters."[18]

Desmond's non-expert excursions into economics stand in sharp contrast to his most widely reported observation, about an impoverished woman who spent her entire month's food budget on one meal:

[Larraine] went to the grocery store and bought two lobster tails, shrimp, king crab legs, salad, and lemon meringue pie. Bringing it all back to Beaker's trailer, she added Cajun seasoning to the crab legs and cooked the lobster tails in lemon butter at 350 degrees. She ate everything alone, in a single sitting, washing it down with Pepsi. The meal consumed her entire monthly allocation of food stamps.

Although Larraine's behavior seems irrational and self-destructive, Desmond offers an explanation:

The distance between grinding poverty and even stable poverty could be so vast that those at the bottom had little hope of climbing out even if they pinched every penny. So they chose not to. Instead, they tried to survive in color, to season the suffering with pleasure . . . . If Larraine spent her money unwisely, it was not because her benefits left her with so much but because they left her with so little.

Desmond has been criticized for seeming to endorse Larraine's improvident use of her limited funds,[19] but his evaluation, in the language of evidence, is "rationally based" on his "first-hand knowledge or observation." In other words, his opinion of Larraine's behavior is helpful because it is sociological.

As much as I respect and agree with Desmond generally, I find some of his policy recommendations "unhelpful," in terms of courtroom evidence, and well outside the purview of sociology. I understand that publishers and readers, and perhaps dissertation committees and grant-makers, want ethnographers to propose solutions to the problems they identify, with or without regard to legal standards of expertise, but it is still worth noting when their opinions venture beyond their discipline. As Charles Bosk has explained, "Ethnographers who occupy specific niches in social science departments . . . have received training in concrete intellectual traditions, and have very definite value commitments regarding the purposes of their work." Thus, "excellence in one domain—ethnography—may make excellence [in another domain] difficult, if not impossible."[20]

Finally, we need to consider the unstated opinions that are frequently wrapped into other observations. Sometimes, the meaning of the opinion is apparent, as when Nicole Gonzalez Van Cleve refers to prosecutors, judges, and public defenders as making up a single "workgroup," meaning that they are jointly responsible for the "racialized punishment" she observed in the Cook County Criminal Courts.[21] The repetition of "workgroup" embodies Van Cleve's strongly held opinion that the bureaucratic objective of the court system is to process defendants—with the complicity of all involved—rather than provide justice, and with only slight attention to separating the innocent from the guilty. There is no mistaking Van Cleve's belief that public defenders are for the most part collaborators with the prosecution, rather than adversaries, and that judges are anything but neutral adjudicators, all of which is neatly summarized by consistently calling them a "workgroup."

Other times, however, the gist of an opinion is opaque. A good example is found in Randol Contreras's *The Stickup Kids*, in which robbery proceeds are called "earnings." Pablo "earned eleven thousand dollars on his first robbery"; soon afterward, "he earned eighteen thousand dollars" on another robbery. A subject named Tukee "once earned one hundred and ten thousand dollars in a drug robbery," and so did Pablo in the same stickup.[22] Most readers would not consider stolen money to have been earned, especially when taken by torture, as practiced by Pablo and Tukee. Contreras could just as easily have referred to the robbery proceeds more neutrally—perhaps they had been obtained, received, or even realized—so it seems that there must be a message embedded in his word choice. We cannot assess it, however, because he does not make his opinion explicit. Is he telling us that robbery is hard work, or that it is the equivalent of a regular job, or that his subjects were getting a good return on their investment in crime?

In real trials, implicit value judgments are often excluded as "characterizations." There is no such objection in ethnography, nor should there be, but it would be better if authors would make a point of explaining what they mean.

DOCUMENTATION

Although eyewitness testimony is revered in popular culture, the law of evidence recognizes that it is often undependable. The witness may have failed to observe salient events or misinterpreted what she saw. Even putting aside the problems of bias and preconception, memory itself can be fatally unreliable. Not only does memory fade over time, but witnesses can also be subject to outside influences that—unintentionally or purposefully—influence, corrupt, conflate, or otherwise alter their recollections.

Psychologists and cognition scientists now understand that a memory is not like a photograph or video that can be retrieved at will in pristine condition. Rather, a new mental image is created—changing slightly or significantly—every time a scene is recalled, depending upon a host of both external and internal factors. Even witnesses who testify

with great certainty may be mistaken, and commonly accepted indica-
tors of reliability—articulate speech, eye contact, upright demeanor—
have been shown to be misleading at best. (The same is true of many
putative signifiers of untruthfulness, such as fidgeting, stammering, or
mumbling; they indicate only that the witness is nervous, rather than
inaccurate or devious.)

The legal system, therefore, places considerable value on documentary evidence, especially when it was created contemporaneously with
an event by someone with no likely incentive to fabricate. Such evidence has, in effect, been frozen in time, unlike fragile human memo-
ries that may change with every retelling. The law of evidence has thus
recognized categories of documentation that are exempt from the hearsay rule because they are thought to be inherently reliable (subject to
certain requirements). Examples include business records, medical and
hospital records, public records and reports, vital statistics, deeds and
other property records, and market reports and published commercial
compilations. In certain circumstances, the absence of an entry may
also be admitted to show the "nonoccurrence or nonexistence" of an
event, as long as it was "of a kind" that would ordinarily have been
recorded.[23] Finally, any document may be excluded from consideration
if it is shown to be untrustworthy.

Ethnographers sometimes rely upon public records and other documentation, although few have been as scrupulous about it as Matthew
Desmond, who made a point of checking building department, court,
and hospital records to confirm the statements of his informants for
Evicted. Many others, I believe, would benefit from greater use of public and private documentation.

In their powerful and compelling account of extreme poverty in
the United States, *$2 a Day*, Edin and Shaefer begin with the story
of "Modonna Harris's" futile efforts to obtain temporary public assistance in Chicago. Modonna had worked whenever possible, but she
had become unemployed at the end of her marriage to an abusive man.

Now on her own, she needed a full-time job. With no college degree
and a sporadic work record, the best position she could find was a
daytime shift as a cashier at Stars Music downtown, which paid $9 an
hour. She would hold that job for the next eight years.

Just as it seemed that things were going right for her, however,

> Modonna's cash drawer at Stars came up $10 short, and she couldn't account for it. She was summarily dismissed, given no benefit of the doubt, despite her years of service and the small amount of money involved. "Ten dollars short, and they found it after they fired me," she says. But no call of apology came, no invitation to return to work.[24]

Edin and Shaefer spent considerable time with Modonna, and Edin even accompanied her to the welfare office when she unsuccessfully attempted to obtain benefits.[25] I have no reason to doubt the general outline of her life history and the desperate situation in which she had been placed. On the other hand, some aspects of the Stars Music story struck me as improbable. Eight years is an extraordinarily long time to work at a retail store. Employee turnover averages 100 percent annually in the retail industry, with many positions having to be filled twice or more each year. Half of all employees last no more than three months on the job. There is an entire sub-industry that counsels stores on sales associate retention.[26] An employee with eight years of experience ought to be highly valued, and not likely subjected to arbitrary firing.

I cannot check with the pseudonymous "Stars Music," but other large retailers apparently do not fire employees for one-time shortfalls in their cash drawers.[27] I provided the Modonna vignette to Caitlin Kelly, a journalist who studies the retail industry, who told me that a productive and reliable employee would "have the goodwill of their supervisors who also know how hard it is to find and retain good staff who work well with others, know the merchandise, etc. In that instance, I doubt they'd fire someone that quickly, as other factors would come into their decision-making."[28]

It is possible that both Modonna and Stars Music were exceptional in their own ways, and that she really did work for eight years without a hitch, only to be precipitously dumped the first time something went temporarily wrong. That would require the combination of an unusually loyal employee and a distinctly faithless employer, but such things can happen. Applying Occam's Razor, however, the simpler explanation would be that Modonna exaggerated the length of her work history, and perhaps the cause of her termination. There are records that could answer this question—the employee file at Stars, Modonna's tax returns, perhaps an application for unemployment insurance—but Edin and Shaefer told me that they did not check for them. In one sense, the precise details of Modonna's employment discharge are inessential to her larger story, which is the centerpiece of a chapter titled "Welfare is Dead." Furthermore, as Shaefer explained to me, they did take measures to "verify the tangible details of the stories to the greatest extent possible (visiting past employers although not interviewing them, looking for records that are consistent with the stories, 'environmental confirmation')."[29]

Nonetheless, Modonna's outrageous treatment by her employer supports one of the main arguments of *$2 a Day*, that the extremely poor show a "high level of attachment to work in the formal economy," but are thwarted in their efforts to maintain employment. One could hardly be more attached to employment than devoting eight years to the same job, nor more thwarted than getting canned for a briefly misplaced ten-dollar bill. Modonna's memory of the events, however, might have been poor, or illusory, or self-serving. She might also have felt the quite understandable need to impress Edin and Shaefer with her conscientiousness (she was very uncomfortable applying for welfare in Edin's presence).[30] Modonna would still be a sympathetic figure if she had spent only a year or two at the music store, and even if she had repeatedly bungled her cash drawer. Her story is thus a good example of the utility of documentation when recollections alone may be misleading.

My consideration of evidence and ethnography has involved substantial fact-checking from multiple sources. Where possible, I sought out original documents, although that has been challenging in the face of ethnographers' commitment to anonymity and pseudonymization (see Chapter Seven). I have also, therefore, turned to secondary sources and the experiences of well-informed individuals—seeking what Edin and Shaefer refer to as "environmental confirmation," and what lawyers call circumstantial evidence.

In some instances I also refer to police reports, prosecution records, and other "establishment" sources, which some ethnographers have considered objectionable per se.[31] So let me say at the outset that I have no great affinity for the police, and I am well aware of the frequent abuses of authority in minority communities. I spent two years as a legal services lawyer on the West Side of Chicago, and another ten years doing juvenile and criminal defense work in Northwestern's Bluhm Legal Clinic. I continue to work on an ad hoc basis with Northwestern's MacArthur Justice Center (which played a leading role in the exposure of police torture in Chicago) and the Center on Wrongful Convictions (which has achieved numerous exonerations in death penalty and other cases), and I am a consultant with the Cook County Public Defender. Recent video revelations of wanton shootings—in Cleveland, Chicago, North Charleston, Baton Rouge, and elsewhere—are appalling, but sadly unsurprising. I recognize that minority communities have good reason to mistrust official investigations of police misconduct, which have often amounted to whitewashes until the production of indisputable dashboard or body camera evidence made further excuses impossible.

Nonetheless, academic responsibility requires facts to be reported as accurately as possible, especially when it comes to policy prescriptions for law enforcement. Sometimes, therefore, police reports are the best source of information. Police do many things that are wrong, but they do not do absolutely everything wrong. As sociology professor Peter Moskos explained, following his year as a police officer in Baltimore, "Overall police integrity is very high."[32] In the aggregate, cops file thousands of reports every day, and they are overwhelmingly as accurate as the officers can make them—if only because it is easier to tell the truth than to fabricate, and in the vast majority of cases there is no incentive to lie. Police reports can thus be as useful as any other documentation, especially when they can be corroborated, or when they were created in circumstances with no motive for invention or misreporting.[3]

As defense lawyers know, the initial police accounts of a crime or encounter can sometimes be the key to the exoneration of a defendant. Such reports are usually created before there is a "theory" of the investigation, and they are therefore unaffected by later suspicion, supposition, or manipulation by the authorities. Thus, the first step for the defense in almost every case is a request for the complete police and prosecution records. Northwestern's Bluhm Legal Clinic has often handled cases in which police files were used to free the wrongfully accused. In one such case, the appellate court cited evidence of innocence in a police report as a reason to reverse the defendant's conviction.[33] In another case, laboratory reports were located after trial that contained exculpatory evidence, leading to an eventual dismissal of charges.[34]

One fundamental obligation of a scholar, in ethnography or any other field, is to separate fact from suspicion and to distinguish rumor from reality, using every available tool, including those that may call for caution. It is ironic that some ethnographers can routinely rely on the questionable recollections of informants—some of whom have reason to shade the truth, and all of whom suffer the inherent weaknesses of human memory—and yet reject contemporaneous documentation as unreliable or irrelevant. A predisposition to disallow all forms of police or other "establishment" evidence can be as detrimental to social science as any other form of confirmation bias.

3

Unreliability

AT ITS BEST, ETHNOGRAPHY reports phenomena that may fall into three broad categories: (1) the researcher's own observations of events; (2) perceptions or stories as related by informants, whether offered for their truth or as impressions; and (3) rumors, folklore, and popular beliefs. Care must be taken to distinguish among these categories and to tell the reader which is which. In the case of second-hand reports, it is important to obtain verification if possible, lest the ethnographer end up recounting misimpressions, shaky recollections, or half-truths.

Lawyers can have similar problems with witnesses, whose testimony may sometimes include both solid observations and questionable, or even damaging or bias-ridden, perceptions and conclusions. There was a time in litigation history when attorneys were said to "sponsor" or "vouch" for all of their witnesses. Having called a witness to the stand, the lawyer was thereafter stuck with the direct examination, which he or she could not challenge or contradict. That rule was abolished in 1975, however, and today a lawyer may call a witness with only a nugget of truthful testimony, while casting doubt on, or flatly rejecting, everything else. Of course, such a selective presentation had better be accompanied by a good explanation for why some of the testimony ought to be believed, even if the rest is dubious or irrelevant. This happens most commonly in criminal cases when one co-defendant accepts a plea bargain to testify against another, and the prosecution has to explain why a suddenly repentant criminal nonetheless deserves some measure of belief.[1]

Ethnographers also rely on informants, some of whose life stories may be filled with errors, assumptions, or biases. Subjects always have their own reasons for cooperating with ethnographers, and strict accuracy may not be among them. No matter how candid an informant seems, it is a "methodological error," as Duneier reminds us, to believe that "apparent rapport is real trust."[2] Or, as Williams and Milton caution, self-reports must be triangulated before they can be believed. At a minimum, unverified stories ought to be clearly identified so that readers may draw their own conclusions.

Ethnographers at times also become unreliable narrators, whose reconstructions of scenes and events are at best approximations. As Northwestern's Gary Alan Fine put it, "we maintain an illusion of omniscience . . . turning near fictions into claims of fact." In reality, the representations of ethnographers—whom Fine likens to playwrights—are "both true and false," in part because memory and observation often fail, and in part because their perspectives necessarily "channel" the data and interpretations they obtain from their informants.[3] Although ethnographers cannot avoid providing partial and imperfect accounts of their field studies, they can at least alert readers to the potential undependability of their subjects.[4]

EXERCISING CAUTION WITH INFORMANTS

It may be impossible to track down the details of a subject's personal history, especially when dealing with marginalized populations. An informant's "life story may be a fabrication," says Terry Williams in *Crackhouse*, adding that "a very real problem in this research is that people often lie." Williams addresses this problem by making his skepticism clear when relating an informant's dubious story. One of his subjects, whom he calls Tiger, claimed to have been a successful professional boxer in his youth. Williams did not fully buy the story, telling it in Tiger's own words while emphasizing the cocaine-infused nature of the reverie: " 'I came back to town and went professional for a while,' " begins Tiger. " 'I beat Gavilan,' he mutters, pushing a stick through one end of the pipe."[5]

Kid Gavilan was the welterweight champion of the world in the 1950s. I looked at every fight Gavilan lost after coming to the United

States in 1947 until his retirement in 1958, and I did not find an oppo-
nent who fit Tiger's description. On the other hand, Tiger also mentions fighting Washington Jones as an amateur, and he provides some
background on Jones's career. Just as Tiger said, Jones did fight as a
middleweight in the 1948 London Olympics, and he was indeed dis-
qualified in his first fight. So there was some truth to Tiger's story,
although, like many ex-boxers, he greatly exaggerated his accomplish-
ments. Williams understood that, of course, making it clear that he was
interested in Tiger's self-image and not in his actual record in the ring.[6]

It took some time to track down Kid Gavilan's opponents, and
I would not expect an ethnographer to make that sort of effort in
every situation. It was more than enough for Williams to express his
skepticism, while using Tiger's boast to illuminate his demeanor and
personality.

Victor Rios is also careful when it comes to crediting his informants
in *Punished*, which is a study of minority youth in the Oakland neighborhood where he had grown up himself. Although Rios is extremely
sympathetic to his subjects, he recognizes that his "insider status" may
have affected his observations and that the participants' responses may
have been biased "to please the ethnographer."[7] Consequently, he makes
a point of distinguishing his own observations—which are narrated in
the first person—from his subjects' stories. In one extended vignette,
Rios describes how a young man named "Tyrell" made the decision to
enter the drug trade, believing that he had no choice. Over the course
of five pages, Rios uses phrases such as "according to Tyrell" and "in
Tyrell's account" twelve times. His point is not necessarily to cast doubt
on Tyrell's stories of mistreatment at school and harassment by police—
which are quite believable—but rather to make his first-hand observations distinct from Tyrell's recollections.

Thus, Rios tells us in one passage that "I watched or heard from
Tyrell about being stopped by police twenty-one times." In another
passage, however, it was "according to Tyrell" that "police threatened
him and his friends with arrest" for trying to watch baseball games from
an overlook near the Oakland Coliseum. At another point, Rios writes,

> Tyrell was homeless for part of his childhood, sleeping in cars, shel-
> ters, crack houses, and in the parking lot of the [housing project]. In

Tyrell's account, the housing authority did not want to provide his father housing. "Because he was not a woman . . . they told him that he had no reason for not having a job." Tyrell's dad was a mechanic but could not find work at the time.[8] (Ellipses in original)

Tyrell's "account" is probably inaccurate; gender discrimination is not officially permitted in public housing, although informal discrimination might still occur. I therefore checked with two long-time housing lawyers in Alameda County, and both doubted Tyrell's story. "I have never heard of OHA refusing to rent to men," said one. "I have never heard of men refused housing as a policy, or even anecdotally," said the other.[9] Perhaps Tyrell was repeating what his father told him, perhaps he misremembered, or perhaps he was rationalizing his homelessness. Whatever the case, Rios trusted and sympathized with Tyrell, but he did not vouch for the accuracy or detachment of his memory.

VOUCHING FOR INFORMANTS

Rios's method may seem obvious, but even exceptionally careful ethnographers do not always take the same approach. In *Evicted*, Mathew Desmond tells the story of a woman named "Vanetta" who was facing eviction, and perhaps even the loss of her children, because her hours were drastically cut at work. She felt "helpless and terrified," as did her friend who had also received eviction papers:

> One day with Vanetta's boyfriend, the two women sat in a van and watched another pair of women walk into a Blockbuster carrying purses. Someone suggested robbing the women and splitting the money; then all of a sudden, that's what they were doing. Vanetta's boyfriend unloaded his gun and handed it to her friend. The friend ran from the van and pointed the pistol at the women. Vanetta followed, collecting their purses. The cops picked them up a few hours later.[10]

Desmond seems to endorse this description as the straightforward recitation of established facts. We learn in an endnote, however, that the source of the story was Vanetta's "own accounting." As defense lawyers know, the first impulse of an arrested criminal is usually to minimize personal involvement, often by shifting some of the blame onto his or her co-defendants. It is therefore fair to ask whether the robbery was really someone else's idea. Was the gun really unloaded, and was it held only by the friend? Was Vanetta's role limited to collecting the purses? Did it truly happen "all of a sudden," or had they planned it in advance? And was Vanetta's confession an attempt to put the best spin on a bad situation (as is almost always the case)? When it comes to the details of a crime, there is no more unreliable narrator than a defendant who is trying to deflect culpability.[11]

Vanetta had been released on bail, and she hoped to be given probation following her guilty plea, figuring that her minimal involvement could mean a lenient sentence. Desmond attended the sentencing hearing, at which Vanetta's public defender argued that she was "younger and 'less street smart' than her accomplices," and that "her friend had held the gun." Vanetta testified that she "took full responsibility" for her actions and apologized to her victims.

> At the time of this situation, me and my kids were going through a difficult time in our lives and on the verge of being evicted and our lights being cut off. I was overwhelmed by the difficulties. But this doesn't excuse what I have done . . . . At this time I'm asking for leniency for me but, especially, for my children. (Ellipses in original)[12]

The prosecutor seemed to reject Vanetta's story about her minimal participation. "It is the state's view that people need to know when you use a gun to take things from other people, you go to prison." The judge agreed with the prosecutor. "This is not . . . a probationary case. I am going to impose eighty-one months in the state prison system. It's going to break down to fifteen months of initial confinement and sixty-six months of extended supervision."[13] Vanetta was handcuffed and taken weeping into custody.

There may well have been more to the story than Vanetta admitted either to Desmond or in her confession. Punishment for armed robbery was strict in Milwaukee in those years, but eighty-one months was still a heavy sentence. About one out of six armed robbers got straight probation, and Vanetta should have been a good candidate for leniency.

She was a female first offender, with children, who pled guilty and accepted responsibility, all of which would typically support a lighter sentence.[14] We don't know why the judge considered the offense non-probationary, but perhaps Vanetta had been more culpable than she let on. Desmond's anonymization prevents me from checking the specifics of the case, but it would not be surprising if the gun had been loaded and at some point in Vanetta's hand.

In $2 a Day, Edin and Shaefer tell the story of an admirable young woman named "Tabitha" who faced extraordinary difficulties while attempting to pull herself out of poverty in the Mississippi Delta region. It had been Tabitha's good fortune in middle school to encounter a teacher named Mr. Patten, an Ivy League graduate who had come to Mississippi with Teach for America. Mr. Patten encouraged Tabitha's interest in education, and he stayed in touch with her after she went on to high school.

In tenth grade, however, Tabitha encountered a teacher of a very different sort. "Her gym teacher messaged her on Facebook and said he had been watching her for years, waiting for her to 'mature,'" and he asked her to meet with him in private. The result was a sexual "liaison that lasted seven months," until Tabitha confided in Mr. Patten. "She blamed herself," but Mr. Patten reassured her that "a sixteen-year-old could not consent to a sexual relationship with a grown-up, especially a teacher."

> Acting on his instructions, Tabitha reported the gym teacher to the county attorney and the high school principal. At first, nothing happened. Finally, after Mr. Patten insisted, the teacher was removed from his post, although they gave him other work at the school. To date, there has been no criminal prosecution by the county attorney. In fact, there has been no response from his office at all.[15]

Tabitha's story is tragically familiar to anyone who follows the news. Far too many children have been sexually exploited by teachers, mentors, and other authority figures. I saw no reason to doubt that the same thing had happened to Tabitha, but I wondered if I could confirm the inaction of the school, and especially the non-responsiveness of the prosecuting attorney.

The Mississippi Delta region described in $2 a Day appears to be real-life Washington and Sunflower Counties.[16] I therefore contacted the prosecuting attorney who was in office during the relevant years. He adamantly denied having been notified of any such case. Dewayne Richardson, who was the district attorney for both Washington and Sunflower Counties, told me that he presents all such accusations to a grand jury, and that he would have spoken to the victim to explain any decision against prosecution. I asked if it was possible that Tabitha's report had been ignored. "Not in my jurisdiction," he said.[17]

I also attempted to contact Tabitha's school, but here I ran into a wall. I wrote to the principal of every high school in Sunflower County, asking if they were aware of such an incident (asking them not to reveal any names). The only response I received was from the attorney for the Sunflower County Consolidated School District, which covers all of the K-12 schools in the county. He informed me that "our District does not provide information on the type of requests as presented; and therefore, we will be unable to satisfy your inquiry at this time."[18]

Mississippi has a strict Child Abuse Reporting Act, which requires school districts to report allegations of sexual exploitation to the state Department of Human Services. I therefore followed up with a request under the state Public Records Act for all records of such reports during the relevant years. I asked for all identifiers to be redacted, and added that I would be satisfied with an assurance that there had been no known reportable incidents. The response again came from the school board's attorney, who stated that my request called for "confidential and/or privileged information not subject to any public records request." I do not agree with that reading of the Mississippi Public Records Act, but the only alternative would have been a lawsuit, so I decided not to pursue the matter further.[19] I did find it significant, to say the least, that the school district—unlike the prosecutor—chose not to deny ever receiving an accusation such as Tabitha's.

I also spoke to Luke Shaefer, who told me about his research method. In addition to Tabitha, he spoke about the events with "someone from the high school and a friendly community member." He also spoke to other people in the community, which generated additional stories "that were equally disturbing about the same school." He was not able to get the principal or prosecutor "on the record."[20]

Based on my contacts with Richardson and several other prosecutors, I think it is reasonable to wonder whether the county attorney really did fail to respond to a report of child exploitation by a teacher. On the other hand, I am far more concerned by the school district's non-denial, and I regret that I was unable to learn more. Of Tabitha's basic story about exploitation by a trusted teacher, as vouched for by Edin and Shaefer, I have no doubt.

USING UNATTRIBUTED STATEMENTS

Verification is even more important when going beyond personal histories and into the realm of social institutions. According to Duneier, it is always tempting for a researcher to tailor the facts so as to support a favored theory, even at the cost of presenting an inaccurate view of social reality. Ethnographers have greatest leeway to tailor the facts when they present unattributed statements or observations.

Consider Alice Goffman's description of the bail system in Philadelphia, which supports her argument that a "web of entrapment" faces young men on the run:

> When the police arrest and process a man, they ask him to provide a good deal of information about his friends and relatives—where they live and where he lives, what names they go by, how to reach them. The more information he provides, the lower his bail will be, so he has a significant incentive to do this. By the time a man has been arrested a number of times, the police have substantial information about where his girlfriend works, where his mother lives, where his child goes to school.

As is not uncommon in ethnography, this observation is unsourced. In evidentiary terms, it would be classified as hearsay: it is evidently based on information obtained from others, and it is offered for its truth value (the reality of dossiers) as opposed to anyone's state of mind ("the cops must have been keeping a file on me"). Although many ethnographers complement their "ethnographic observations with other validating sources," others often present their conclusions as unattributed and undocumented generalizations of this nature.[21]

Because such summaries are highly dependent on the reliability of both the author and the unnamed sources, the statement about extensive bail-related dossiers is precisely the sort of assertion that should be tested in an ethnographic trial.

I therefore consulted two former Philadelphia public defenders, both of whom were in the office during the period of Goffman's field work. They confirmed that her description of the bail system is highly inaccurate, especially regarding the role of the police. One of the former PDs told me that there was no connection between providing information to the police and obtaining lower bail, because bond is set by commissioners rather than the cops. "I have never heard of providing more information about other people mean[ing] lower bail," he said.[22]

The other former PD told me that Goffman's description of the bail system "appears to take several things that have a grain of truth to them and turn it into something that collectively appears far more nefarious than it actually is." The police do not use bail as a means of gathering information for future harassment of friends, mothers, and girlfriends, he explained. Although he had spent ten years as a defense lawyer, including stints as a supervisor and a major crimes trial lawyer in the public defender's office, he had never heard of "any type of scenario in which you are told by a detective that if you tell the police where your kids go to school the commissioner who sets the bail will look at that more favorably."

I also obtained the form used by bail commissioners to set bond amounts. In addition to personal details—age, race, sex, height, and weight—it asks only for the following: living arrangements, marital status, number of children, employment or other support, military service, and length of residence in Philadelphia. There are no general questions about friends and relatives, much less "where his girlfriend works, where his mother lives, where his child goes to school."[23] The obvious objective of the questionnaire is to obtain information about an individual's "community ties" for the purpose of determining the likelihood of flight. Although this might be interpreted by some defendants as the creation of a long-term dossier, a responsible researcher could easily discover the actual use of the bond-setting interview.[24]

My informants are former public defenders who collectively spent two decades representing poor people in and around Philadelphia. Far from apologists, the two of them have cross-examined hundreds, if not thousands, of cops, doing their best to catch them in contradictions and inconsistencies in order to keep their clients out of jail. Based on years of relevant experience, they both reject the claim that bail applications are used to develop a profile of friends and family to be used for the purpose of later warrant enforcement. Said one of them, "It seems like the passage suggests that once you've been arrested the police can just go and open a file and say things like, 'the person's known associates are or, the person is known to frequent the following places.' Like it's a movie. This is not to say that the Philadelphia Police Department is this great bastion of civil rights, but they are also not the East German Stasi."[25]

Most ethnographies include at least passing references to the need to be wary of undependable informants, but it is much less common to see serious skepticism toward research subjects. One such example is Randol Contreras's uncertainty about an episode related by one of his subjects, who described robbing a drug dealer in the Bronx (the italics are original):

This nigga, Neno, he even raped a bitch that was inside the apartment.
Word? I asked.
Yeah, he did bro, Gus responded, matter-of-factly. *He's done that shit before.*
How did it happen? I asked.
While we were torturin', Gus explained, *he just took her to a bed-room and raped her. . . .*
I shook my head in disbelief. I knew that these men were brutal robbers, but I never thought of them as "robber-rapists." Troubled, I tried to verify the story.

Contreras first attempted to learn more from David, who had taken part in the robbery, but he couldn't get a straight answer. Years later, Contreras finally confronted Neno:

I heard that sometimes guys rape women during robberies? Have you ever seen that happen?
. . .

No, I never saw that happen, he responded, with raised eyebrows. *We always say, if we find women and children, we don't lay a hand on them.*

Oh, this is the first time I heard that, I said.

Contreras did not believe Neno's denial, but he realized that his subject "was not going to admit that he had sexually assaulted a woman—or any other women—during a robbery." Contreras makes his own belief clear, however, that Neno had raped the woman, "using his body to degrade her in the ultimate violation."[26]

But that was just one episode. Throughout the rest of the book, Contreras mostly takes his informants, including Neno, at their word. He relays uncritically their stories of robbery and mayhem, including their unverifiable exploits in Ohio and Georgia.

In *Crook County*, Nicole Gonzalez Van Cleve expresses skepticism toward an entire class of informants. As discussed in the Introduction, Van Cleve conducted an ethnographic trial to test her own impression of the public defenders who, she wrote in her field notes, had "mocked Gideon's promise" of universal representation by "standing as ineffectual puppets that emboldened this court culture and the racism that fueled it." Van Cleve therefore obtained a position with the Cook County Public Defender, which allowed her to conduct interviews with defense lawyers. "There was no shortage of attorneys who wanted to explain their version of justice in the court system to a young female clerk." Her standard question was, "Do you believe that defendants are treated fairly within the court regardless of their race or class background?"[27]

Although some of the defense attorneys "were straightforward about describing the courts as bastions of racial bias," Van Cleve believed that most of them hedged their answers in a "rhetorical dance." One lawyer opined that "judges have equal contempt for all defendants," and another said, "I don't know any judge who is not trying to be fair; whether they can be is another story." A third respondent attributed bias to the "fact of 'being human.'" Van Cleve considered these answers as "evasive and apologetic," which therefore "required weeding through the semantic moves or rhetorical strategies" necessary to uncover her subjects' true attitudes. She concluded that many of the defense lawyers' responses had been "evasive and apologetic" attempts to defer blame for complicity "in the practices of the courts."[28]

I do not share Van Cleve's disdain for public defenders and other defense lawyers, most of whom, in my experience, do the best they can in very challenging circumstances.[29] I do agree strongly with her view that the statements of research subjects should not routinely be taken at face value. As Colin Jerolmack and Shamus Khan have explained, it is always risky "to draw conclusions about people's behaviors based on what they tell us."[30]

Undependable informants can be impossible to detect in ethnography, given the discipline's extreme commitment to masking and anonymity (discussed in Chapter Seven). The potential for embarrassment, or even disaster, can be seen more clearly in journalism, where the accounts of named sources are more readily investigated. Gay Talese, for example, spent over forty years researching his book *The Voyeur's Motel*, in which he told the story of an Aurora, Colorado, motel owner named Gerald Foos, who claimed to have spied on the sexual activities of his guests at a property called The Manor House. Talese visited Foos and interviewed him extensively, and even joined him watching an unsuspecting couple in bed. Much of the book was based on Foos's notebooks, which he claimed to have kept from 1966 to the mid-1990s. Talese's book was already printed and ready for distribution when it was discovered that Foos had lied about key details in his story.

It turned out that Foos had sold the motel in 1980 and had not owned it for the next eight years (he re-purchased it in 1988). Some of the dramatic events described in *The Voyeur's Motel* purportedly occurred during this interregnum—in other words, they were untrue—which could have been discovered if Talese had simply fact-checked the county property register. Instead, he learned about it only when confronted by a reporter.

The author was forced to disavow his own book on the eve of publication, telling *The Washington Post* that he could not stand behind it. "How dare I promote it when its credibility is down the toilet?" he said. "The source of my book, Gerald Foos, is certifiably unreliable." "He's a dishonorable man, totally dishonorable."[31]

Tellingly, Talese ignored red flags along the way, naively accepting explanations—and even inventing excuses—that he never should have believed. For example, Foos recounted in his journal that he witnessed the strangulation murder of a young woman at The Manor House on November 11, 1977, claiming that he had anonymously reported the murder to the police. Talese investigated this claim, but he could find no record of a murder on that date. There was nothing in police files, no coroner's report, no death certificate, and nothing in the local newspapers. Rather than disbelieve his informant, however, Talese attributed the missing records to bureaucratic error. It would "not be impossible," he wrote, "for there to be no remaining police records," because "two former officers" told him they might have disappeared over time. If Talese had investigated further, however, he would have discovered that a young woman named Irene Cruz had been strangled at a different Denver motel, not far from The Manor House, on November 3, 1977— only eight days before Foos's journal entry. The Cruz murder was covered in the Denver press, and the police record of her death is still easily obtainable, raising the obvious suggestion that Foos had appropriated the story for his journal.[32]

Talese's credulity—a willing suspension of disbelief for the sake of a good story—was his undoing. Where he should have been skeptical of his informant, he was far too trusting, or even enabling. Law, journalism, and social science must equally demand a standard of proof greater than "not impossible." Like all narrators, ethnographers must wrestle with the temptation to credulity, as we will see in the next chapter.

4

Credulity

IT IS ESSENTIAL TO understand that informants' "own account of their social reality is also a social construction."[1] The story of even the most sincere subject, or witness, may be affected by bias, self-importance, poor memory, or the desire to please—and sometimes they may even lie. Thus, researchers (like lawyers) must always be on guard against their own naiveté or credulity, lest they accept an imagined or embroidered story as actual fact. In *The Con Men*, Terry Williams and Trevor Milton recognized that "self-reports have always been problematic for ethnographers," who must do their best to "understand why subjects talk to them. What's in it for them? What is the quid pro quo in the enterprise, and what is the psychological motivation?"[2] This will not always be complicated, especially when the "social construction" is the very subject of the research. In her book *Scream*, for example, the sociologist Margee Kerr was easily able to report sympathetically on her observation of ghost hunters without endorsing their belief in the supernatural.[3]

As noted in Chapter One, I am skeptical of Kimberly Hoang's claim that bars featuring sex work played an indispensable role in bringing sizeable foreign investment to Vietnam. I realize that she bases her conclusion on extensive field work and many interviews, but it is hardly unusual for movers and shakers, in every country and culture, to characterize their vices as socially and economically beneficial. In that regard, Hoang's elite Vietnamese businessmen may not be very different from the Italian racketeers of Whyte's Cornerville, who claimed that their illegal gambling proceeds provided valuable capital in their neighborhood, and that their "tough" sales methods—bullying and coercion—were essential to local businesses that were "struggling to get ahead."[4] The same could also be said of contemporary Chicago gang leaders, as described by Laurence Ralph, who entice thirteen-year-old kids to deliver drugs "with a pistol and a pocket full of cash." "Whether or not community outsiders buy into the idea that the gang provides both jobs and protection," explains Ralph, the leaders use "this rationale to help justify the gang's existence."[5]

Did Hoang truly uncover a "hidden currency" that has been crucial to Asian capital development? Although I do not doubt that she has accurately conveyed the statements, values, and beliefs of her subjects, opposing counsel in an ethnographic trial could readily tell a completely different story based on the identical facts and interviews.

Where Hoang sees sensible, trust-building business practices, someone else might see extravagant boasting over outsized male prowesses. What Hoang accepts as a reliable account of the international money flow, someone else might interpret as self-justification and the "performance of masculinity."[6] No matter how many deals were consummated in expensive nightclubs, it remains the case—in both law and social science—that coincidence does not imply causation. Determining the actual relationship between foreign investment and the sex trade would be an empirical challenge for even a sophisticated macroeconomist. Although I am not able to look further into the details of the Vietnamese economy, it will be possible to interrogate some similar sorts of claims that arise closer to home.

It is not unreasonable to fully accept the word of one's informants on passing or relatively unimportant details (what the law calls collateral matters). Thus, there was no great reason for Elijah Anderson to inquire further when he was given an explanation for the reluctance of some unmarried women to name the fathers of their children:

> There is sometimes an incentive for the young woman not to identify the father, even though she and the local community know "whose baby it is," for a check from the welfare office is much more dependable than the irregular support payments of a sporadically employed youth.[7]

Had he looked into welfare law at the time, however, Anderson would have learned that a woman would not have jeopardized her public assistance check by naming her child's father. In fact, quite the opposite was true; a woman's benefits could have been terminated for refusing to cooperate with the authorities by identifying the father. Under the system in effect at the time, however, any payments then extracted from a child's father would have gone directly to the welfare department, with no impact one way or the other on the mother's grant. From the couple's perspective, it would simply be lost money; he would have to pay, and she would receive nothing more.

What was really happening, of course, is that many of the young men were making under-the-table payments to the mothers. The result was a form of understandable double-dipping, in which the young women received both their regular welfare checks as well as occasional money from the fathers. Had the women formally identified the men, it would have ended an arrangement that was preferable for everyone except the welfare department. The behavior was unlawful, though widely accepted and seldom prosecuted, which probably explains why Anderson was told only a sanitized version by his informants.

I would never fault Anderson for slightly missing that point, or for trusting his subjects, given that it was not essential to his description of the community under study. Comparable passages can be found in almost every ethnography. Some are more significant than others, and not every unreliable hearsay statement can be as easily uncovered.

In the next section, therefore, I will show how secondary and circumstantial evidence can be used to controvert an informant's fictive statement that was somehow credited by the authors of an otherwise exceptionally well-documented ethnography. The discussion is lengthier that it might merit if our only concern was the accuracy of the account, but it is offered instead for two important, and related, purposes: first, to show the particular difficulty of disproving an unsourced hearsay statement, even when it seems unbelievable on its face, and second, to demonstrate how opposing counsel in an ethnographic (or any other) trial would go about accomplishing the task.

USING CIRCUMSTANTIAL EVIDENCE

In *$2 a Day*, Kathryn Edin and Luke Shaefer tell the story of an idealistic middle-school teacher in the Mississippi Delta who arranged for his sixth-grade class to take a school trip to Washington, D.C.

The children, all of whom were poor, had grown up in the hamlet of "Percy," on the outskirts of Greenville. So isolated is the Delta region that Edin and Shaefer title their chapter "A World Apart," describing it as "a world unto itself, with a unique history and a distinctive set of social conditions" characterized by "record poverty rates of well over 40 percent."[8]

The trip to Washington, D.C., was the highlight of the children's lives, remembered with delight even years later. "It was so exciting," said one of Edin and Shaefer's informants. "We were on an airplane! Saw the White House, the Washington Monument . . . It was so cool because a lot of white people actually were the ones would talk to us." So far, there is no reason to question the description of the trip, but the following passage provides a good lesson in the pitfalls of both hearsay and unexamined testimony. Edin and Shaefer continue,

> Also on this trip, many of the children saw an elevator for the first time. Initially, some of them didn't believe that the box behind the doors could actually transport them from one floor to another. They honestly thought it was some sort of joke that the teachers were playing on them.[9]

The school trip occurred some years before Edin and Schaefer's ethnographic work, probably in about 2007. Thus, the authors are obviously relating a second-hand account that was provided to them by a teacher, chaperone, or student. In other words, it is hearsay, with all of the attendant hearsay problems.

I find it virtually impossible to accept that several American sixthgraders ("some of them") were unaware of the very existence of elevators in the twenty-first century, and that they did not believe their own teachers about taking one to a higher floor. Every middle-school student would have had at least some knowledge of automobiles, airplanes, satellites, cell phones, and other routine features of modern technology, so a simple elevator could not have come as such an incredible surprise. Disproving the story, however, requires the always challenging proof of a negative. How is it possible to show that the existence of elevators did not come as an astonishing revelation to a group of Mississippi schoolchildren?

The Mississippi Delta may be a world apart—and there are probably no elevators in Percy itself—but they still have television, which, at the very least, renders the story of the students' wonderment highly implausible. The first passenger elevator went into service in 1857, making the technology older than air travel by fifty years and older than home television by nearly a century. Surely the word had spread to Percy, Mississippi, by 2007. Edin and Shaefer's anecdote should have set off alarm bells. But because it is based on hearsay, we have no access to the originator of the story (the "declarant"), and therefore no means of assessing his or her reliability.

In an ethnographic trial, however, we can look to circumstantial sources. My first step was to contact Heather McTeer Toney, who was the mayor of Greenville at the time of the school trip. I provided her with the passage from *$2 a Day* and asked for her reaction. Her reply was understated. "I find it highly unlikely that the MS sixth graders would not be familiar with an elevator," she said. I also spoke to Rebecca Madison, who works for the state Department of Child Protection Services. After I read her the passage, she said, "I would not find that to be true," adding her distress at the thought that "people think we are antiquated, that we live in the Third World." Summer Graves made the same observation about the "preconceived notion that we are backward" in Mississippi. Graves holds a doctorate in education, specializing in millennials, and she currently teaches high school in Jackson. "I find it inconceivable within the last ten years that a child would not know about elevators," she told me. I did not find a single Mississippian who believed the elevator story; most were offended by it, some thought it was just silly.[10]

"Percy" itself is a pseudonym and therefore unlocatable, so I could not interview anyone from the subject middle school. It was possible, however, to impute the experience of students elsewhere in Mississippi by looking at the circumstantial evidence of widespread elevator awareness. For that, I turned first to television. There is no resource that lists television shows with elevators, but I was able to identify the most popular shows during the several years preceding the school trip—that is, when the students were about eight to twelve years old. Many of the top broadcast shows during that period had at least occasional scenes in buildings with elevators, including *House, Friends, Will & Grace, NCIS,*

Grey's Anatomy, The Office, Criminal Minds, 30 Rock, and *The Big Bang Theory*—the last of which is set in an apartment building that prominently features a non-working elevator secured by bright yellow police tape.[11]

Children would not necessarily watch all of those shows—especially the ones aimed at mature audiences—so I also looked up the television shows most popular among African Americans during that time period. They included *House of Payne*, which is set in contemporary Atlanta and probably showed an elevator now and then, and *Law & Order*, with a courthouse elevator in many episodes.[12] Two of the most popular black-themed television shows in history were *Good Times* and *The Jeffersons*, which were shown in syndication during the relevant time period. Both shows were set in high-rises—a Chicago housing project and a "deluxe apartment" on Manhattan's East Side—thus requiring elevators. *The Jeffersons'* famous theme song, "Movin' On Up," was a double entendre, referring both to their improved economic status and their elevator-accessible apartment "in the sky."[13]

If not quite ubiquitous, elevators are a regular presence in popular television and film. There is a website listing the situation comedies in which babies have been born in elevators—a sufficiently frequent occurrence to have become a meme—and another with the most exciting elevator scenes in action movies.[14]

Finally, I learned that the elevator safety door—a feature that keeps passengers from falling into the shaft—had been invented by Alexander Miles, an African American, in 1887. Although that fact is generally obscure, it is often included in the national materials for Black History Month.[15] I found a reference to Miles's invention in the curriculum for Oxford, Mississippi, but there is no curriculum posted for the Sunflower County Consolidated School District, which is where I believe Percy is located.[16] Students who have read about Miles would not need to remember his name in order to be aware of the existence of elevators.

My conclusion from the overwhelming circumstantial evidence is that the claim of elevator bafflement was indeed a joke—but it was played by the students who feigned ignorance, not by the chaperones who appear to have fallen for it. The story could have been easily unraveled by interviewing the declarants—that is, the schoolchildren—more closely, or by subjecting them to imaginary cross-examination in an ethnographic trial. Do you have a television set in your house? What sorts of shows do you watch? Have you or your parents ever been to Greenville? Have you ever seen pictures of New York or other big cities with tall buildings? Does your school observe Black History Month?

The story of the students' excitement at visiting Washington, D.C., would have been just as compelling if Edin and Shaefer had been appropriately skeptical of the farfetched elevator vignette, which is mostly inconsequential to the compelling insights of $2 a Day. Nonetheless, the authors' desire to underscore the isolation of the Mississippi schoolchildren seems to have resulted in their unquestioning acceptance of some anonymous kid's mischievous banter.

Most readers will not care one way or the other about whether the elevator story was a prank, but it exposes a flaw in the practice of ethnography. If such glaringly implausible hearsay can slip through unnoticed by such admirably meticulous authors and their editors and reviewers, then what other dubious—but less conspicuously questionable—facts might be found in other studies if one were to take the time and energy necessary to look? Most ethnographies include many anonymous assertions about an informant's experiences, background, or local social conditions, presented in a context that makes them impossible to verify. We must therefore depend on the author's acuity to separate real events from exaggerations and tall tales. That is usually a sufficient guarantee of reliability, but what happens when it fails?

There can be circumstances in which an ethnographer's credulity undermines the credibility of an entire project, especially when it is occasioned by the researcher's own unacknowledged agenda. As Nikki Jones put it, ethnographers must always "interrogat[e] the assumptions and perspectives that we bring to our research."[17]

SUSPENSION OF DISBELIEF

There is a point at which reliance on informants turns from willing naiveté into a strategic blind eye. We see this most clearly in *On the Run*, where Alice Goffman tells the story of the brothers Chuck and Tim. In Goffman's account, eighteen-year-old Chuck was driving eleven-year-old Tim to school when they were pulled over by the police. It turned out that the car had been stolen, and Chuck was arrested for receiving stolen property, even though he had only borrowed the car from his girlfriend's uncle. Young Tim was also arrested, according to Goffman, and later placed on three years of juvenile probation on the charge of "accessory to receiving stolen property."[18]

This story is pivotal in Goffman's description of over-policing, as she uses Tim's ordeal to argue that it is nearly impossible for her subjects to avoid acquiring criminal records at an early age. Although I do not question her general observation about the toils of the judicial system, these particular events could not have happened as Goffman recounts them in her book and lectures.

I provided Tim's story to a current Philadelphia prosecutor and two former public defenders, all of whom worked in juvenile court during the period of Goffman's research on 6th Street. All three said that it was virtually impossible that an eleven-year-old would be arrested, much less charged with a felony, for nothing more than riding in a stolen vehicle. According to the prosecutor, a child of that age would not even be taken into custody, other than "to get him home safely." Riding in a stolen car is not a crime in Pennsylvania, he said, so even an adult passenger would not be charged under those circumstances. In fact, there is no such crime as "accessory to receiving stolen property" in the Pennsylvania Criminal Code. "That is a term you might hear on television," the prosecutor told me, "but not from a juvenile court judge."[19]

The public defenders were likewise unconvinced of Tim's alleged conviction and sentence. There had to be more to it, one of them said, "like maybe if the kid had popped the ignition with a screwdriver." The other PD explained that Pennsylvania does not even have fixed probation terms for juveniles, so there could not have been a three-year "probation sentence." A total of three years of probation would only result from repeated violations over a period of years, irrespective of the original charge.[20]

We do not know what actually happened to Chuck and Tim, but neither does Goffman, who appears to have uncritically accepted her informants' version of the events. The story that an eleven-year-old passenger was arrested and sentenced for nothing more than riding in a stolen car, however, stretches credulity to the breaking point. Even Goffman's sympathizers in the media doubt its credibility. *New York Magazine*'s Jesse Singal cites "a longtime Philadelphia public defender [who] said he found the Tim story extremely unlikely."[21]

Chuck's story about his girlfriend's uncle is equally shaky, as would be immediately apparent to any experienced criminal defense lawyer. Auto thieves routinely claim the car was borrowed, if not from a girl-friend's uncle, then from an uncle's girlfriend. Although such stories are not always contrived, they are highly suspicious and they frequently fall apart after investigation or cross-examination. (I have obtained police records of Chuck's and Tim's auto theft arrests, which flatly contradict the key details in Goffman's account.[22])

It is understandable that Chuck and Tim wanted to present them-selves to Goffman in the best possible light, perhaps withholding what one legendary ethnographer has called "dark secrets."[23] Although their stories are useful as reflections of their attitudes toward courts and the police, they are not reliable accounts of the underlying events. In evi-dentiary terms, they should not be accepted for their truth-value, but only for the declarants' state of mind.

It was easy to identify the fault lines in the story of Chuck and Tim. Goffman could have checked it just as easily, but she instead chose to use it as a cornerstone of her case against the judicial system.[24] The great irony is that the Philadelphia courts, as American courts everywhere, no doubt entrap the innocent and the minimally culpable of all ages, especially in minority communities. Goffman's case would only have been stronger if she had premised it on solid evidence.

Ethnographers are not the only professionals who must wrestle with the credibility of their sources, but many have expressed reluctance to question their informants. Goffman herself says that it is objectionable to challenge "the perspectives and experience of people at the bottom" even when they are contradicted by other sources.[25] A lawyer in the same position would run a practice cross-examination of her witnesses before putting them on the stand. Journalists are also cautious when confronted with implausibilities. "Ordinarily when a journalist discov-ers profoundly discrediting testimony like this, he utters 'Whoa,' item-izes the discrepancies, and digs deeper."[26]

CONFIRMATION

Let me add that the outcome of such fact-checking is not at all prede-termined, and some potentially questionable stories can be confirmed.

I researched more accounts than I have included in this chapter, and many of them turned out to be accurate (or indeterminate). I began at the beginning, with W.E.B. Du Bois's 1899 classic *The Philadelphia Negro*. It is full of data and figures that would be impossible to fact-check today, but there are also vignettes about identifiable individuals, including this one:

> An ex-minister to Hayti moved to the northwestern part of the city and his white neighbors insulted him, barricaded their steps against him, and tried in every way to make him move; to-day he is honored and respected in the whole neighborhood.[27]

Because of my earlier work on the black abolitionist John Mercer Langston (who was also an ambassador to Haiti), I knew that the United States' first black ambassador was Ebenezer Don Carlos Bassett—but I had not known the details of his life.[28] It turns out that he indeed lived in Philadelphia in the nineteenth century, and there is a historical marker at his home site on North Twenty-Ninth Street, where he and his wife lived "alongside European immigrants as well as white native-born families." Bassett's only biographer does not say anything about the reaction of the neighbors, and his State Department biography refers to his "courageous service" as a "pioneer in race relations." Bassett had at one time been associated with John Brown, however, which obviously could have accounted for the hostility of some white neighbors. That is probably the only one of Du Bois's anonymous anecdotes I can investigate after almost 120 years, but it checks out well.[29]

In *Code of the Street*, the sociologist Elijah Anderson tells of his efforts to help one of his subjects, a young black man whom he calls John Turner, escape from the grasp of the Philadelphia criminal justice system. Turner's problems started when he was caught by the police with an illegal handgun he had been carrying for protection in a tough neighborhood. Although the cops were sympathetic to Turner's situation, they had no choice but to arrest him. In court, Turner declined his attorney's advice to deny that the gun was his (it was found next to him on the street), and he was sentenced to five years of probation and a $1,500 fine. Turner had not been able to pay the fine, which is why he sought help from Anderson.[30]

Turner's sentence seemed excessive to me, given his claim that it was his first offense, and that he had cooperated with the police. I wondered if there was more to the story than Turner had shared with Anderson, or if Anderson had been mistaken (or misled) about the nature of the crime and the sentence. My research disclosed, however, that five years of probation was well within the allowable range for unlawful firearm possession in Pennsylvania in the 1990s (when *Code of the Street* was published), and the maximum fine was $10,000.

But still, Turner claimed that he had never even been arrested before. Wouldn't a year or two of probation, and a more manageable fine, have been more likely for a first offender? Once again, I called upon two former Philadelphia public defenders. While both thought that Turner's sentence was toward the high end, they agreed that it was certainly possible in the circumstances. Gun violence and street crime had been serious problems in Philadelphia in the 1990s, and stiff sentences were not uncommon, even for first offenders. Neither one doubted that a defendant could have been sentenced as John Turner claimed.[31]

In *Code of the Street*, Anderson himself eventually discovers Turner to be unreliable and deceptive. He begins to regard Turner with skepticism, and ultimately decides that he must cut off contact with his subject, in one of the most poignant episodes in the book. But the basic starting point of Turner's story—that he was harshly punished for a minor crime—appears to have been accurate, at least to the extent that such things can be investigated and confirmed.

I also questioned a vignette in Randol Contreras's *The Stickup Kids*. Pablo, one of Contreras's subjects, had been sentenced to a year at Rikers Island, "the infamous jail where chaos reigned." After watching inmates being "slashed and stabbed" for two months, and participating in a few fights himself, Pablo realized that the correctional officers had given up keeping order, and he needed to find someplace safer in order to survive.

After two months of Rikers chaos, Pablo requested a transfer to a prison in upstate New York. After approval, he was bussed to the Watertown Correctional Facility, about six hours north, near the Canadian border.[32]

This passage drew my interest because Rikers Island is New York City's jail complex, used to house prisoners awaiting trial or those with sentences of a year or less. It is not part of the New York state prison system and, in my experience, prisoners are not able to divide their sentences, and certainly may not request transfers, between local jails and state prisons. Although inmates may be moved back and forth between jails and prisons for administrative reasons—to attend court hearings, for example—I had never heard of an option to serve part of a one-year sentence in a long-term facility. Although I didn't doubt that Pablo had spent some time at Watertown, I suspected that it was for reasons other than a requested transfer.

It turns out that I was wrong. In the late 1980s and early 1990s, the New York City Department of Corrections was under a court order to reduce the population at Rikers Island, which had soared well beyond the jail's safe capacity. As a remedy to overcrowding, the NYC DOC leased space at two state prisons, one of which was Watertown. Prisoners who had already been sentenced to longer terms—as opposed to those waiting for trial, or who would only be in custody for a month or two—were transferred to the state prisons to serve their time in what had essentially become extensions of the local jail. Given his one-year sentence, which was the maximum at Rikers, Pablo was an obvious candidate for the program, with or without a request.[33]

In *Blue Chicago*, David Grazian tells the story of a blues musician with the nickname Tail Dragger, who "rhapsodizes mournfully" about his latest stint in prison. "Oh, why was I in jail? Oh, I remember, because I shot somebody and killed them."[34] Prison is a familiar theme in blues and country music, from "The Midnight Special" to "Folsom Prison Blues," though rendered by different artists with greater and lesser degrees of authenticity. Huddie "Lead Belly" Ledbetter actually did serve time in Texas, for killing a relative, and again in Louisiana, for stabbing a man in a fight. Johnny Cash, on the other hand, did not kill a man in Reno (nor did Bob Marley ever shoot a sheriff). In fact, Cash never spent more than a night or two behind bars for misdemeanors, despite the outlaw persona he affected during his prison concerts.

It doesn't take a guilty man to sing a murder song, so it was hard to know on first reading whether Tail Dragger was actually a killer, or had instead adopted a role from the "myths of the stage." Many musicians, as Grazian explains, "play characters familiar to the world of blues and jazz," but he obviously believed his informant, writing that "Tail Dragger murdered fellow Chicago blues performer Boston Blackie over a financial dispute" in 1993.[35] And sure enough, the Chicago newspapers reported that James Yancey "Tail Dragger" Jones shot and killed Benny Houston, also known as "Boston Blackie," on July 11, 1993, in a dispute over payment for their performance at the Chicago Blues Fest. The two musicians had known each other for about twenty years, and the shooting occurred during a performance on an outdoor stage called the Delta Fish Market, which would have provided great material for a blues number. Although Jones pled self-defense, he was convicted of second-degree murder following a jury trial and sentenced to four years in prison.[36] If Tail Dragger ever expressed remorse for the killing, Grazian does not tell us about it.

The results of my investigations were mixed. Some narratives checked out and some did not. In the end, there is simply no way to know how many embroidered, sanitized, prankish, or made-up stories have been retold in ethnographies due to the authors' reluctance to dig more deeply into the facts. Based on my research—which considered only examples that raised obvious questions—the phenomenon is not isolated, and it can include accounts that are both collateral and essential to an author's theory.

DISCONFIRMING EVIDENCE

Short of actual cross-examination, the remedy for this problem, if there is one, is scrupulous fact-checking. Mario Small, for example, supplemented his observations in Boston's Villa Victoria with newspaper articles, archival records, and census data; Bettylou Valentine verified interview information for *Hustling and Other Hard Work* with "multiple cross-checking"; and Robert Jackall's *Wild Cowboys* drew heavily from police reports and court transcripts.[37]

Nearly all ethnographers acknowledge the need to seek disconfirming evidence, but fewer seem to have made a point of personally investigating informants' dubious claims. Patricia Adler had good reason to mistrust the drug dealers and smugglers she encountered when researching *Wheeling and Dealing*, so she "adopted a hard-nosed attitude of suspicion" that led her to check out their stories against hard facts in "newspaper and magazine reports; arrest records; material possessions; and visible evidence," although she provides no examples.[38]

Many more ethnographers generalize about fact-checking than give specific instances of how they have done it. Among the latter are the co-authors Terry Williams and Trevor Milton, who wrote *The Con Men*. In his research for the book, Williams encountered a hustler whom he called "Alibi." Realizing that Alibi's stories might or might not be true, Williams simply wrote them all down "as grist for the ethnographic mill." After all, Alibi's stories, even if phony, were still "a significant aspect of who he is." One of Alibi's stories was about training to be a jailer at Louisiana's infamous Angola Penitentiary, where he claimed to have been a guard on the toughest cell block with "the meanest prisoners in the country." This struck Williams as implausible, given that Alibi had a criminal record for drug dealing, and he confronted his subject with his doubts. The answer, according to Alibi, was that his "connections" made it possible. Williams investigated and reports that "after a bit of digging I found the Angola Correctional Academy and discovered a certificate Alibi received from there." Williams continued to wonder whether Alibi's other stories were genuine, "but he *was* telling the truth in this case." Later in the book, Milton tells of being suckered by one of his subjects—a rare admission among ethnographers.[39]

By far the most scrupulous approach to fact-checking was effected by Matthew Desmond in writing *Evicted*. A number of Desmond's subjects, for example, were on various forms of public assistance, but he did not simply assume the accuracy of their stories. Larraine, who was receiving disability assistance (SSI), told Desmond that she could not save money because "when you're on SSI you can only have so much money in the bank, and it's got to be less than a thousand dollars. Because if it's more . . . they cut your payments until that money is spent." Desmond both confirmed the existence of SSI's "resource limit" and corrected Larraine's misimpression of the amount. "She was allowed to have up to $2000 in the bank, not $1000 as she thought, but anything more would result in her losing benefits."[40] The difference was probably meaningless to Larraine, who rationally believed that she was better off buying "something worthwhile" than risking her benefits by banking her money, but it demonstrates Desmond's care to ensure that he was providing accurate information and not merely the impressions of his subjects.

Desmond also checked out a story that was more consequential to his informant, a woman named Arleen who received Temporary Assistance for Needy Families (TANF). Having fallen behind on her rent due to a family emergency, Arleen had made a deal with her landlord to catch up by paying $650 a month, which was twenty-two dollars more than her entire welfare check, while hoping to make up the balance with the help of a social service agency. When the first payment was due, however, Arleen called the landlord to report that her "check didn't come." According to Desmond, "this was a half-truth":

> Arleen had received a check, but not for $628. She had missed an appointment with her welfare caseworker, completely forgetting about it. A reminder notice was mailed to [one of her previous addresses]. When Arleen didn't show, the caseworker "sanctioned" Arleen by decreasing her benefit.

Rather than give her landlord the reduced check, Arleen "thought it was better to be behind and have a few hundred dollars in her pocket than be behind and completely broke."

Desmond did not take Arleen at her word. Instead, he turned to the TANF regulations and determined that they indeed required "suspending all or some" of the benefits of recipients who were "found to be noncompliant." In Wisconsin, "nearly two-thirds of those who entered the program were sanctioned at some point during the first four years." He even accompanied Arleen to a meeting with her caseworker to "sort out the details," later corroborating the nature of TANF sanctions with "emails and phone calls." Even though Desmond could not determine whether Arleen's noncompliance had been an innocent mistake—exacerbated by a misdirected reminder letter—he had been able to confirm "the possibility of something happening, if not the thing itself."[41]

Fact-checking did not always lead Desmond to such certain results. Several female residents of a Salvation Army shelter called "the Lodge" reported to him that "some of the maintenance men propositioned the residents for sex, offering fresh sheets, snacks, or extra shampoo." Desmond had never witnessed such an occurrence, however, and the shelter staff denied it. Even so, Desmond quite reasonably decided to include the allegation because he heard it from "Crystal, Vanetta, and other women I met at the Lodge." The existence of multiple sources made the claim credible, as Desmond explained in his notes.[42]

In another instance, however, Desmond omitted a story that he was unable to substantiate. A subject named Natasha Hinkston told him that she stopped going to high school after there was a shooting in the cafeteria. The story well fit his theory, and he was "eager to include it," but he first sought confirmation. Desmond spoke with three Milwaukee Public School administrators, none of whom could verify "that a shooting occurred around the time Natasha said it did." Realizing that the "gist (if not the details) of Natasha's story" might or might not still be true, Desmond nonetheless chose to exclude it as insufficiently corroborated.[43]

It is rare enough for an ethnographer to explain the omission of an unreliable story, but it is even more exceptional for an author to explain that it had been a theory-driven choice. Charles Bosk did just that, however, in a revised appendix to his 1979 book *Forgive and Remember*. In the second edition, published in 2003, Bosk explains that he had initially decided against including the story of a bigoted senior surgeon because it "would draw attention away from the book's central thesis— that in surgical education technical norms are subordinated to moral ones." In what he titled "An Ethnographer's Apology," Bosk concedes that his concern to avoid the appearance of "doctor bashing" led him to conceal the lead surgeon's use of racial and anti-Jewish slurs in the operating room because acknowledging the boorish behavior would have undermined his "central thesis about the dominance of normative over technical standards" in surgery.[44]

Few ethnographers make even passing mention of the research material they have chosen to leave out of the finished book, let alone explain their reasons for the exclusion. Nonetheless, it is obvious that months and years of field work, and thousands of pages of field notes, must be severely winnowed if there is to be a readable text. As we have seen, there is a constant danger that the ethnographer's choices will be too strongly influenced by what lawyers call the "theory of the case," with preference given to supporting facts and with contrary evidence minimized or obscured. Desmond cautions that ethnographers must learn to mistrust the impulse to emphasize their favored stories, and they must likewise take care not to gloss over data that do not fit their hypotheses. Bosk is almost unique in having recognized that he had suppressed certain information because it conflicted with his central thesis, and he came to that realization only two decades after first publishing his work.[45] Therefore, it is to the problem of selectivity that we turn in the next chapter.

5

Selectivity

A LAWYER PREPARING FOR trial is in many ways similar to an ethnographer writing a book. The research has been completed, the witnesses have been identified and their statements have been recorded, the notes have been taken, the data are assembled, and the sources have been explored. The remaining task is one of marshaling. What is the best way to organize and present the material? Which facts are essential and which are unnecessary? Who are the best witnesses, and which testimony is too boring or redundant to use? How much documentation will be necessary, and at what point will it become overwhelming? And how can it all be organized for maximum effect?

There are also crucial differences between trying a case and writing an ethnography, one of which is the need for comprehensiveness. Lawyers in an adversary system are obligated to represent their own clients zealously, and to present—with few exceptions—only the evidence that advances their side of the case.[1] It is the job of opposing counsel to produce counter-evidence. In theory, and for the most part in practice, this dialectic produces a comprehensive picture from which the fact-finder can draw a sufficiently reliable conclusion. It may be strategically wise for a lawyer to preemptively concede flaws and weaknesses—sometimes using what is called defensive direct examination or "drawing the sting"—but that is not a requirement.[2] Such tactics aside, lawyers are generally free to include or exclude evidence as the needs of the case demand; judges and juries know better than to rely on either side to present a full account of the facts.

The author of an ethnography, however, is responsible for providing all information that the readers will see. Careful researchers will no doubt make a point of presenting evidence both pro and con, but even the most objective scholar is nonetheless subject to cognition errors such as anchoring, framing, and belief perseverance, which can result in an unintentionally one-sided picture. Some urban ethnographers have quite intentionally put aside objectivity in favor of advocacy, asserting that their job is to allow marginalized subjects "to speak for themselves about the reality they face" without regard to contrary evidence from "officials or middle-class people." Others see their task as putting "a human face" on their subjects, no matter what their behavior.[3] That is all well and good, so long as it is openly acknowledged. It is important to tell the stories of the disenfranchised—although there ought to be a discernible line between oral history and social science—which naturally results in emphasizing one perspective on facts to the exclusion of others.

But whether omission is intentional or unintentional, a question remains. Has the author shaded the story through the strategic representation of details, sources, and data? One needn't believe that all ethnographies are "fantasy documents [that] emplot and narrativize" their subject matter for the sake of affectivity—as suggested by the anthropologist John Jackson—to recognize that selection bias is a constant problem.[4]

Some ethnographers resolve this dilemma by deliberately seeking both sides of the story. Desmond, for example, includes both landlords and tenants in his study of eviction, making a point of showing the difficulties faced by property owners in low-income neighborhoods. In *Wild Cowboys*, Robert Jackall attempts to provide the perspectives of police, victims, and criminals, just as Elijah Anderson's *Code of the Street* includes the viewpoints of both "street" and "decent" subjects.[5] Sudhir Venkatesh's books on Chicago's Robert Taylor Homes include observations of tenants, gang members, housing officials, police, and social service workers, as does Laurence Ralph in his study of gangs on Chicago's West Side.[6]

Nonetheless, even the most well-rounded ethnographies are necessarily selective, because no author can include everything he or she learned during years of field work. Edin and Shaefer followed eighteen families while researching *$2 a Day*, although they ultimately wrote about only eight of them in their book.[7] Desmond "conducted more than one hundred interviews with people not featured" in *Evicted*, "including thirty landlords."[8] The authors' intention was to tell the stories of subjects who can best illustrate the situation under study—in these cases, extreme poverty and the housing crisis—and I have no reason to doubt that they did their best to identify representative examples. Even so, it is fair to wonder whether other factors—fascination, simplicity, accessibility, diversity, drama—may have influenced their choices. As Wendy Chapkis put it, "There is perhaps no other aspect of so-called 'qualitative research' that so clearly reveals (or, by sleight of hand, conceals) the power of the writer as that of editing interview material."[9]

The author's standpoint in most urban ethnographies is further limited by the nature of the community under study. Randol Contreras and Philippe Bourgois could hardly go to the police for a second opinion about the robbers and drug dealers they studied, nor could Peter Moskos reasonably interview the criminals whom he arrested during his year as a participant-observer on the Baltimore police force.[10] Readers of such books must understand and accept that certain questions will be unanswered and critical voices will not be heard.

Even under these circumstances, however, an ethnographer might do more to complete the picture. In *In Search of Respect*, for example, Philippe Bourgois tells the story of an East Harlem drug dealer named Primo whose inability to find and hold a straight job left him no alternative to lawbreaking. "This book's argument," explains Bourgois, is that people like Primo "have not passively accepted their structural victimization. On the contrary, by embroiling themselves in the underground economy and proudly embracing street culture, they are seeking an alternative to their social marginalization." As evidence of such victimization and marginalization, Bourgois describes Primo's "humiliation" during the eight months he worked as a mail clerk for a professional trade magazine.

"I had a prejudiced boss. She was a fucking 'ho,'" said Primo about a woman called Gloria Kirschman. Primo complained that he had been reprimanded for attempting to show initiative by answering the telephone when his supervisor was away from her desk. "That boss was a bitch, because I answered the phone correct." Even worse, Primo was constantly being disrespected, as when "my supervisor told me to do a job one way, but I thought it was best to do it another way. She dissed the shit out of me a coupla times. That lady was a bitch." Even her suggestion that Primo go back to school was greeted with anger. "My boss, she wanted me to go to school too. Well fuck her, man!"

Bourgois grants that Gloria Kirschman may have had good intentions. "Reading between the lines of Primo's vilifying account, one suspects that she cared about the future of the bright, energetic high school dropout working for her," he allows. Nonetheless, Bourgois opines that the working relationship showed "institutionalized racism at work in how the professional service sector unconsciously imposes the requisites of Anglo, middle-class cultural capital." As proof, he repeats Primo's complaint that he had been forbidden to answer the telephone "because objectively a Puerto Rican street accent will discourage prospective clients and cause [the company] to lose money."

Perhaps it was Primo's accent that led to his banishment from the telephone. Then again, it might have been his penchant for profanity or his all-too-obvious hostility. "I used to look at her and want to kill her; wanted to burn her," he told Bourgois.[11] Maybe Kirschman overheard him calling her a ho and a bitch, and she was worried about what he might say to customers, or perhaps there was simply an office protocol that she wanted to enforce. I do not want to discount institutional racism as the potential root of the problem between Primo and Kirschman—there is certainly plenty of that in many offices—but there are other possible explanations as well.

Bourgois could not explore the alternatives, however, because (as far as we know) he did not talk to Kirschman or anyone else in a similar position. He did not interview any of Primo's coworkers to see if there was a different story, nor did he seek out any of the "thousands of East Harlem residents" who are "successfully employed [and who] work downtown and adapt to high-rise office culture." According to Bourgois, "48 percent of all males and 35 percent of females over 16" from East Harlem were "employed in officially reported jobs" during the years of his field work.[12] The number is depressingly low, about fifteen points below the citywide average, but it demonstrates that an accent is not an absolute impediment to straight employment, and an unhappy job experience may not always be attributable to racism.

In other words, Bourgois is arguing a case. Not unlike a trial lawyer, he sets out his theory and presents the witnesses who support it, while minimizing or discounting contrary evidence. He engages in a bit of "defensive direct" by describing Kirschman as a "well-meaning liberal," while still crediting Primo's description of her as "a cheap bitch."

Trial lawyers are advised to "bury" inconvenient or unhelpful facts in the middle of an examination (or argument), so that the fact-finder will have an opportunity to "make friends" with a witness before learning anything harmful or damaging. I advise my students to "give the judge or jury every possible reason to like your witness before offering anything that might have a contrary effect."[13] Bourgois does that too.

It is only on page 203—fifty pages beyond Primo's story of mistreatment by Kirschman—that are we are told of the "gang rapes" that Primo and his friends "used to organize" in abandoned buildings. Well before that revelation, we learn of Primo's ambition, aspirations, generosity, and resourcefulness, while his crimes are explained as reflective of his "oppositional identity."[14] Would Gloria Kirschman have appeared more sympathetic if she had been juxtaposed to Primo the serial rapist, rather than Primo the diligent but misunderstood worker?

This is not a criticism of Bourgois, but rather an observation about the nature of his method, which is not unusual in ethnography. To his credit, Bourgois lets us know at the outset that his book is an extended argument, with evidence marshaled to support his conclusions. More importantly, the gaps or inconsistencies in the story are apparent on its face, thus allowing a critical reader to recognize disparities and evaluate the strength of his claims. Although the evidence in *In Search of Respect* is selective, it is transparently selective. In a fairly unusual move for an ethnographer, Bourgois even tells us about evidence he omitted from his book. Over the course of a year, he collected "dozens of accounts and versions of [his subjects'] direct participation in sexual violence," but he provides only one extended and gut-wrenching description of "five or six guys" holding down and raping a seventeen-year-old girl. Bourgois also tape-recorded several rape survivors "to obtain alternative perspectives," but he did not include any of their accounts in the book. "I did not have the same kinds of long-term relationships with these individuals to allow for the detail and confidence of a meaningfully contextualized life-history interview or conversation," he says, without explaining why a life history would be necessary to relate the impact of a gang rape.[15]

We might wish that Bourgois had been more inclusive in his writing, or that he had tracked down more "disconfirming evidence," as the sociologist Annette Lareau puts it. Who knows what an ethnographic trial might have revealed about the telephone story if Gloria Kirschman had been called as a witness? And the reaction of a rape survivor would certainly have added to our understanding of Primo and his friends, even if it may have caused readers, as Bourgois recognizes, to become "disgusted and angry . . . and deny them a human face."[16] Nonetheless, we can still understand his commitment to a strongly argued, if one-sided, case.

A different sort of selective reporting—sometimes called the "file drawer problem"—poses a more difficult question in social science. In quantitative studies, this is most often accomplished by omitting negative, inconsistent, or non-confirming results while reporting only those data that support the researcher's conclusions.[17] In ethnography, a researcher will always be tempted to emphasize only the favorable evidence, to the exclusion of unhelpful or contrary facts. In every ethnographic project, as Duneier points out, "there are phenomena that are extremely inconvenient from the standpoint of the line of thinking or theory that has emerged from the fieldwork."[18] The omission of unfavorable evidence is extremely difficult to detect, but diligent research can sometimes reveal meaningful discrepancies.

Duneier himself uncovered contradictory evidence when he reviewed the findings in Eric Klinenberg's *Heat Wave*. In brief (and necessarily over-simplifying), Klinenberg had posited that differential death rates during Chicago's killer heat wave of 1995 had been the consequence of social conditions that varied from neighborhood to neighborhood. As proof, Klinenberg compared two adjacent communities, both poor but with different ethnic majorities. In predominantly African-American North Lawndale, there were nineteen heat-related deaths, for a rate of forty per 100,000 residents. In nearby South Lawndale, which was mainly Latino, only three people died, for a rate of four per 100,000. From these numbers, and follow-up interviews, Klinenberg arrived at a "broken spaces, broken families" theory of heat wave death.[19]

The conclusion "didn't seem right" to Duneier, who looked further into the data. He located a third adjacent neighborhood—predominantly white Archer Heights—that had suffered a far greater death rate of fifty-four per 100,000, notwithstanding its greater prosperity and social cohesion. Duneier thus criticized Klinenberg for his selection of neighborhoods, which seemed to have been chosen to prove a point about ethnicity and the local power structure. In fact, "we may have been looking at . . . a myth in *Heat Wave*," wrote Duneier.[20] (Klinenberg disagrees.[21])

Heat Wave identified the neighborhoods Klinenberg considered, and by extension the ones he excluded, thus allowing Duneier to challenge his conclusions. It is far more problematic when the underlying events in an ethnography are papered over or concealed by the author, and can only be discovered through secondary research.

RUNNING FROM POLICE

Alice Goffman's *On the Run* begins—on the first page of the first chapter—with a poignant story about two brothers in the Philadelphia neighborhood she calls 6th Street. "On quiet afternoons," writes Goffman, "Chuck would sometimes pass the time by teaching his twelve-year-old brother, Tim, how to run from the police."

"What you going to do when you hear the sirens?" Chuck asked.
"I'm out," his little brother replied.

Chuck finished the lesson by telling Tim that it was best to hide where nobody knew him. Their home was out of the question, because the police would be "tearing down that little door."

This vignette is central to Goffman's theory of over-policing, in which community members are routinely arrested for petty or meaningless offenses. Nearly everyone in her story is on probation or parole, or wanted on a warrant, and they are relentlessly hunted by police who use both fair means and foul to find them. Tim himself is on juvenile probation—having been unfairly convicted, according to Goffman, for riding in a stolen car—which makes it essential for him to avoid the cops. "So Chuck began teaching his little brother how to run from the police in earnest: how to spot undercover cars, how and where to hide, how to negotiate a police stop so that he didn't put himself or those around him at greater risk." Goffman admires Chuck's concern for his younger brother, and approves of the lesson in "dipping and dodging," which she believes to be a necessity for their survival.

But the narrative is radically incomplete. As Goffman knows—and as I have confirmed from newspaper stories, police reports, interviews, and court records—Tim's aversion to the police almost had devastating consequences in real life, although the full story is not disclosed in *On the Run*. Chuck was murdered on July 22, 2007, when he was standing outside a Chinese take-out joint in Philadelphia's Wynnefield neighborhood. Tim was standing at his brother's side when two rival gang members drew their guns and fired five or six rounds, one of which hit Chuck in the forehead. The killers ran, but not before Tim got a good look at them. According to Goffman, "Tim had seen the shooter from only a few feet away," and probably knew his name. Goffman's account of the shooting ends there, with no mention of the subsequent events—most of which were known to her prior to publication of *On the Run*—that eventually led to arrests, trial, and convictions for Chuck's murder. It was only by obtaining the contemporaneous police reports, and other records, that I have been able to complete the story.

When the police arrived, they saw Tim on the ground, holding his wounded brother in his arms with blood soaking his pants and shirt. As he had been taught, Tim took off running when he spotted the cops. Realizing that the teenager was a witness, the officers chased him, finally catching up after two blocks. Tim refused to cooperate, however, at first telling conflicting stories, and ultimately denying that he had even seen the shooting.

It took detectives five years of police work to track down Chuck's killers, during which time they got very little help from people in the neighborhood. From the beginning of the investigation, Goffman's friend "Mike"—who is a central character in *On the Run* and Goffman's mentor on 6th Street—invoked a "no snitching" ethos, and warned (or intimidated) people away from cooperating with the detectives investigating the case.[22] In the lobby of the hospital where Chuck had been taken, Mike told potential witnesses to leave without speaking to the police, and he continued to interfere with the investigation until the detectives stopped him. He later showed up in Chuck's hospital room when the police were interviewing Chuck's girlfriend. Once the witness saw Mike, she refused to talk any further. Goffman claims to have been present in the room when the detectives were there, but she does not mention Mike's intrusion.[23]

To this day, Tim has not given a formal statement about the killing, and he refused to testify at the trial of the two men who were eventually convicted of Chuck's murder. Although she claims herself to have "a pretty good idea" of the killer's identity, Goffman also declined to come forward with any information for the police. (*On the Run* mentions only one shooter, though in fact there were two.[24])

The lead detective on the case told me that it could have been solved much sooner if Goffman and others had been willing to provide helpful information. As it was, however, the accused killers remained at large for years, in part because Tim had learned his lessons too well.[25]

Running from the police, in Goffman's account, is an almost charming coming-of-age story, as one brother teaches another the art of survival in their cop-ridden neighborhood. There is another side to the story, however, in which the enforced norm of police avoidance may allow murderers to go free, no matter whom they killed. As Nikki Jones observed of other Philadelphia youth in similar circumstances, Tim and his friends were "deeply committed to a value system that they think is protective, but that . . . is also potentially destructive." Although Tim may have been adhering to the "code of the street," it was, as Elijah Anderson has observed, an ethic "that promises security while in fact it exacerbates violence and homicide rates on the inner-city streets."[26]

Throughout her discussion of Chuck's murder and its aftermath, Goffman omits or alters numerous facts that might otherwise be seen as reflecting well on the Philadelphia police. She portrays them as almost indifferent to Chuck's death—saying that they "rolled right past" her at the hospital, and "left the neighborhood" after a few days—while mentioning nothing of their years-long, and ultimately fruitful, investigation of the crime. Much of her narrative is contradicted by the police reports and court records, which were created when no one could have imagined that Chuck's murder would be a subject of a bestselling book about police oppression. No detective had an incentive to falsify his police report regarding the events in the hospital or to advance any particular account of the murder.

Goffman has explained that her "goal here wasn't to describe the crime and its legal aftermath—the goal was to explain what Chuck's death meant for his family and community during the years I knew them, and for me personally," which is another way of saying that she advanced her narrative by providing only a selective account of the events.[27] Thus, the police in *On the Run* are described as the constant source of "routine stops, searches, raids, and beatings," but virtually never as public servants or crime-solvers. In other words, Goffman purposely excluded what Duneier would describe as the inconvenient facts that had negative implications for her overarching theory.

In a trial, ethnographic or otherwise, the above discussion would be called an "impeachment by omission." An "omission" is the intentional elision of significant information that is essential to the completeness of the story. An "impeachment" casts doubt on the reliability of the witness or narrator, who chose to include only those facts that conveniently fit one version of the story.

On the Run is unique among urban ethnographies because it involves an identifiable murder, thus making definitive documentation available from police and other sources. I also looked into three shootings described in other books where there seemed to be enough data for investigation—meaning at least approximate dates and locations. To avoid my own selection bias, I discuss those cases below.

OTHER MURDERS

In *Renegade Dreams,* a moving and expressive study of life on the West Side of Chicago, Laurence Ralph tells of the years he spent in a neighborhood he calls "Eastwood," where he came to know members of a street gang he calls the "Divine Knights." The neighborhood is easily recognized as North Lawndale from the many identifiable details in the book; Ralph mentions, for example, that Sears moved its headquarters out of the neighborhood in 1974.[28]

In a chapter titled "Framing," Ralph begins with a long excerpt from his field notes, dated March 3, 2009:

This morning Mr. Otis tells me that the police are going to check the blue-light footage from his street to try and figure out why the eighteen-year-old Eastwood boy was shot last week. Mr. Otis paces in front of me, gripping the community newspaper, the *Eastwood Gazette*, which features a photograph of the slain teenager. Glancing at the paper, then shaking his head, Mr. Otis tells me the part of the story that is not in the newspaper. "Police say the boy ran from them"—he says, still pacing—"ducked and dodged through an alleyway when he saw them, right? When the officers cornered him, they say he pointed a gun at them, so they shot to kill. And believe me, they succeeded. But, get this, man: The kid was shot in the back. The boy's mama says he was scared stiff of the police. A couple days ago, before he was shot and all, she said some cops told the boy, 'We're gonna get you.' So, now she's trying to sue the city."[29]

The Chicago police have a long and disreputable history of unjustified shootings of young black men, and of covering up afterwards.[30] I thus expected to confirm this incident easily, given that Ralph provides the date of his field note, and says that the shooting occurred "last week." I searched official records for police-involved shootings in the second half of February 2009, but could find nothing even close to a fatal encounter on the West Side.[31] In fact, I found only one police-involved shooting of any sort during late February 2009, and it was on the South Side, far from Eastwood/Lawndale. The victim (or "subject," as he was called in the police report) was a nineteen-year-old black male, who was shot in the thumb by an off-duty officer, and was treated and released at Jackson Park Hospital.[32]

I therefore reviewed the reports for every fatal police shooting in the year preceding Ralph's field note, and not one of them occurred in North Lawndale, or anywhere near Mr. Otis's street on the West Side. Two African-American teenagers were killed by police the previous August, but both were on the South Side.[33] There is also a late June 2008 report of a teenager shot in the back, but it was a male Hispanic on the Northwest Side, three or four miles from North Lawndale.[34] The other fatalities were all older "subjects" in different neighborhoods.[35]

It is always a good idea to doubt police accounts of their own shootings, but it seemed almost impossible that they could suppress the existence of a fatality—especially one that appeared to have been reported in the community press. I therefore contacted Ralph to ask if I had missed something. He explained that "the actual shooting had taken place a couple of years prior," and not the previous week as stated in *Renegade Dreams*. The community newspaper article had been about a neighborhood protest aimed at the Independent Police Review Authority, rather than the shooting itself.[36] The relevant issue of the community newspaper (presumably the *North Lawndale Community News*) is missing from the archive, but I found a report of the demonstration in the *Chicago Sun-Times*, which provided the date of the shooting, the block in North Lawndale where it occurred, and the justification claimed by the police.[37]

Mr. Otis was right about the family's planned lawsuit. The case went to trial in 2013, and the family won a jury award of $8.5 million. Testimony indicated that the cops had planted the gun that was found next to the teenager's body, although there does not appear to have been any evidence that he was shot in the back or that he had earlier been threatened by the police. It took the jury less than three hours to reach its verdict.[38]

I was unable, however, to confirm two murders described by Sudhir Venkatesh in *Off the Books*, which is set in a Chicago neighborhood called "Maquis Park," but which is revealed in the endnotes as the Grand Boulevard area around 47th Street and King Drive. In February 2002, according to Venkatesh, a hustler named "Babycake Jackson" was sleeping in an "abandoned building" when he was shot twenty-two times because he refused to continue acting as a lookout for a drug dealer. A review of Chicago Police Department homicide records, however, locates only two late-night murders in the relevant neighborhood that February, but neither was in an abandoned building, or even indoors. (There was one Chicago murder in an abandoned building that month, but it was a woman who was strangled to death about two miles from "Maquis Park.")

In the second case, which is said to have occurred in "late fall" 2003, Venkatesh's main informant, Big Cat, was murdered in a drive-by shooting "in a small park" in the neighborhood. According to police records, there were no outdoor murders in the "Maquis Park" vicinity in the late fall. I had hoped to fact-check Venkatesh's statement that no arrests were made for either killing, but *Off the Books* does not provide sufficient information for me to dig more deeply, and Venkatesh did not respond to my multiple requests for additional details.[39]

Ralph's incorrect date is an understandable (and truly minor) error, which I was able to correct when he graciously provided me with the victim's real name.[40] The discrepancies in Venkatesh's account may be attributable to the ethnographic convention of extensive anonymization, in which not only names but also dates, locations, and details are changed for the "protection" of sources. I do not find this rationale convincing, precisely because it impedes verification and raises questions about reliability, as discussed in Chapter Seven. Venkatesh criticizes the Chicago police for oppression and fecklessness, so the shooting stories provide support for his overall theories. His general observations about the police are accurate, in my opinion, but that is not a good reason to obscure the underlying facts.

Goffman's case, on the other hand, is extreme, and I was able to obtain the omitted facts only because murders create extensive paper trails. It is therefore impossible to know whether, or to what extent, other ethnographers have also suppressed information that contradicts or undermines their essential theories. My assumption, though, is that nearly all have told their stories in good faith, and many have made a point of including at least some contrary evidence. Speaking as an attorney, however, I am aware that the temptation to advocacy—on behalf of a client or a grounded theory—is ever-present, and it is never more powerful than when there can be no challenge or rebuttal. From time to time, this may even result in reporting rumors as fact, to be addressed in the next chapter.

6

Rumors and Folklore

RUMORS APPEAR TO BE impossible to avoid in ethnography. Every community has its own set of beliefs—some of which are anchored in fact, some of which are folk tales—and it is the task of the researcher to discover and describe them. Careful ethnographers will make rigorous efforts to separate rumor from reality, especially in circumstances where there is a likelihood of overlap or confusion. It is not unheard of, however, for rumors to be presented as statements of fact, particularly when they tend to reinforce the author's theory. Although this can be relatively benign as a passing comment, there are circumstances in which the validation of rumors can be positively harmful.

In *Whispers on the Color Line: Rumor and Race in America*, Gary Alan Fine and Patricia Turner define rumors as "truth claims" based on plausibility but lacking authentication. "The power of rumor is that it is seen as something that could have happened" according to the "cultural logic" of the group among which it spreads.[1] Some rumors have bases in fact, while others amount to urban legends that are "true-sounding but utterly false."[2]

As Fine and Turner explain, different communities are disposed to believe different rumors, based upon their particular experiences. In many African-American communities, for example, it was once accepted that the Ku Klux Klan had purchased a fast-food chain featuring fried chicken. The corresponding phenomenon in affluent white neighborhoods was a story about a planned invasion by minority street gangs. Neither rumor was remotely true, but both were widely credited because they reinforced longstanding fears and were derived from pre-existing attitudes.[3] In any case, as Jeffrey Pfeffer and Robert Sutton explain, "Half-truths are more difficult to debunk than total nonsense because arguments can always be mustered about times and places they are correct."[4]

Common rumors can be useful to illustrate community attitudes, so long as they are clearly identified. Mitchell Duneier, for example, observed that his African-American informants were "very cynical about the motives of the powerful institutions in their society," and were thus susceptible to stories about control and manipulation by secret forces such as "the government" and "the CIA." Duneier recounts rumors that Martin Luther King had been "assassinated in a government conspiracy," that the Gulf War had been "an effort to eliminate the race by placing a disproportionate number of young black men on the front lines," and that the University of Chicago was able to suppress the news of murders committed in the Hyde Park neighborhood.[5]

No thoughtful ethnographer would ever give credence to the rumors of Klan-owned restaurants or an imminent street gang invasion—patently false as they are—other than to illustrate their subjects' attitudes or beliefs. Sometimes, however, more subtle rumors and legends do become embedded in ethnography when they are used, probably unthinkingly, to advance an overall narrative.

BENIGN RUMORS

In *$2 a Day*, Kathryn Edin and Luke Shaefer tell the important stories of eight families who struggle at the very edge of survival, attempting to make ends meet with almost no cash income. As the authors explain, even the poorest of the poor have a "high level of attachment to work in the formal economy," and they often go to extraordinary lengths in their attempts to obtain steady jobs with predictable hours. Their efforts, however, are frequently undermined by factors such as ill health, inadequate education, domestic violence, unstable housing, alcohol or drug abuse, lack of interviewing skills, and sometimes volatile temperaments. "They've had their share of hard luck; they've made their share of bad moves; they have other personal liabilities; [and] their kin pull them down as often as they lift them up." One recurring problem is the need to care for children, especially when they are sick or very young, which often prevents parents from meeting work obligations. Edin and Shaefer's central theme is that "the $2-a-day poor envision themselves first and foremost as workers," but it is overwhelmingly difficult for them to find and hold jobs, given the complicated, and often chaotic, nature of their lives and the lives of their children.[6]

One of Edin and Shaefer's exemplary subjects is Susan Brown, a young African-American woman who lives with her husband and infant daughter, along with several other family members, in a crumbling house "deep on the South Side of Chicago." There is seldom enough food for everyone, and the canned infant formula Susan receives from a government program is not enough to last the entire month. To explain her difficult circumstances, Susan told Edin and Shaefer that "a lot of things don't go my way," beginning with an unplanned pregnancy during her senior year of high school. She was forced to drop out "when the pregnancy became high risk," eventually delivering a stillborn child in her eighth month.[7]

Susan was determined to go back to school. "I kept saying I was never gonna get pregnant again," she told Edin and Shaefer. She completed her GED and enrolled in a community college, hoping to earn an associate's degree in early childhood education. Before she could finish, however, she became pregnant again, and her plans for the future were derailed. According to Edin and Shaefer, "antibiotics she had been prescribed had apparently neutralized her birth control." In Susan's words, "They told me, 'You have to read the packets.' But who reads the packets?" Susan's unintended pregnancy had prevented her from following through on her career objectives, which supports Edin and Shaefer's general narrative of the working poor as resolute people who are buffeted by unkind fate. "My luck sucks," said Susan Brown, as she explained how she became pregnant.[8]

According to both Planned Parenthood and the American College of Obstetricians and Gynecologists, however, the commonly prescribed antibiotics do not diminish the effectiveness of hormonal birth control such as the pill, despite rumors to the contrary.[9] It seems likely that the coincidence of taking antibiotics, and the prevalence of the rumor, allowed Susan to rationalize her unplanned pregnancy in her interview for $2 a Day. Perhaps she viewed it with some embarrassment, perhaps she assumed that Edin and Shaefer would think less of her if she had been inattentive to contraception, or perhaps there is another good reason for her presentation of self. In any case, antibiotic interference would have provided a more comfortable explanation than forgetfulness, and Susan evidently wanted to believe—and wanted Edin and Shaefer to believe—that she had become pregnant only because of a misprescribed medication.

There is no harm in accepting a subject's explanation of her pregnancy, especially given Edin and Shaefer's nonjudgmental sympathy for their informants.[10] No one reading *$2 a Day* is likely to further spread the rumor about antibiotics and contraception, much less forego prescription medications of one sort or the other. I have used this example only to show that rumors are everywhere—even in exceptionally well-sourced books such as *$2 a Day*—and they do not come with labels attached. It is otherwise of small importance in this instance, but repeating rumors can be extremely dangerous in other circumstances.

HARMFUL RUMORS

In *On the Run*, Alice Goffman tells us that many young male residents of 6th Street believe that it is risky to go to the hospital, even when in dire need of medical care, lest they be arrested on outstanding warrants. This belief has serious consequences, which can be seen in Goffman's own harrowing stories of young men who suffer greatly rather than be taken to the nearest emergency room. One of her subjects, whom she calls "Alex," had been pistol-whipped in a robbery, leaving him with a lacerated face, broken jaw, and missing teeth. Nonetheless, he refused to go to the hospital because he was on parole at the time and had been out past his curfew. On another occasion, a fourteen-year-old boy had broken his arm when running from the police. Rather than take him to the emergency room, the boy's mother located a hospital janitor who, according to Goffman, arrived with a bagful of medical supplies, including a syringe with "some kind of anesthetic." The janitor stitched up the wound and set the boy's arm, while Goffman herself turned up the radio to drown out his screams. Their fears were warranted, according to Goffman. In Alex's words, "I'm not just going to check into emergency and there come the cops."[11]

Black communities may be uniquely susceptible to medical rumors because they have "been ill served by the medical establishment" for decades—the Tuskegee Experiment having been the most infamous and despicable example of callous treatment of African Americans by mainstream physicians.[12] Corresponding rumors therefore have an inherent ring of truth, such as the stories, related by Fine and Turner, that the AIDS virus had been invented by white scientists in order to decimate the black community. Duneier heard the same story from some of his informants, who believed that the AIDS virus was "created in a government or CIA laboratory" as part of an attempt "at genocide."[13] Another common rumor held that the Centers for Disease Control (sometimes in cahoots with the Klan) had been responsible for the Atlanta child murders of the early 1980s.[14]

Medical rumors can be especially dangerous. According to Fine and Turner, many black AIDS patients once refused to take AZT, which was the most effective HIV drug at the time, because of a rumor that it actually accelerated the rate at which the disease developed among African Americans. This was "particularly tragic for pregnant women, among whom research has found that taking AZT can reduce the baby's chance of being HIV-positive."[15]

Goffman's Philadelphia hospital story has all of the same attributes, with the additionally credible feature of overbearing police. It has also led to similar results, with young black men allowing broken arms, fractured jaws, and deep lacerations to be treated by amateurs because they do not trust emergency room doctors. That is a steep price to pay for believing a rumor.

Goffman repeatedly assures her readers, however, that these gruesome measures are really necessary because hospitals are indeed perilous places for black men on the run. "To round up enough young men to meet their informal quotas and satisfy their superiors," she writes, "the police wait outside hospitals serving poor Black communities and run the IDs of the men walking inside." She describes "the cops who crowd the local emergency room and run through their database the names of Black young men walking in the door." Claiming to have seen it herself, she calls this the "standard practice in the hospitals serving the Black community." Goffman thus endorses self-treatment as a necessary alternative. To this day, she says, one of her subjects "still finds it difficult to breathe through his nose and speaks with a muffled lisp," but at least he did not risk prison by seeking medical attention in an emergency room.[16]

Goffman has evidently related an urban legend, rather than something she truly observed about law enforcement conduct. While there is no doubt that young men are sometimes arrested in hospitals—thus tethering the rumor to a plausible "truth claim"—my research has located no person other than Goffman who has ever reported seeing a police checkpoint at the hospital door. Routine police screening of patient lists, moreover, would violate HIPAA, the federal medical privacy law.

No trial lawyer would accept Goffman's claim in the absence of corroboration. I therefore contacted every hospital that plausibly fit Goffman's description of "serving the Black community" of West Philadelphia, and they unanimously denied sharing patient or visitor information with the police.

In an interview, the director of security for Jefferson Hospital said "it is certainly not our practice to release names of patients for warrant checks," adding that Philadelphia police officers do not hang out in front of the hospital to check anyone's identification. If that happened, he would "call their captain" to tell them not to do it. Hahnemann University Hospital responded to my inquiry by email, stating that "It is not the practice or policy of Hahnemann University Hospital to share patient or visitor information" with police. The University of Pennsylvania Hospitals likewise confirmed in writing that they do not routinely "share patient or visitor information with police," other than to cooperate in a specific "ongoing investigation." Mercy Philadelphia Hospital made a similar statement: "We do not release patient names or provide external parties access to our patient lists. If the police present to our hospital with a warrant for a patient, they are not allowed to execute that warrant until the patient is discharged and no longer in our facility. In addition, we do not provide police with visitors' names." Finally, Temple University Hospital replied that it "does not engage in the conduct described in [On the Run] nor does it allow such conduct on its property." In addition, the Children's Hospital of Philadelphia (CHOP) provided this statement to Philadelphia Magazine: "No information is shared beyond hospital security. CHOP is not aware of any instance in which representatives of any law enforcement agency have requested access to our electronic visitor database."[17]

For good measure, I also contacted Everett Gillison, a former Philadelphia deputy mayor and director of public safety, who served as a public defender for 28 years before joining the administration of Mayor Michael Nutter in 2008. I provided Gillison, who is African American, with the relevant quote from *On the Run*, to which he replied, "The passage about hospitals is NOT in any way a standard practice . . . . It is not a practice, period."[18]

Is it possible, as one young sociologist suggested to me, that the police and the five hospitals are all lying? After all, we have seen repeated incidents of egregious police cover-ups in recent years, and some hospitals have been known to violate both law and procedures. Still, a social scientist ought to be able to distinguish things that are somehow imaginable from things that are truly real. Invoking a faint possibility—"everyone else is lying"—is not convincing in either law or social science.

In a trial, we would say that the burden is on the proponent of the evidence to substantiate her claim—which in this case would be that the hospitals of Philadelphia have conspired with police to arrest young men rather than treat them, and to deny it afterward. If that were indeed the case, we might expect at least one doctor, nurse, or ambulance attendant to come forward, given the difficulty of keeping such conspiracies secret over a period of years. But that has never happened. Other ethnographers have studied the African-American communities of Philadelphia, including the hospitals, but no one has mentioned seeing a police cordon at an emergency room entrance.[19]

It does seem that certain informants told Goffman about their fear of hospitals, which was real although in most cases needless. But it is the job of a social scientist to dispel dangerous rumors, not to spread them.

WELFARE RUMORS

Poor people are justifiably mistrusting of public agencies, often as the result of mistreatment and other unhappy personal experiences. Sometimes, however, stories metastasize into rumors that take on lives of their own. Such a rumor might have its origin in a few occurrences or a long-defunct regulation, to be repeated for generations until it eventually makes its way into academic writing. Because such rumors are highly plausible—who would doubt the hard-heartedness or irrationality of a bureaucracy?—they are understandably accepted by ethnographers who hear them from informants.

Here is an example from *Promises I Can Keep: Why Poor Women Put Motherhood Before Marriage*, by Kathryn Edin and Maria Kefalas. In a section on paternal responsibility, the authors observe that Pennsylvania has one of the "toughest child-support enforcement systems in the nation," in which a delinquent father can lose his driver's license and a substantial percentage of his wages. Then they add,

> Couples who remain together usually manage to avoid child support, unless she claims welfare and is thus forced to participate so the state can reimburse itself for her benefits . . . . If he doesn't pay, the police will visit him on his job and harass him in full view of his employer and coworkers.[20]

It is true, as noted in Chapter Three, that the public welfare agency will pursue fathers for reimbursement of child support payments. It is not the case, however, that police will routinely enforce the obligation by job-site harassment. I confirmed this with two experienced child-support lawyers in Philadelphia. One of them said, "The police absolutely do not enforce child support orders and/or show up at the workplace of people who have child support arrears." The other explained that a "bench warrant" may be issued if a father is found in contempt for non-payment (or more likely, for failure to appear for a court date), but it is "rare that anyone follows through on bench warrants and it only comes up if the payor is picked up on another offense." It is certainly possible that some men may have been arrested at their jobs for non-payment of support, leading to the spread of a story throughout the community. In reality, though, such arrests are practically nonexistent. As one of the lawyers put it, "outstanding warrants for failure to appear for family court child support proceedings are not exactly top priority given all the people who fail to appear in criminal court."[21]

More widespread is the rumor that public assistance agencies police the romantic lives of women on welfare. There was once truth to this story, but it is long outdated. Nonetheless, it continues to turn up in ethnographic writing.

In his classic ethnography *Tally's Corner*, first published in 1967, Elliot Liebow quoted an unmarried mother named Lena who explained that she had not applied for Aid to Dependent Children because "you can't live your own life" if you accept public welfare. "You can't have any boyfriends or nothing," she said, "and I sure like my boys." Liebow added an explanatory footnote:

> A reference to Washington's "man-in-the-house" rule which excludes women from receiving Aid to Dependent Children if there is an employable male in the household. This grotesque paternalism was enforced by special investigators who made unannounced searches— at all hours of the day and night—for evidence of a "man in the house." Thus were "cheaters" weeded out; that is, undeserving children whose mothers continued to want love or sex even though they had received a check from the Department of Welfare.[22]

Liebow's description of the welfare system was accurate at the time of his field work, which was conducted in Washington, D.C., in 1962–63. In 1968, however, the U.S. Supreme Court held that the rule—called MARS, or "man assuming the role of spouse"—was invalid under federal law. In a powerful opinion, Chief Justice Earl Warren stated that "immorality and illegitimacy should be dealt with through rehabilitative measures rather than measures that punish dependent children, and that protection of such children is the paramount goal of AFDC." The ruling applied to every state, as well as the District of Columbia, and it prohibited the "den[ial] of assistance solely on the basis of the substitute father regulation." Because only a child's actual father (biological or adoptive) could be legally compelled to provide support, the income or presence of a non-father could not be used to terminate welfare payments. In other words, the man-in-the-house rule, which had never even applied to transient boyfriends, was defunct throughout the United States.[23]

Nonetheless, the image of welfare snoops as sexual police continued to exercise a strong grip on the public imagination. The MARS rule was a major plot point in the 1974 film *Claudine*, set in Harlem and starring James Earl Jones and Diahann Carroll.[24] More significantly for our purposes, it was alluded to in Carol Stack's widely admired ethnography *All Our Kin* (also published in 1974).[25]

Stack's inclusion of the man-in-the-house rule may account for its appearance in much more contemporary ethnographies. Sudhir Venkatesh repeats it in *Off the Books* (2006) and *Gang Leader for a Day* (2008).[26] Most recently, he provides a seemingly contemporary version of the welfare mother's dilemma in *Floating City* (2013). Venkatesh tells the story of his encounter with a group of young Manhattan philanthropists—the children of business moguls and investment bankers—who were interested in helping the disadvantaged. They sought Venkatesh's advice on how to do it effectively, and he decided to take them "to Harlem for a crash course in living poor." Noting that "they had all been social science majors," Venkatesh "assumed they were already familiar with the basics of low-income life—a painful error, it turned out."

Their first stop was the home of "Silvia McCombs," a single mother of three. Following introductions, Venkatesh told Silvia that "we've been reading about bureaucracies. You know, welfare offices, health clinics, caseworkers who make sure you aren't making money and getting rich off welfare. These guys don't understand the 'man in the house' rule."

"I don't understand it either," replied Silvia. "It's *bullshit*." She explained the difficulty of living on welfare to the naive trust-funders. "I spend every other minute I have trying to scrounge up a little more money, babysitting and cleaning and helping people out—all off the books, of course, so I'm committing a crime too, just to keep from losing my welfare. Just like I commit a crime if I dare to have a man stay."[27]

It is hard to understand why Venkatesh led off by asking his informant about a rule that had been invalidated forty years earlier, or how Silvia McCombs had even heard about it (unless she'd been prompted beforehand). Inexplicably, Venkatesh does not correct her misimpression—or his young friends' or his readers'—that a New York welfare mother is currently in jeopardy if her boyfriend spends the night. Not only had the U.S. Supreme Court long ago invalidated the MARS rule, but a federal district court, in 1969, prohibited the New York welfare department from making any home visits at all, so there was no possible way that McCombs could ever have experienced a threatening intrusion. According to an experienced New York welfare rights lawyer, "by 1969, there was no risk that having a boyfriend stay overnight would be a problem, or even discovered."[28] If McCombs actually lived in fear of a nonexistent rule, she was held captive by a rumor from which Venkatesh ought to have released her.

Welfare recipients experience many difficulties that deserve the attention of young philanthropists. Chief among these is the impact of the 1996 Personal Responsibility and Work Opportunity Reconciliation Act, which President Bill Clinton touted as putting an end to "welfare as we know it." Following the reform, assistance to families with children became temporary and in many cases virtually impossible to obtain, as Edin and Shaefer cogently explain in a chapter titled "Welfare is Dead."[29] In contrast, the MARS rule endures today only as a dim memory, of historical interest but with no present effect on anyone's life.

FOLKLORE

Many communities share stories of iconic individuals, some of whom are real and some of whom exist only, or mainly, in myth. The legendary exploits of these characters can tell us much about the aspirations, values, or fears of the community under study, even though fact cannot always be distinguished from fiction. Law has little use for such folklore, other than perhaps to provide the context for someone's state of mind, but it can be significant in ethnography, so long as it is clearly identified. It is always revealing to learn the sorts of people who are idolized or scorned by one's informants.

In *Slim's Table*, Duneier uses the story of an astute judge to illustrate his subjects' respect for community traditions. One of the regulars explained the outcome of a case in which an elderly woman was accused of hitting her grandson:

> This little social worker had a grandmother in front of the judge, who was black. And she said, "She beat him unmercifully." She wanted the court to take the kid from the grandmother. And the judge said to the grandmother, "What did the child do?" Grandma said, "I came out from the bathroom and I caught him with his

hands in my purse." "Say what?" said the judge. "Case dismissed."
The little social worker was enraged. "This is brutality." Judge said,
"You do not understand the black experience. You do not steal from
your grandmother. That is the one looking after you. And he steals
from his grandmother? I ought to put him in jail. Case dismissed."[30]

Juvenile court proceedings in Illinois are closed to the public, so
Duneier's informant could not have had first-hand knowledge of the
event. Nor did he even claim to have heard about it from the people
involved, whom he characterized only as "a grandmother" and a "kid."
Most likely, he heard the story from someone who had heard it from
someone else, perhaps ultimately traceable to a lawyer or bailiff in juvenile court. While it is hardly implausible that a Cook County judge
chewed out an overzealous social worker, it is likely that the incident
had been exaggerated through its retellings. By the time the story got
to Valois, it would have been embedded in local folklore, thus being
more significant for the respect attributed to the black judge and grandmother than for the truth or untruth of the dismissed child abuse case.

In a complementary example, Randol Contreras, in *The Stickup Kids*,
asks a subject named "Pablo" about the limits of acceptable violence.
Pablo himself made a living by robbing and torturing drug dealers, which
sometimes involved cutting off someone's finger or burning him with a
hot iron in order to get information about a hidden stash.[31] Even so, Pablo
did not consider himself "an animal," which was a description he reserved
for others. "Who would you call an animal?" Contreras once asked him.

> There used to be this guy called Bobo. Gus used to hang with him.
> That nigga used to just shoot people for the hell of it. If he killed
> them, he killed them, whatever-whatever. That's the type of nigga
> who just didn't give a fuck . . . . Like Sammy the Bull, he's an ani-
> mal. That nigga killed like eighteen murders *[sic]*, bodies, bro. He's
> a snitch and all, but he was an animal, ha-ha. You know people like
> that. They just got bodies and to them it's just like breathin' to kill
> somebody, you know.[32]

Bobo, or someone like him, is probably a real person. But his exploits—
related by Gus, and not seen by Pablo—seem at least partly mythical.

He is invoked as a foil by Pablo, who uses violence as an instrument, and only as much as necessary to accomplish his goal. An animal, on the other hand, kills people "for the hell of it." Whatever the truth of Bobo's wanton shootings, the story provides us with meaningful insight into Pablo's self-regard.[33]

Another of Contreras's torturer-subjects regarded Bobo as a role model rather than a foil. Neno described himself as an animal:

> I mean, people say that to me, you know. The way they see me doin' my job when I go to do that. People say, 'Nigga's a animal. Nigga's crazy. I abuse those niggas [victims]. I grab those niggas, 'Get on the floor motherfucka!' Niggas be like, 'This nigga's a animal.'

Contreras points out, however, that Neno was projecting a violent persona that was inconsistent with his actual reputation and behavior, in which he was at best a secondary figure in the torture-robberies. Thus, his self-image as someone "brutal, chaotic, a heart like a stone" was reinforced by reference to a figure who really did, or was said to, act that way.[34]

In *The Con Men*, Terry Williams and Trevor Milton report on various hustlers who operate in New York City, including those who fleece unsuspecting tourists in the Canal Street commercial district. "This location is begging to vacuum money out of people's pockets," said an informant, whom they called Daniel, adding that "Everyone's got a hustle. You just have to create the need." Rich tourists were the easiest to "slam," he explained, meaning to sell them something at an inflated price by making it seem like a bargain. "Study people. Start up some conversation and find out what makes them feel pleasure, then treat him special. Boom! I got you."[35]

Daniel told the story of a man named "Mr. Badesh," whom he called a "hotshot European tourist," who showed up in an electronics store with money to spend. Recognizing a mark when he saw one, the store owner called in his "slam team," whose job it was to separate Mr. Badesh from his funds with "props, bait, and distraction." Eventually, a combination of trickery, flattery, and alcohol led to the purchase of $350,000 worth of cameras, watches, video equipment, and other gadgets. The owner had to call three cabs just to get the stuff back to Mr. Badesh's hotel, but that was not even the best part of the slam.

So the owner knows that Mr. Badesh is flying out of New York the next afternoon. So before this guy can sober up and figure out what just happened, the owner shuts down the store for the rest of the day and then shuts it down the entire next day . . . . So when Mr. Badesh shows up the next morning, the gates are down, and he's stuck with that stuff. And what's he going to do, call the police? He has a receipt saying that he spent $350,000.

The story, told in a conspiratorial whisper, has all the signs of an urban legend. The "owner" is anonymous, "Mr. Badesh" is a generic European, the store is unnamed, the goods are unspecified, and the events took place long in the past. Given the nature of the merchandise sold on Canal Street, it is hard to imagine that $350,000 worth could fit into three cabs, let alone be taken home on a passenger flight. And why close the shop in any case, given that the owner had proof of the sale? Of course, there is no mention of Mr. Badesh's method of payment. If it had been by check, then closing the store would not have prevented him from stopping payment. Likewise if it had been by credit card—although it is doubtful that even preferred clients had $350,000 credit limits in those days. Or did Mr. Badesh walk around lower Manhattan with an enormous wad of cash? It would have taken a fifteen-inch stack of hundred-dollar bills to amount to $350,000.[36] Daniel, an admitted con man, knew enough to deflect the authors' skepticism. "That was back in the day, though," he said. "Write that one down."[37]

However much truth there was in Daniel's tale—perhaps the inebriated tourist spent $3,500 or $35,000—the story is still a valuable illustration of the con man's larcenous heart. He revels in the extravagant slam, including the employment of a team whose "job is to roam around on Canal Street until they are called" into action. And he takes special pleasure in the ultimate humiliation of the mark, who shows up at a gated storefront in the cold light of day. When it comes to insight into Daniel's own character, self-image, and aspirations, there is no better exemplar than the story of the easily cheated Mr. Badesh.

Nicole Gonzalez Van Cleve tells a far more sympathetic story in *Crook County*, about a "mythical figure" in the criminal defense bar:

One private attorney warned me about a seasoned public defender who committed suicide and became a cautionary tale. The devout Catholic filled his bathroom sink with holy water and slit his wrists because the burden of defending was too much to handle. Tragically, and poignantly, his family found a prayer card for Saint Jude, the patron saint of lost causes and cases, floating in the red water.[38]

Like many such myths, this one is partially grounded in fact, although the most poignant details were evidently added in the course of successive retellings. A seasoned Cook County public defender did commit suicide in the early 1990s. I spoke to one of his close friends and colleagues in the public defender's office, who happened also to have attended parochial high school with him. My informant confirmed that the deceased had indeed been a devout Catholic, married with four children. He was a stalwart on the "murder task force," who was a conscientious advocate with a "strong commitment to his clients." The rest of the story, however, is inaccurate. The man had suffered depression for many years, and his suicide—which was by hanging—had not been "job related" according to his friends and family. There was no sink full of holy water, no slit wrists, and no bloody prayer card.[39]

It is easy to understand how the true story would metamorphose into the cautionary tale recounted by the attorney to Van Cleve. Public defenders and other defense lawyers are pushed around every day in the Cook County criminal courts, by judges, by prosecutors, and even by sheriffs who hold "disobedient defense attorneys in lockup, humiliating them in front of their colleagues, [and] preventing them from seeing their clients by lying or creating undue barriers." In that atmosphere, "fear breeds paralysis and then perhaps shame."[40] Defense lawyers thus search for heroes, such as the intrepid defenders who have been able to win trials against the odds, and they also need martyrs in the form of colleagues who have actually given their lives in the cause. As one longtime public defender told me, "there are guys spilling their blood for their clients" every day in the Cook County courts.[41] There is not much distance between figurative blood in the courtroom and the legendary blood of a suicidal colleague.

Van Cleve sets an example for other ethnographers by plainly identifying the tragic public defender as a mythical figure. His fate, however much embellished, obviously exerts a powerful influence on other defense lawyers and perhaps even on prosecutors and judges. The precise details of the story are thus less important than the faith people have in it, which is something that Van Cleve makes clear in her exposition. In other words, she separates myth from fact, and keeps each in its proper place.

Law has little use for folklore, except in narrow and unusual circumstances. Ethnography, on the other hand, can benefit from the exploration of rumors and legends, but that should not relieve an author from the obligation of distinguishing between myth and reality. Sometimes, unfortunately, the convention of anonymity results in a troubling confusion of the realms, which will be covered in the next chapter.

7

Anonymity

ANYONE WHO HAS EVER been in a courtroom—or has seen a lawyer show on television—will recognize the opening line in virtually every direct examination: "Please state your name." With only a few seldom-used exceptions, witnesses at trial are required to identify themselves as the first step in establishing their credibility. A witness who refused to provide his or her name would be mistrusted; a witness who lied about it would be subject to perjury.[1]

Almost every problem we have seen in the preceding chapters is compounded by anonymity. When all identities are thoroughly masked, it becomes nearly impossible to separate reliable informants from storytellers and rumor-spreaders, much less to determine whether the author has omitted or distorted essential information. Nonetheless, it is standard practice in ethnography to conceal the identities of research participants by using pseudonyms for people and locales, as well as by changing personal characteristics, altering facts, and rearranging or eliding time sequences. Anonymization of human subjects is generally thought to be required by federal regulations and university institutional review boards (IRBs)—although that may not actually be the case—and the assignment of pseudonyms has therefore been relatively uncontroversial.[2]

At some point in the introduction or appendix to nearly every ethnography, there is an almost obligatory reference to anonymization—either with or without an explanation of the reason. Randol Contreras's subjects resorted to torture and mutilation in their drug robberies, so it seems obvious that he "used pseudonyms to protect them all" from arrests or "drug dealer retaliation." Even so, he discloses that his field site was the High Bridge neighborhood in the South Bronx and provides "character descriptions" based on his personal knowledge, adding, "That, I hope, is enough."[3] In contrast, Shamus Khan tells us only that he "changed every student name" in his study of St. Paul's School, though perhaps the necessity is evident from the fact that his subjects were minors and he was a teacher.[4] Nicole Gonzalez Van Cleve says that "protecting the anonymity of those described in this book—be they attorneys, judges, or defendants—is imperative," which she extends even to events that occurred in open court. Thus, Van Cleve does not name the judge who berated a defendant "in a manner so harsh it [resembled] domestic abuse," even though he certainly deserved to be exposed as a bully.[5] In most cases, however, anonymity is simply said to be "necessary for the approval of universities' Human Subjects Committees."[6]

The renaming of subjects is seldom questioned among ethnographers, although, as we will see, it is not actually required in every case by university protocols. Other commonly used forms of masking can be even more problematic, as many ethnographers disguise their research sites and some also alter "dates and ages and other characteristics, as well as the details of particular events and who was present for them."[7] The result of such extreme anonymization can be a "pseudo-generalizability" that deprives readers of "information that *they* consider crucial for independently evaluating the ethnographer's analysis."[8]

NAMES

The use of fictitious names has long been the default approach in urban ethnography, dating back at least to Whyte's *Street Corner Society* and Drake and Cayton's *Black Metropolis*. Some ethnographers have lately challenged the basic assumption of anonymity—beginning with names—on the ground that it is not always necessary for the protection of subjects, and it may even be harmful to their perceived self-interest.

According to Colin Jerolmack and Alexandra Murphy, "masking is a *convention*" that may speed IRB approval of ethnography projects, but it is not "an *ethical necessity* in every case from a university IRB's perspective."[9] In other words, pseudonyms need not be employed mechanically, but rather according to the needs of the situation. While some research subjects may benefit from or require anonymity for their own well-being, others would not be harmed by the use of their real names—and some would even prefer it if given the option.[10]

In courtroom trials, it is often said that jurors cannot decide what to believe until they have first decided whom to believe. Consequently, the personalization of witnesses is a crucial first step in building a credible case. The same ought to be true in ethnography, but the pervasive use of pseudonyms threatens to reduce individuals to types, or even stereotypes. While some characters are well drawn and stand out in clear relief, others may appear as stick figures and some are in fact composites (acknowledged or otherwise; discussed below). Although every author insists that all essential information has been provided, there is no good way for a reader to be sure. Moreover, the author's conception of importance may differ from a reader's. We see this in courtroom trials as well, where a seemingly minor witness, as far as the lawyers are concerned, may turn out to be outcome-determinative for the jury.

The use of pseudonyms (or the omission of names) can prevent re-interviews or re-investigations in situations where facts may be in doubt. As Mitchell Duneier has pointed out, the ethnographic method succeeds by "finding *actual* people whose lives correspond to the theories that sociologists employ to explain the social world," which cannot easily be done when facing fictitious or undisclosed identities.[11] Or as Harvard's Christopher Winship told *Slate*, "It makes it really hard to verify—you don't even know if the people exist," adding, "the discipline thinks it's fine and that's probably totally wrong."[12]

We can be confident that ethnography's fictional names generally correspond to real people. Nonetheless, masking can raise unresolvable problems of verification, even when several ethnographers have explored the same terrain. In his 1999 classic *Code of the Street*, Elijah Anderson devotes a chapter to "The Mating Game" among young African Americans in Philadelphia. "Each sexual encounter," he observes, "generally has a winner and a loser," in which "the girls dream of being carried off by a Prince Charming" while the boys "desire either sex without commitment or babies without responsibility for them." Anderson continues,

To the young man the woman becomes, in the most profound sense, a sexual object. Her body and mind are the object of a sexual game, to be won for his personal aggrandizement. Status goes to the winner, and sex is prized as a testament not of love but of control over another human being. The goal of the sexual conquests is to make a fool of the young woman.[13]

More recently, several other ethnographers—including Alice Goffman (2014), Nikki Jones (2010), and Kathryn Edin and Maria Kefalas (2005)—have written about sexual and romantic relations among young African Americans (and others) in Philadelphia, but none of them described a situation in which males make a contest out of turning young women into fools.[14] Many of the depicted relationships are strained or exploitive, but they do not appear to involve the sort of heartless trickery that Anderson describes as typical. There is no doubt a reason for the discrepancy. It may be due to the time lag between the studies, which ranges from six to fifteen years, and there are many other possible explanations for the differing observations. But in any case, the anonymity of the informants makes it impossible to draw meaningful comparisons. Even if they had wanted to, Goffman, Jones, and Edin and Kefalas could not have compared their informants directly to Anderson's, and a follow-up researcher would be at an even greater disadvantage.

Important information can be discovered when anonymity is relaxed. As we saw in Chapter Five, Lawrence Ralph did not name the victim of a police shooting, while unintentionally stating a mistaken date for the killing.[15] Initially, therefore, I was unable to confirm the occurrence, despite the existence of extensive public records. At my subsequent request, Ralph readily provided me with the victim's name, which allowed me to learn that the shooting and cover-up had been just as his informant described it (if not worse). The effort turns out to have been worthwhile—and, in my opinion, there was no compelling reason to omit the name in the first place.

A different problem arises from Ralph's acknowledged use of composites for "Pastor Tim" and the gang leader "Kemo Nostrand," who are two of the main characters in *Renegade Dreams*.[16] Pastor Tim and his Eastwood Community Church—which is also a composite—are mentioned a combined forty-six times, involving multiple activities and events. Kemo shows up thirty-two times—sometimes fighting, sometimes making peace, sometimes keeping other gang members under control, and sometimes meeting personally with Ralph. Given the breadth and extensiveness of their exploits, it would make a difference to know the extent to which Pastor Tim and Kemo are discrete individuals.

Kemo, for example, is described as his gang's "commanding officer" who—at 6′4″ and at least 250 pounds—is admired and feared by his subordinates. He has a "massive presence," his "voice booms," and his words "pierce the air like bullets." He is known for "violent incidents and venomous outbursts," as well as for "acts of chivalry and kindness." But how many actual people do those characteristics represent? Does the gang have multiple commanding officers? If so, are they all physically dominant, or is one tall and thin and another short and hefty, adding up to Kemo's size and weight? Is one of the Kemos mostly violent and another relatively chivalrous in comparison? By creating a composite in such an important and finely described role, Ralph has given us the worst of both ethnographic worlds. We have neither a generic "gang leader" nor a wholly real person. Instead we are left to guess which traits are attributable to the character under discussion and which are grafted from others in similar roles.[17]

Ralph presents Pastor Tim as a composite of "four white males operating in the neighborhood," but how can such an amalgam work? It seems impossible that all four ministers would always have fully agreed with one another about community issues, such as dealing with gangs, cooperating with the police, responding to the AIDS epidemic, reacting to the establishment of charter schools, working within the political structure, or promoting various forms of economic development. They must surely have competed with one another for grants, donations, programs, parishioners, and influence, and they no doubt have theological differences as well. Yet this significant dynamic is obscured by Ralph's merger of the four men into a single character. The ultimate depiction suppresses the inevitable disagreements among the four, and substitutes a seeming clerical consensus where none is likely to have existed in real life. Composite characters are necessarily inaccurate, which is why they are prohibited in mainstream journalism and strongly disfavored in other forms of narrative nonfiction.[18]

It also matters whether the Eastwood Community Church is just one place, or the combination of three or four locales. Does a single church administer "more government-sponsored programs than any other nonprofit in the neighborhood," or is that an aggregate amount for the entire composite group? Was the church that held a black-tie banquet at the DuSable Museum the same one that has the "Stable Work" program, or is it the one with the "Rebirth Center" and the "Delivery Development Corporation"? Is it the church with the "hip-hop worship service," or is it the one with the pickup basketball games? How many churches had their doors kicked in by angry gang members, and how many offered HIV testing in their libraries? A neighborhood where such key events and programs are spread out over multiple churches is quite different from one where they are confined to a single venue (with only one spiritual leader), which brings us to the subject of masking research sites.

LOCATIONS

There is a tradition of masking research sites in ethnography, from William Whyte's "Cornerville," which was said to be in "Eastern City," to Carl Milofsky's "Smallville." In other cases the locale is central to the story, and it would therefore be absurd to assign a fictional site. Mitchell Duneier's *Sidewalk* could be located only on New York's Sixth Avenue; Victor Rios's *Punished* is necessarily set in the Oakland neighborhood where he grew up; and Sudhir Venkatesh's *American Project* would make no sense if he did not identify Chicago's Robert Taylor Homes.[19]

The more recent trend is to disclose at least the city under investigation, even while continuing to disguise the neighborhood. Thus, Alice Goffman locates "6th Street" in Philadelphia and Laurence Ralph places "Eastwood" in Chicago. The masking of place, however, even if only at the neighborhood level, is not unchallenged within ethnography. UCLA's Jack Katz has called on ethnographers to "reflect carefully on the costs of invoking supposed ethical gains from concealing place," specifically explaining the need to identify city neighborhoods for the sake of transparency and plausibility.[20]

Colin Jerolmack and Alexandra Murphy go further. Recognizing that many in "the academic community [deem] the particularities of a place . . . to be more or less irrelevant," they argue against the use of "fake place names" that hide the "distinct features" of the particular locale. The consequence, they warn, may be "pseudo-generalizability," in which the ethnographer's claims of typicality may not be reliably tested or evaluated.

The contrary view has been championed by Charles Bosk, who argues that masking the research site renders an ethnography "more convincingly sociological." Disguising the locale, he says, "generalizes our descriptions . . . and makes them more universal."[21] As lawyers know, it can be tempting to build a case by "assuming facts not in evidence," but many readers would prefer more rigorous proof, or at least the opportunity to decide for themselves. The appearance of generalizability—created by withholding information—is not the same thing as generalizability itself. And even a general description of the locale—with details chosen by the author—enshrines "ethnographic authority" and risks erasing "sociologically significant information" that is inconsistent with the study's underlying theory.[22] Bosk named his site "Pacific Hospital" because "it was deliberately misleading," which is a serious imposition on readers for the sake of a sociological impression.[23] Or, as Duneier put it, the more difficult it is to identify the field site, the greater the "likelihood of misrepresentation."[24]

The virtue of neighborhood identification is well illustrated by the opening vignette in John Jackson's *Harlemworld*, which finds the author standing in line at a McDonald's restaurant in northern Manhattan. The man at the head of the line—whom Jackson calls "Dexter"—is arguing with the cashier about the validity of a newspaper coupon for a ninety-nine-cent Big Mac. The small print on the coupon, however, excludes "the borough of Manhattan" from the deal, where the still-discounted price is a slightly higher $1.39. The cashier patiently explains the differential to Dexter, who would have none of it. He is willing to pay only ninety-nine cents, plus another dime for tax:

> "This is Harlem," he stated with electrified finality, "not Manhattan! If they meant Harlem, if they meant Harlem, they should have written Harlem! Harlem is not Manhattan! So I'm paying $1.10 for my Big Mac."

The cashier ultimately relents and accepts the lower price, although more to get the line moving than to acknowledge the force of Dexter's reasoning. As Jackson explains, there was much more to the situation than a forty-cent difference in the price of a meal:

> I open with this seemingly trivial transaction—a customer haggling over the cost of a specialty hamburger at an iconic fast food joint—because Dexter's geography-warping interpretation of Harlem's relation to the rest of New York City hints at something important about the place.[25]

The Big Mac story is powerful because it elucidates—as only ethnography can—the relationship between a neighborhood and its residents. Dexter is asserting that Harlem is a distinct and special environment; it is in Manhattan but not of it. In a few short paragraphs, we are provided with "ethnographic evidence for a rendition of race and place" that would not have been possible if the author had located the events in a fictional or unnamed neighborhood. Harlem occupies a unique place in the cultural history of the United States, but every field site is also unique in its own way, and that quality may be obscured when the location is hidden from readers for the sake of generalization.

Perhaps the greatest scholarly problem with field site masking is that it makes re-interviews or revisits, or even reappraisals, nearly impossible. Successive ethnographers are unable to conduct longitudinal studies to determine whether conditions have changed over time. Equally important for evidentiary purposes, the use of fake neighborhood names prevents, or at least inhibits, verification or falsification of the ethnographer's reported observations.

In addition to her story of a police gantlet outside Philadelphia emergency rooms, Alice Goffman also says that she witnessed three new fathers arrested on a maternity floor, on a single evening, by officers who were following their "custom" of running "the names of the men on the visitors' list." I have found nobody who is aware of even one such arrest in Philadelphia and, as discussed in Chapter Six, the relevant hospitals have all denied making visitor information available to the police. Nonetheless, the story of the three arrests would be easy to fact-check if Goffman would identify the hospital in question. Although a search of police records might reveal the real name of her informant—a 6th Street Boy whom she calls "Alex"—a general inquiry to hospital security could preserve his anonymity while still determining whether there had ever been three maternity floor arrests on the same night.[26] Nonetheless, Goffman has steadfastly refused to disclose any of the particulars of her research site, regarding this incident or others.[27]

Whatever imperatives might require pseudonymizing individuals, they do not carry the same force when it comes to locales. Edin and Kefalas identified the "eight hardscrabble neighborhoods" in and around Philadelphia where they interviewed "poor single mothers," and they even included maps, with no compromise of confidentiality. Khan made no secret of his study location at St. Paul's School in Concord, New Hampshire. Both Contreras and Bourgois, who studied drug dealers and other criminals in New York City, also named their neighborhood research sites, to no evident ill effect on their informants.[28]

DETAILS

How much further should an ethnographer go in the name of anonymity? If it is acceptable to change the names of people and neighborhoods, is it likewise permissible to rearrange dates or even to alter the nature of actual events? One prominent ethnographer described the practice this way:

> My strong belief here is that I've got the right as well as the obligation to change identifying details on things like dates and ages and other characteristics, as well as the details of particular events and who was present for them, to disguise and thus protect people.[29]

The problem with this assertion is evident, assuming that we are discussing social science rather than fiction or memoir. Such tinkering with facts can render the resulting work completely irreproducible or untestable. Which details, precisely, have been altered, and whose presence has been added or omitted? We have only the ethnographer's word that the changes are inconsequential, but how much can we trust it? As Jerolmack and Murphy explain,

> This practice enshrines ethnographic authority: while the ethnographer may disclose all the details that she deems necessary in light of

her particular theoretical interests, for readers masking may withhold information that they consider crucial for independently evaluating the ethnographer's analysis and considering alternative explanations.

Scrambling facts is most effective when it is least acknowledged, so there are few documented instances of the practice.[30] The best example was provided by Charles Bosk, in a reappraisal of his 1979 study of surgeons at an elite hospital. Writing more than twenty years after the first publication of *Forgive and Remember*, Bosk allowed that in creating "a version of reality that would in Levi-Strauss' memorable formula be 'good to think with,'" he might have slighted the importance of "literal or even interpretive truth." One particular change—undertaken for the sake of anonymity—bothered him greatly, even though it had seemed "not just morally justifiable but [also] morally necessary" at the time. In retrospect, he came to realize that the altered fact was not a minor detail, but instead had significant "theoretical consequences" for his study.[31]

As Bosk explained, a second-year surgical resident whom he called "Jones" had not been allowed to advance in the program due to "technical maladroitness [and] an inability to admit mistakes." So poor was Jones's performance, and so tenuous was his stability, according to the senior surgeons, that "he will not be allowed to return to duty until he is investigated by someone in neuropsychiatry." In fact, "he was a total problem that attendings wished to rid themselves of entirely by shifting responsibility to the psychiatry department."

Notwithstanding the pronouns in Bosk's original account, it turns out that "Jones" was "the sole female in the cohort of surgical residents" under observation. Bosk admits that he "did not think twice about changing Jones's gender" in order to preserve his promise of confidentiality, and he realized only much later that he had been blind "to the impact of gender." Bosk now recognizes that turning Jones from female to male "theoretically impoverished" his book, and prevented him—and thus his readers—from recognizing that she had been working in a "hostile environment," which of course might well have accounted for her dismissal by the senior surgeons.

Bosk's realization is both admirable and cautionary. "When we alter our data to protect our subjects," he now asks, "how do we know that the data we alter is not critical? What is an innocent change and what is not?" The greatest pitfall of switching Jones's gender "is that it makes the critique I did not make impossible for others to make." To Bosk's credit, he offers no excuses: "To say I was a prisoner of my times seems too convenient, too exculpatory." In that, he is surely correct. We are all prisoners of our times in one way or another, and therefore unable to predict which facts, though seemingly fungible today, may be crucial to social scientists in the future—or even to contemporaries with differing perspectives.

AUTHENTICITY

Courtroom evidence is subject to a requirement of "authenticity," meaning that there must be some proof that it is "what it purports to be." Is that the actual contract between the parties? Are we look-ing at the real murder weapon? Does the photograph "truly and accu-rately depict" the location of the cars after the accident? The facts that establish authenticity are collectively known as the "foundation" for the evidence. The basic foundation for eyewitness testimony, for example, is the witness's presence at a relevant time and place, coupled with an adequate opportunity to observe the scene.

For our current purposes, the most analogous foundation may be the one for a conversation, which goes like this:

Q. Did you hear a conversation between the parties?
Q. When did it occur?
Q. Where did it occur?
Q. Who was present?
Q. What was said?

Even in the complete absence of hearsay problems, a witness must first state the time, place, and persons present, before testifying to the content of a conversation. The function of the foundation is both to demonstrate authenticity—to show that it really happened—and to enable the cross-examiner to challenge the witness's account. Without the necessary details—locating it in time and place—the conversation could have occurred anywhere and involved anyone, which makes it impossible to question and thus renders it too suspect for admissibility.[32]

Radically masked ethnography presents a similar problem, because it is not tethered to identifiable individuals or anchored in a particular place, and in some cases even the events themselves have been uprooted and rearranged. The more deracinated it is, the more unreliable it becomes.

Nonetheless, it appears that many ethnographers approve of altering facts—even beyond disguising names and locales—in pursuit of radical anonymity. As Leon Neyfakh explained in *Slate*, their approach is not always to capture discrete "truths about specific individuals but general truths that tell us how the world works [in which] the need to maintain strict adherence to real details could take a back seat." In an interview for the same article, Harvard's Christopher Winship put it this way:

> If you told a sociologist they got a particular fact wrong, they'd say, "Well, that doesn't matter—what's important is that it's true in a bigger sense." We can talk about a piece of fiction as being true or not—as in, would real people actually act that way?—and I think sociologists and ethnographers fall back on that.[33]

The masking of subjects thus underpins the view that distinct facts are less important than epistemic truths. Once subjects have had their names and other data changed—perhaps including appearances, ages, backgrounds, jobs, and histories—they risk becoming vessels for the ethnographer's observations, rather than actual individuals. Every ethnographer will deny having gone to extremes, while insisting that only inconsequential details have been altered, but that is inevitably a matter of interpretation. As the British sociologists Rosalind Edwards and Susie Weller put it, anonymizations "that change or remove personal characteristics, location references, or people's roles and relationships to each other . . . may undermine the integrity of the data." Philip Gerard, a professor of nonfiction writing, goes even further when it comes to "changing details about the place or circumstances." Such adjustments, he says, are "tricky devices tending toward fiction."[34] What is inconsequential in one author's view might be quite meaningful to another—and perhaps even more so to a critical reader. Biographical facts are still facts, after all, and scrambling them would be anathema to any responsible lawyer or journalist.

Nonetheless, many prominent ethnographers, including UCLA's highly regarded Jack Katz, seem to take a flexible view of discrete facts when they appear to be secondary to the sociologist's theoretical perspective. Speaking at a conference at New York University, he told the audience that "the demands for fact checking that are often made are about issues that readers find controversial, but are not central to the story that the ethnographic writer is trying to get across." Fact-checking makes sense in journalism, he explained, "but it's not our way and for very good reasons in academic social sciences."[35]

I cannot accept Katz's view, and I doubt that he could defend that position in an ethnographic trial, much less under actual cross-examination. Yes, narrative arcs are important in both law and sociology, and stories can be told from many perspectives. Lawyers are famously able to argue different sides of the same case, but their interpretations, as I teach my own students, must not rest on doctored evidence. Anonymization presents challenges for ethnographers that lawyers seldom face, but it should not be used as an excuse for presenting a less-than-rigorous account of events.

JOURNALISM

Ethnographers often assert that blanket masking is essential to their work because informants would not agree to cooperate with them otherwise. This is sometimes made explicit, as when Laurence Ralph informs his readers that "anonymity was the condition that made much of my work possible."[36] Most of the time, however, the subjects' insistence on masking is assumed and unexplained, with no mention of any attempt to negotiate the use of real names or locations. As Charles Bosk puts it, anonymity may be employed as "virtually an unthinking reflex."[37]

It must be noted that journalists, often working under similar conditions, do not encounter the same resistance to naming. As Jerolmack and Murphy point out, reporters are regularly able to obtain on-the-record stories from named informants, including outsiders such as "jihadists" and "Somali pirates." It turns out that many people are eager to tell their stories to journalists and others, and they are "no great respecters of their own confidentiality and anonymity."[38] Venkatesh,

Goffman, and Ralph, for example, all encountered gang members who were hoping to publish memoirs or to have their biographies written. If ethnographers have been unable to obtain consent to conduct unmasked research, it may be only because they did not ask.

Journalists on occasion rely upon anonymous sources, but they do not change other details, such as locations or biographical descriptions. For example, a leak from a presidential advisor might be attributed to "a knowledgeable source in the administration," but not to "an official in the White House" unless the informant actually worked there. Moreover, anonymous sources may be used only when there is no alternative.

The Code of Ethics of the Society of Professional Journalists provides that sources must be identified with "as much information as possible," and that individual promises of anonymity should be separately negotiated only with informants "who may face danger, retribution or other harm, and have information that cannot be obtained elsewhere." In addition, the reporter must "explain why anonymity was granted."[39] The published policy of the *New York Times* is to grant anonymity only as "a last resort [when] The Times could not otherwise publish information it considers newsworthy and reliable." Reminiscent of the credulity problems discussed in Chapter Four, the *Times* policy holds that the "level of skepticism should be high" because "without a named source, readers may see The Times as vouching for the information unequivocally." As explained by the public editor, unnamed sources are potential "journalistic I.E.D.'s" that are liable to explode when fact-checked by outsiders.[40]

The publishers of ethnographies seem to have no qualms about the routine use of masked informants and altered details. To my knowledge, no trade or university press requires the internal disclosure of subjects' real names, even regarding essential elements of the story. The risk involved should be obvious, given that two of the most significant scandals in the history of journalism were occasioned by reliance on anonymous sources that were not vetted by the relevant editors.

In 1981, *Washington Post* reporter Janet Cooke was awarded a Pulitzer Prize for a front-page article titled "Jimmy's World," in which she told the story of an eight-year-old heroin addict who had been introduced to drugs by his mother and her boyfriend. Just two days later, the *Post* announced that the story was contrived—Jimmy did not exist at all—and the Pulitzer was returned. Soon afterward, the *Post* published a front-page analysis explaining how the paper had missed obvious warning signs.[41]

It turned out that no editor had ever demanded to know "Jimmy's" true identity, relying instead on Cooke's insistence on anonymity. As the *Post's* ombudsman later put it, the supervising editor "did not ask the mother's name or the family's street address. He had promised Cooke confidentiality for her sources. The jugular of journalism lay exposed—the faith an editor has to place in a reporter."

Other editors—including the legendary Ben Bradlee and Bob Woodward—also took a hands-off approach to Cooke and her sources. On the rare occasion that she was asked for more information, Cooke responded that "Ron," the invented lover of Jimmy's mother, had threatened her life and therefore could not be approached. "In a way, both [Cooke] and the story were almost too good to be true," explained Woodward. "This story was so well-written and tied together so well that my alarm bells simply didn't go off."

But there were doubters from the beginning. Dr. Alyce Gullattee, of Howard University's Institute for Substance Abuse and Addiction, said she did not believe that Jimmy's mother "fired up" in front of Cooke. Junkies "just don't trust reporters like that," she said. Even Washington's Mayor Marion Barry—who turned out to know a thing or two about drug use himself—expressed doubts. "I've been told the story is part myth, part reality," he said. Speaking of the police, he continued, "We all have agreed that we don't believe that the mother or the pusher would allow a reporter to see them shoot up."

Confronted by implausibilities in the article, the *Post* editors did not initially demand confirmation or documentation. Instead, the *Post* editors backed their reporter, even when she was not able to show them the house where Jimmy allegedly lived. For as long as it could, the *Post* "stuck by its story and what it described as its First Amendment rights to protect its sources."

It was only when Cooke won the Pulitzer Prize that other journalists started asking questions, at which point the story began to unravel. Cooke's editors at last confronted her about discrepancies in her account, which they finally realized "cast serious doubts on her honesty [which was] the only thing that held the 'Jimmy' story together."

For a while, Cooke insisted that that story was true. Fortunately for the *Post*, Cooke's notes and tape recordings had been preserved and she was required to bring them into the newsroom. There was nothing in them about a child addict. Cooke had no choice but to confess the fraud. "There is no Jimmy and no family," she said. "It was a fabrication," she admitted, acknowledging what the *Post* later called a "journalistic felony." The story was retracted and the Pulitzer Prize was returned.

The fraud was Cooke's alone, but the *Post* could not deny shared responsibility. "This business of trusting reporters absolutely goes too far," the ombudsman admitted. "There is a point when total reliance on this kind of trust allows the editor to duck his own responsibility. Editors have to insist on knowing and verifying."[42]

If the Janet Cooke debacle was a cautionary tale about over-reliance on unidentified sources, the lesson was later lost on the editors of *Rolling Stone*. In November 2014, the popular-culture magazine published an article titled "A Rape on Campus" that told the story of a woman called "Jackie" who had been gang raped at a University of Virginia fraternity party. Written by veteran reporter Sabrina Rubin Erdely, the story recounted Jackie's rape in detail, including the callous response of three of her friends who had also attended the party. Although the fraternity was identified, all of the other names in the story—including Jackie's date, who had lured her into a trap—were pseudonyms. It turned out, however, that the story was untrue. There had been no party at the fraternity on the date in question, there was no member of the fraternity who fit Jackie's description of her date, and Jackie's friends, once located by other reporters, contradicted essential aspects of her story.

Forced to retract the article, *Rolling Stone* retained Steve Coll, the dean of the Columbia School of Journalism, to lead an investigation of the errors "in reporting, editing, and fact-checking" that led to the fiasco. The report was devastating. Although Erdely had interviewed Jackie multiple times, she had never revealed her source's true name to her editors at *Rolling Stone*, and they had not taken steps to confirm her story. Erdely herself had never learned the real name of Jackie's alleged rapist, nor of the three friends whom Jackie claimed had been with her on the night of the incident. According to Coll and two co-authors, *Rolling Stone* had "set aside or rationalized as unnecessary essential practices of reporting." Moreover, "the published story glossed over the gaps in the magazine's reporting by using pseudonyms and by failing to state where important information had come from."[43]

Unlike "Jimmy's World," the *Rolling Stone* article was not a journalistic fraud. Jackie was a real person who had in fact told Erdely the story of a gang rape. The problem, as revealed by a review of Erdely's notes, was that she had "relied solely on Jackie's information" without confirming it from other sources, and the *Rolling Stone* editors had agreed to allow the use of pseudonyms for alleged witnesses and participants whose true identities they never learned. As one editor explained to Coll and his co-investigators, Erdely was "a writer I've worked with for so long, have so much faith in, that I really trusted her judgment in finding Jackie credible . . . . I asked her a lot about that, and she always said she found her completely credible."

Alas, Jackie was not telling the truth, for reasons that no one may ever understand. Both Erdely and her editors, however, had missed obvious warning signs—including Jackie's refusal to provide real names and contact information—while disregarding basic tenets of accurate reporting. The Coll report attributed this to "the problem of confirmation bias—the tendency of people to be trapped by pre-existing assumptions and to select facts that support their own views while overlooking contradictory ones."

It is not hard to see how the missteps of editors at the *Washington Post* and *Rolling Stone* could be repeated in ethnography, given the field's strong emphasis on preserving anonymity, extensive masking of research sites, and resistance to editorial confirmation. The untruths in the Cooke and Erdely articles were eventually exposed because the stories included sufficient details for others to fact-check. That would have been impossible, however, if either reporter had been allowed to follow the standard conventions of ethnography.

Speaking at a conference at New York University, the journalist Eyal Press recognized that ethnographers have "strong intellectual and philosophical reasons" for extensive anonymization. "But to be very frank," he said, "I don't buy them. I don't find them convincing enough to allow for the level of anonymization that exists." "If I were given license to anonymize in my magazine work," he explained, "I would very quickly, and probably not even noticing it, leave out all the inconvenient details that didn't conform with the assumptions I had going into the story. Why report them?"[44]

The example of journalism notwithstanding, ethnography's extreme commitment to anonymization is usually explained by the researchers' ironclad obligation to "do no harm." Even hinting at a subject's identity, or revealing the research site, it has been argued, may cause all manner of emotional or psychological distress, including embarrassment, regret, or self-doubt. In some cases, ethnographers have been concerned about more substantial consequences for their informants, including ruptured relationships, loss of public benefits, and even prosecution for crimes. We therefore turn to the interplay of ethnography and criminality as our final chapter.

8

Criminality

ETHNOGRAPHERS HAVE LONG RECOGNIZED the need to observe, and even engage in, certain crimes, in order to understand the communities they study. There is a genre of urban ethnography devoted to the effects of crime and the criminal justice system on minority and low-income populations, and another devoted to what was once called "deviance studies." Researchers in other areas of ethnography—from housing to health care—also encounter unlawful behavior and must therefore decide how to approach it in their field work and how to address it in their writing. This chapter will discuss two related issues: ethnographers' participation in criminal activity, and their obligation, if any, to provide evidence to law enforcement and the courts.

In the research for *Street Corner Society*, William Foote Whyte accepted an offer to hang out at an illegal "gambling joint," as a means of access to Cornerville. He recognized that he would risk arrest by his very presence, and expressed his willingness to commit perjury in order to beat the rap. Fortunately, his resolve in that regard was never tested.

Whyte did, however, confess to committing voter fraud when one of his subjects recruited him to "steal the election," lest their rivals "steal it from us."[1] He willingly accepted the role of "repeater," by voting four times under assumed names. Audaciously, he attempted to vote twice at the same polling place, which was almost his undoing. After receiving a ballot and filling it out for the preferred candidate, Whyte was approached by a "checker" who questioned his identity. Although he did not match the official description of the person whose name he was using—a Sicilian fisherman twice his age, who was away at sea—Whyte attempted to bluff it out. He gave false answers for his age and height, and he made up names for his two "sisters." All the while fearing an imagined tabloid headline—"HARVARD FELLOW ARRESTED FOR REPEATING"—he continued the deception. Eventually, a senior "warden" stepped in and required Whyte to sign the back of the ballot, and to "swear that was my name and that I had not voted before." Whyte nervously complied, although he was so disoriented that he provided the wrong first name. Now truly fearful of arrest, he contemplated "trying to run for it," only to see the warden—who was evidently in on the fix—scratch out the erroneous signature and place the ballot in the box.[2]

Whyte went free, but he was shaken by the experience. He was most upset by the realization that he had not actually felt guilty "until I had thought that I was going to be arrested." To his credit, Whyte did not rationalize the experience as necessary to his research. "I had been observing these activities at quite close range before, and I could have had all the data" without breaking the law. "Actually, I learned nothing of research value from the experience, and I took a chance of jeopardizing my whole study."

Upon reflection, Whyte was deeply remorseful. "When I discovered that I was a repeater, I found my conscience giving me serious trouble . . . . I could not laugh it off simply as a necessary part of the field work." He also avoided the temptation to excuse his conduct as harmless, given that his candidate lost and the phony votes therefore had no impact on the election. A field worker must refuse to engage in "immoral" behavior, he wrote, in order "to continue living with himself."[3]

Other celebrated ethnographers have expressed no comparable regrets over breaking the law, perhaps because they did not share Whyte's self-image as "a respectable, law-abiding, middle-class citizen," and no doubt because they believed that their participation in certain minor crimes was essential to their research. It seems obvious that the study of crime and deviance requires a certain amount of leeway for an embedded researcher—especially when it comes to victimless or minor crimes—but how far does the latitude extend?

Clifford Geertz was unconcerned about the illegality of cockfighting when he and his wife arrived in a Balinese village in 1958. Although the practice had been outlawed by the newly independent Indonesian government, Geertz considered that an unfortunate "result of the pretensions to puritanism radical nationalism tends to bring with it." In his view, cockfighting was part of the Balinese way of life, and the ban was entitled to no respect. The occasional police raid, he said, was little more than a nuisance, and the cockfights, like drinking during Prohibition, were bound to "go on happening, and with extraordinary frequency."

Undaunted by illegality, Geertz and his wife attended a cockfight on the tenth day of their stay, and it turned out to provide a fortuitous entry point into Balinese life. Contrary to Geertz's expectation, the fight was raided by "a truck full of policemen armed with machine guns," who evidently took the law more seriously than the ethnographer had assumed. The authorities began to arrest both the participants and the spectators.

Rather than take advantage of their status as foreigners, the Geertzes decided to run away along with the villagers. That act of solidarity opened many doors, both literally and figuratively, and the Geertzes were soon transformed from barely tolerated interlopers into welcomed guests. Geertz eventually attended fifty-seven cockfights, collecting data on wagering patterns and social relationships among the bettors. For him, "getting caught, or almost caught, in a vice raid" was the key to "that mysterious necessity of anthropological field work, rapport."[4]

In his classic essay "Becoming a Marihuana User," Howard Becker explains precisely how to "get high" (the quote marks, which are original, were evidently necessary in 1953), but he does not once mention the illegality of the drug. Instead, he refers only to "considerations of morality and expediency, occasioned by the reactions of society." Even those considerations, however, were irrelevant to Becker's exploration of the "social character of drug use." His personal experience is evident from the considerable detail in which he describes "the sequence of changes in individual attitude and experience which lead to *the use of marihuana for pleasure.*" The taste for marijuana is "socially acquired," says Becker, "not different in kind from acquired tastes for oysters or dry martinis." The user feels intensely hungry, dizzy, and thirsty. "His scalp tingles; he misjudges time and distance." These sensations may not be enjoyable at first. A user must learn, "in short, to answer 'Yes' to the question: 'Is it fun?' "[5]

Becker's immersion in the drug and jazz culture is today held up as a prescient model for the ethnography of "outsider" behavior. *Becoming a Marihuana User* was recently re-issued in booklet form by the University of Chicago Press, with an unapologetic cover blurb calling it "a famous timestamp in weed studies." If there was ever any professional criticism of Becker's illegal drug use, it has long been forgotten. These days, everyone is in on the joke.

Some oppressive laws will never be a laughing matter, even after their enforcement has ended. In 1970, Laud Humphreys published *Tearoom Trade*, a path-breaking study of male homosexuals in St. Louis. Humphreys explained that he had posed as a "watchqueen," or voyeur, in order to observe the behavior of men who met in public bathrooms for clandestine and anonymous sexual encounters. By recording license plate numbers, he was able to obtain many of the men's names and addresses, and he then used the ruse of a community health study to interview many of them about their lives and families.[6]

Humphreys, who conducted the study while a graduate student at Washington University, was severely criticized by sociologists and journalists for deceptively invading the privacy of his subjects. He was staunchly defended by several senior colleagues, who praised the work for its "principled humaneness [and] the constructive contribution that it makes toward our understanding" of what was then called "deviant behavior."[7]

In a 1975 retrospect, Humphreys conceded that he had been wrong to trace license numbers for the purpose of interviewing his subjects in their homes. He also responded to charges that he had "committed numerous felonies" by facilitating "some 200 acts of fellatio." "Was I not guilty as an accomplice to the acts?" he asked rhetorically. In fact, it was not a crime to watch men engage each other sexually, or, as Humphreys's critics argued, to fail to report their then-illegal activities. It was a crime, however, to tip them off to passing police cars, which was the role Humphreys acknowledged as a watchqueen. A lookout is as guilty as a principal in ordinary crimes, such as holdups or burglaries, and the same would have been true for so-called sodomy offenses in the 1960s. Nonetheless, Humphreys forthrightly rejected the accusations. "There are many laws I have never had any intention of obeying," he wrote, "including most of those governing victimless 'crimes' against 'public order.' "[8]

Humphreys's defiance was addressed only to the charge of facilitating fellatio, but there is reason to believe that he had been not only a lookout, but also a participant in acts of "criminal sodomy," as they were branded at the time. He later came out as gay—although he was "married and closeted" at the time of the research—and explained that his "sexual outlets were largely furtive and impersonal," and that the tearooms, therefore, "held both sexual and intellectual fascination for me."[9] Humphreys's biographers revisited the public restrooms where he conducted his research, and concluded, based on the architecture and lighting, that he "could not have served as a watchqueen while observing the behavior inside," and they questioned whether the role of "watchqueen" had been invented by Humphreys to conceal the extent of his involvement with his subjects.[10]

Humphreys's status as a participant in sex acts, rather than an observer, would change the ethical evaluation of his project. He gives no indication that his partners consented to be the subjects of a research study, or to have their license plates tracked by Humphreys's assistant, whom he identified only as "a trusted, mature graduate student."[11] It also adds meaning to his disdain for laws against victimless crimes.

The sodomy laws of the time were cruel and oppressive. They were thankfully declared unconstitutional by the U.S. Supreme Court in 2003, over thirty years after Humphreys had concluded his research, and after they had been repealed by all but fourteen states.[12] As Humphreys understood, and as most today would surely agree, no blame can attach to someone who frequented tearooms, or who protected gay men from harassment and arrest. No matter which laws he violated, Humphreys's research was a crucial step forward in the sociological treatment of gay people. His familiarity with tearooms allowed him to gather information that no one else had ever collected in what became "one of the first major studies of homosexuality in America."[13]

Much has changed over the years, but the works of Geertz, Becker, and Humphreys (and others) continue to be cited for the proposition that ethnographers may, and sometimes should, break the law in the course of their research. It is easier to make that argument when the particular laws are seen as foolish, outdated, inconsequential, or inhumane, but Howard Becker opined that studying lawbreakers in their "natural setting" would always entail the "moral decision" that one must "break the law himself."[14]

Are there any aspects of law that sociologists feel bound to respect? Or do they avoid committing crimes simply as a matter of expedience? In all my reading of urban ethnography, I have seen very few articulations of an inherent obligation to obey the law (there may be some that I have missed). In *Gang Leader for a Day*, Sudhir Venkatesh recounts his overdue realization—after four years of embedded research with gang members in Chicago—that he needed to consult counsel about his own possible involvement in crimes. It happened almost by accident when, in a "casual conversation" with some professors, Venkatesh described his observation of the preparation for a drive-by shooting. According to Venkatesh, his subjects had "sent a young woman to surreptitiously cozy up to the rival gang and learn enough information" to launch a "surprise attack." Fortunately, if belatedly, this revelation sent off alarm bells in the University of Chicago sociology department, and Venkatesh was ordered to suspend his research until he obtained legal advice. Venkatesh did consult a lawyer, from whom he learned the following:

> [I]f I became aware of a plan to physically harm somebody, I was obliged to tell the police. Meaning I could no longer watch the gang plan a drive-by shooting, although I could speak with them about drive-bys in the abstract.

"It wasn't as if I had any intention of joining the gang in an actual drive-by shooting," he continued. "But since I could get in trouble just for driving around with them while they *talked* about shooting somebody, I had to rethink my approach."[15]

Randol Contreras, who had made an unsuccessful attempt at drug dealing as a teenager, studied a gang of robbers who specialized in torturing drug dealers into giving up their proceeds. Although Contreras had grown up with some of the "stickup kids," he was careful not to get too close to their crimes. The stories of their exploits—which included beating, maiming, and burning their victims with hot irons—are related second-hand by the participants, and not described by

Contreras himself, who declined to accompany the robbers even when they urged him to "tag along."[16] Contreras sometimes uses italics to set off the scenes that he did not observe, and he sometimes uses quotes, as when he asked "Gus" to provide a glimpse into how drug robbers transitioned into torture:

> "You tell them, 'Look, I'ma ask you what to do. If you don't tell me what I wanna know, I'ma cut your ear.' So, when you tell 'em that shit, you gotta do it. Or they gonna start fuckin' with you, 'Ah, this nigga's bullshit. He told me he was gonna cut my ear off and he didn't cut it.' So I asked him what he had on 145th Street and Broadway. He said that he doesn't know. I didn't even ask him again. I just cut his earlobe off."[17]

It turns out that avoiding crime is not so easy when studying it up close. Venkatesh participated in a beat-down in a stairwell at the Robert Taylor Homes, and he incited another during his day as a surrogate gang leader.[18] Contreras did not actively encourage his friends' robbery and torture spree, but his deep interest might well have been taken as approval. On at least one occasion, he appeared to make that explicit, when Gus, who was the most violent of the crew, was explaining his use of a young woman to lure a drug dealer into a trap:

> "Yo, that nigga's an old man and he thinks he gonna get some young ass tonight! That nigga's gonna get a big surprise, bro! What you think, Randy?"
> "He's goin' d-o-o-o-w-w-n," I answered, inebriated.
> After a few hours of such updates, the driver appeared and drove Gus, Jonah, and David to the apartment where they would later sequester and brutally torture the dealer.[19]

To Gus, who was waiting for the trap to spring, it might well have seemed that Contreras was affirming his impressive scheme of sexual trickery and brutality, or at least confirming his expectation that the plot would succeed as planned.[20]

The study of outlaws always requires a certain suspension of judgment. Drug dealers, robbers, and gang members could hardly be expected to share their experiences with ethnographers who hectored or lectured them about lawbreaking. An expression of disapproval would risk shutting off the source of information, without any certain impact on the subjects' behavior. Venkatesh and Contreras therefore had to draw a line that would allow them to continue their research without crossing into overt criminality. One might disagree with their placement of the line, or wonder how scrupulously they respected it, but the authors, and most other ethnographers, have recognized that serious crimes are off limits. Although the boundary may be imprecise, it would surely have to lie well short of facilitating a murder plot. But apparently not.

ON THE RUN

The heart of the criminal controversy over Goffman's *On the Run* lies in her multiple versions of the events following the murder of "Chuck," her friend and subject. In Goffman's first telling, as found in the book's Methodological Appendix, Chuck's killing provoked his friends to prepare for a gang war, as they "acquired more and more guns." Once armed, several of the 6th Street Boys spent "many nights [driving] around looking for the shooter, the guys who were part of his crew, or women connected to them who might be able to provide a good lead." Goffman was not a mere spectator to these events.

> On a few of these nights, Mike had nobody to ride along with him, so I volunteered. We started out around 3:00 a.m., with Mike in the passenger seat, his hand on his Glock as he directed me around the area. We peered into dark houses and looked at license plates and car models as Mike spoke on the phone with others who had information about the 4th Street Boys' whereabouts.

She did this, wrote Goffman, not because she wanted to learn firsthand about violence, but because she "wanted Chuck's killer to die." Then,

> One night Mike thought he saw a 4th Street guy walk into a Chinese restaurant. He tucked his gun in his jeans, got out of the car, and hid

in the adjacent alleyway. I waited in the car with the engine running ready to speed off as soon as Mike ran back and got inside.[21]

These events, as Goffman recounts them in *On the Run*, constitute a conspiracy to commit murder under the laws of Pennsylvania and virtually every other state. In her own words, she agreed to assist in the commission of a crime, and she engaged in multiple "overt acts" in furtherance of the scheme. Thus, she committed a felony, even though the potential victim was never located. According to one former Philadelphia prosecutor, to whom I provided the relevant passages, "She's flat out confessed to conspiring to commit murder and could be charged and convicted based on this account right now."[22] If this were the subject of a first-year criminal law exam, it is unlikely that any student would get it wrong (although some might wonder if it was a trick question, given the obviousness of the answer).

But even for those who would discount the severity of a crime in which no one was harmed, Goffman's behavior was still profoundly immoral and unethical. It was immoral because she endangered the lives of her potential target and any bystanders who happened to be in the vicinity; it was unethical because she violated any conceivable standard of conduct for a sociology graduate student engaged in field work.

Goffman defended herself by changing her story. In her second telling, posted on her webpage at the University of Wisconsin, Goffman claimed that the late-night manhunts had been conducted only "to satisfy the feelings of anger and pain" caused by Chuck's murder. "They were a way to mourn a dear friend, and showed people in the neighborhood that Chuck's friends were doing something," she wrote, adding, "I knew these drives were about expressing anger and about grieving, not about doing actual violence."[23]

It is understandable that Goffman would recant her satisfaction at having "learned what it feels like to want a man to die," and replace it with the story of an elaborate mourning ritual in which no one was to be harmed. It is impossible to know which version is actually true. An ethnographic cross-examiner, however, would point out that the two accounts are entirely inconsistent. If the only purpose of the late-night ride was to demonstrate grief for the benefit of the neighborhood, why was Mike's "hand on his Glock" when only the two of them were in the car? Why were they "peering into dark houses and looking at license plates and car models," with no one else present, if they had no real intention of finding someone? Why did Mike speak "on the phone with others who had information about the 4th Street Boys' whereabouts"? And why was it that Mike "tucked his gun in his jeans, got out of the car, and hid in the adjacent alleyway" when he thought he'd seen "a 4th Street guy walk into a Chinese restaurant"?[24]

None of Goffman's original details can be squared with the later story of a mourning ritual, as is evidently obvious even to her supporters. Writing sympathetically in the *New York Times Magazine*, Gideon Lewis-Kraus suggested that "what her critics can't imagine is that perhaps both of the accounts she has given are true at the same time," meaning that Goffman would have done the driving as both a participant in an armed "manhunt" and as a "detached" observer in a ritual. Such a dual intention, however, would not change the criminality of the activity. A mixed motive is still a motive, and a detached conspirator is a conspirator nonetheless.[25]

Mitchell Duneier, who was Goffman's dissertation advisor at Princeton, frankly acknowledged that she crossed an ethical line in what has been called the "Glock ride."[26] Others agree. Michele Goodwin, who has appointments in both law and public health at the University of California at Irvine, expressed her dismay that "In Goffman's desire to kill a rival 4th Street Boy, she also exposed the children and women on 6th Street to harm, because their lives might likely have come under threat in the aftermath of a shootout."[27] UCLA's César Ayala told me, "I do not think it is ethical to drive the car in a conspiracy to commit murder, as Goffman claims she did in her book," adding his concern that her supporters "are sending a message to graduate students that this type of research behavior is acceptable."[28]

Still, Goffman has her adamant defenders. UCLA's Jack Katz told the *Chronicle of Higher Education* that "The ethical line she crossed, in a way, was honesty," evidently because other ethnographers have concealed their own crimes rather than acknowledge them. "Most of the time, people doing research on drugs and crime and the police don't report the incidents that potentially compromise them," he explained. John Van Maanen and Mark de Rond agree, stating that "the line Alice crossed is therefore one of being too honest, coming forward when the unstated norm is to hold back."[29] In a book review, Harvard's Laurence Ralph writes that "were she to be charged with conspiracy . . . a cadre of academics (myself included) would have been willing to come to her defense by testifying in court about the greater merits of urban ethnography."[30] The Pennsylvania statute of limitations has expired on the events of *On the Run*, so we can only wonder what the cadre might say on the witness stand. But even granted its many virtues, how does urban ethnography justify driving the getaway car in a murder plot? And how could that possibly be explained in a trial? Although we may never know Ralph's answer, there would certainly be one hell of a cross-examination.

REPORTING CRIMES

Should ethnographers ever cooperate with police and other authorities, or does their commitment to anonymity preclude reporting or providing other evidence of crimes? There appears to be no professional consensus on this question. Many ethnographers seem to agree with Goffman that participant-observation includes an implicit promise to keep mum about any and all criminal activity. As we saw in Chapter Five, she declined to offer information to the police about the murder of Chuck, her friend and informant, even though she had "a pretty good idea" of the killer's identity.[31] Gary Alan Fine told me that reporting a crime, including murder, would depend in part on "whether there is a sense that the community would wish this speculation shared with the police, and how that would affect the research."[32]

Others have at least implicitly endorsed reporting serious crimes. In *Gang Leader for a Day*, Sudhir Venkatesh wrote that he was "obliged to tell the police" about any plans "to physically harm someone," and he later told me that he kept his lawyer and advisors informed "if I heard of something being planned that was criminal or if I wanted to study something that was questionable." He added that "I personally don't think the police expect all crimes to be reported—jaywalking, for example, which seems obvious enough."[33] As far as I know, Venkatesh never found it necessary to get in touch with the authorities concerning a crime—either trivial or severe—and there are no such instances in his books. Other sociologists do appear to share the view that major crimes cannot be kept secret. "I do NOT think it is ethical to withhold information in a murder investigation," said César Ayala in an email.[34]

It is impossible to know how many ethnographers, if any, have actually cooperated in the investigation of crimes or reported a subject's intended violence. It is unlikely that anyone would include such an episode in a book. I have seen only one example that comes close.

In *Evicted*, Matthew Desmond tells of an attempt by two women— Crystal and Vanetta—to rent an apartment together. When they arrived for their appointment, however, the landlord saw that they were African American and suddenly realized that "his partner" had already rented the place. One of the women was shaking with anger by the bigoted treatment, while the other was more fatalistic. "He just like, 'Oh, they black,'" she said.[35]

Desmond, who had been assisting in the apartment search, was waiting in the car with Vanetta's three children. When the two women returned, they told him about the discrimination they had encountered, which spurred him to become more participant than observer:

> I copied down the landlord's number from the rent sign and called him up the next day. Meeting him in the same unit Vanetta and Crystal had been shown, I told him I took home about $1400 a month (Vanetta and Crystal's combined income), that I had three kids (like Vanetta), and that I'd really like a unit with a bathtub.

The landlord gladly showed the apartment to Desmond (who is white), even though he had just turned away the two black women on a pretext. Angered by the illegality, Desmond "reported him to the Fair Housing Council," using his real name and contact information. "They took down my report and never called me back."[36]

It is deplorable, though probably unsurprising, that the Fair Housing Council took no action on Desmond's report. For our purposes, however, it is more relevant that he breached anonymity—of both the landlord and the would-be tenants—so that he could lodge the complaint. In order to make a meaningful case for housing discrimination, it would not have been enough for Desmond to explain his own welcoming treatment by the landlord; he also had to describe how the two black women were turned away only a day earlier. Even if he had not included their names in the initial report to the authorities, he implicitly indicated that he would disclose them in the event of a follow-up investigation. (There would have been no point to filing a complaint only to withhold proof of the violation.) I raised this issue with Desmond, who replied,

> The book does not reveal the discriminating landlord's name or address. So in that way his confidentiality is upheld in print. I did report him to the Fair Housing Council because I felt it was the right thing to do.[37]

The landlord might have been less aggrieved by inclusion in a book than by getting a summons from the Fair Housing Council, but I respect Desmond's judgment about making the report. I hope that I would have done as much in similar circumstances. I asked Desmond whether doing the right thing would extend to reporting a violent crime, and whether he would urge other ethnographers to follow his example, but he declined to answer.[38]

The practice of ethnographers is elastic, to say the least. Many appear, as Fine told me, to place their research needs on the same plane as civic duty. Desmond's complaint against the landlord was admirable—he spent a full day setting up an appointment and viewing the apartment—but it involved no risk to his research, which would have continued no matter what the outcome. Other ethnographers have been aware of crime after crime—drug dealing, robbery, domestic violence, law enforcement mayhem—without intervening, because that was the very behavior under study.

James Marquart worked as a Texas prison guard for nineteen months in the 1980s, during which time he "witnessed fifty incidents in which guards beat inmates." By his own account, he saw "officers punch, kick, and knock inmates senseless with riot clubs as they screamed and begged for mercy." He watched guards beat one inmate for ten minutes, using a blackjack and "kicking his legs and genitals." He said nothing about these events to anyone in higher authority, because that "would have violated the implicit research bargain . . . not to use information to injure the subjects," which evidently meant protecting the guards rather than the vulnerable prisoners.[39] In addition to Chuck's case, Alice Goffman claims to have personally witnessed two other murders—including one committed by police officers—which she did not report to authorities. In the many glowing reviews of *On the Run*, in both academic and popular outlets, not one person even remarked upon, let alone questioned, her decision to refrain from coming forward with evidence of these homicides.[40]

Lawyers are privileged to withhold evidence of past crimes, but only when communicated by a client in the course of representation. Even for defense attorneys, no privilege attaches to the planning of future crimes or the observation of crimes in progress. Along with all other citizens, lawyers are also expected to comply with subpoenas and to provide testimony when ordered by a court.[41]

SUBPOENAED TESTIMONY

Many ethnographers have expressed concern about the potential for law enforcement to seize their field notes or compel their testimony, but the actual threat is remote. Even ethnographers who have written of serious crimes—from organized drug sales to multiple rapes—have not been subjected to subpoenas. The great exception is Rik Scarce, who spent 159 days in jail in 1993 for refusing to testify before a federal grand jury.

Scarce had been a graduate student in sociology at Washington State University, conducting research that followed up on his book about radical environmentalists, when a university laboratory was vandalized by members of the Animal Liberation Front, causing about $100,000 in damage.[42] Scarce and his family had been out of town on the day of the incident, having left their home in the care of a friend and research subject named Rod Coronado, who also happened to be a prime suspect in the crime. The authorities traced Coronado to the Scarce residence, and Scarce was eventually placed under subpoena.

After months of unsuccessful legal maneuvering, Scarce was finally called to testify before a grand jury in March 1994. He spent over seven hours on the witness stand while the federal prosecutor asked him thirty-two questions about his possible knowledge of Coronado and the break-in. Scarce resolutely refused to answer, and would neither "confirm nor deny" that he had any information concerning the events. He based his refusal on his "ethical obligations as a member of the American Sociological Association and pursuant to any privilege that may extend to journalists, researchers, and writers under the First Amendment."[43] Ruling that no such privileges applied, the judge found Scarce in civil contempt and ordered him into custody until he would agree to testify. The ruling was upheld by the appellate court, and Scarce was sent to jail. (Civil contempt is intended to be coercive in nature, meaning that the "contemnor" will be incarcerated until he or she complies with the court's order; there is no fixed sentence.[44])

Throughout his five-month-long ordeal, Scarce insisted that the government had no right to ask him *any questions at all* about his research (italics original).[45] That would have amounted to a privilege broader than anything granted to lawyers, doctors, or clergy, all of whom may be required to testify about events they observed, as opposed to confidential communications from their clients, patients, or parishioners.

In the only other known case of a social scientist jailed for contempt, the political scientist Samuel Popkin was subpoenaed before a grand jury in 1972 to answer questions about the Pentagon Papers, which disclosed a previously secret history of the Vietnam war. Popkin did not claim a blanket privilege, and he agreed to testify concerning any "direct evidence about a crime," including his awareness of "the possession, copying or dissemination" of the documents, which had been surreptitiously photocopied and given to the press. He refused, though, to answer questions about communications from his confidential sources, insisting on further hearings before a federal judge. The government would not agree to the limitation and Popkin was jailed for contempt. He was released after a week, however, due to the U.S. Solicitor General's embarrassment at the government's handling of the case.[46]

We can all respect Scarce's sacrifice in the name of principle, while still recognizing that he was mistaken about the scope of First Amendment law. In a democracy, citizens may occasionally be called upon to provide evidence of crimes, and the default rule is that everyone has to testify. Certain exceptions have been recognized by either common law or statutes, but none of them—other than the Fifth Amendment privilege against self-incrimination—is as extensive as the right claimed by

Scarce to refuse to answer "any questions at all" about his research. Even the broadest conception of privilege would still have required Scarce to answer questions about whether he had seen the instrumentalities of vandalism—say, spray paint or burglar tools—in Coronado's possession. (The prosecution was on the right track; Coronado was eventually arrested and later pled guilty to the offense.[47])

It is not only prosecutors who may seek testimony from ethnographers. James Marquart was approached by an attorney investigating prison brutality, who was seeking evidence for use in a lawsuit against the Texas Department of Corrections. Marquart declined to cooperate, telling the lawyer he had "nothing to say." Even though he had seen plenty of relevant incidents, Marquart "envisioned going to jail for contempt of court" rather than testify on behalf of abused prisoners. Push did not come to shove, and it appears that there was never a subpoena.[48]

Richard Leo had a different experience with a different outcome. In the early 1990s, while a graduate student at Berkeley, Leo spent hundreds of hours as a participant-observer at a "large, urban police department." After developing a rapport with the detectives in the Criminal Investigation Division, he was allowed to observe the custodial interrogations of arrestees in major crimes, including murders.

Leo was aware from the outset that he "could be called to testify about anything I observed," but the issue only arose once when he was subpoenaed "to testify in court as a percipient witness." As Leo describes the events:

> During his brief interrogation, the suspect in this case had provided detectives with a full confession to his role in the armed robbery of a local food chain store and the physical assault on one of its employees. The suspect had confessed virtually spontaneously to his full participation in the crime; his interrogation lasted less than thirty minutes.

The suspect later alleged that his statement had been coerced and that the detectives has "prevented him from invoking his *Miranda* rights," which, if true, would have been grounds for suppressing his confession.

When the public defender learned of the unusual presence at the confession of a sociologist, he subpoenaed Leo to produce his notes and to testify at the suppression hearing. It would have been "legal malpractice," explained the public defender, not to seek Leo's testimony, when "his client's freedom hung in the balance." The police and defendant had given different versions of the events, but Leo, as a neutral third party, could describe "what *really* transpired during that interrogation" (italics original).

Leo attempted to quash the subpoena. His lawyer (provided by the University of California) argued that Leo's research had been "uniquely predicated" on maintaining confidentiality, and that he could therefore assert the same "limited First Amendment right" to withhold testimony that is allowed to journalists. Even the prosecutor did not accept that argument, thus joining the public defender's demand to compel Leo's notes and testimony.

The court ruled that "the defendant's due process rights clearly outweighed any public interest" in Leo's research, because the testimony was necessary to "provide the accused with a fair trial." The judge informed Leo that "failure to testify would leave me in contempt of court, a penalty that carried a renewable five-day jail term (at least until the end of the jury trial) and a $1000 fine."

Unlike Scarce, Leo decided to comply with the court's order, and he proceeded to testify at the suppression hearing. "I will always regret this decision," he later wrote.[49]

I contacted Leo to see if he had perhaps changed his mind about testifying. He is now a law professor and a leading authority on police interrogation and false confessions. "In retrospect, now twenty years later, I don't especially regret my decision to testify," he replied. "With hindsight, I would rule the same way the judge did. The defendant's due process right to the information in my notes clearly outweigh[ed] any research interest in keeping the information confidential, with or without a limited journalist/researcher privilege."[50]

Whether one agrees with Scarce or Leo, actual subpoenas for research data have been very few (and contempt citations fewer yet). Consequently, subpoenas hardly represent a significant threat to the practice of ethnography. Even among those who study criminals, there is no compelling need, and certainly no requirement, to destroy field notes or take other extreme steps to avoid the production of evidence—which, as we have seen, may sometimes be sought by prisoners or defendants, and not only by the government.[51] A greater problem is probably created by over-promising, as field researchers routinely make blanket commitments to extreme confidentiality that they may not be able to maintain.[52]

Conclusion: Toward Evidence-Based Ethnography

THE EVIDENCE IN A courtroom trial is subjected to many forms of adversarial testing. Most notably, there is cross-examination, which probes for inconsistencies, gaps, implausibilities, contradictions, and exaggerations. In addition, a case may be shown to rest on previously omitted, overlooked, or conflicting evidence, as adverse witnesses call earlier testimony into question. Finally, opposing counsel may present counter-arguments, either by exposing the weakness of contrary claims or assertions, or by developing an alternative interpretation of the known facts.

A similar dialectic is engaged in the quantitative sciences, where results are questioned or reinterpreted, experiments are replicated, and other efforts are made at falsification. Both systems are salutary, even if imperfect, because they consistently challenge claims and contentions by holding them up to a standard of provability. Neither law nor science invariably gets things right, but at least they do not routinely allow questionable assertions to go unexamined.

Ethnography seems seldom to employ comparable correctives. This is no doubt caused in some part by the extreme labor intensity that ethnography requires, and the consequent difficulty of replication. Whatever one thinks of Mitchell Duneier's *Sidewalk* (which is widely admired and unquestioned by me), no one else would ever venture to spend a year, or even a month, selling used magazines in New York simply for the sake of testing his conclusions. Nonetheless, there are devices that could be used far more often to interrogate the evidentiary bases of ethnographic studies, including fact- and citation-checking, revisits and re-interviews, and examination of field notes.

FACT-CHECKING

As we have seen, it is sometimes possible to fact-check ethnographies even when they have been heavily masked. Murders and other serious crimes are reported in newspapers and generate extensive official paper trails. Other sorts of facts—such as vital statistics or housing and welfare regulations—are also documented in public records and reports.

Mitchell Duneier was able to compare the death rates in adjacent Chicago neighborhoods during the devastating heat wave of 1995, and thereby raise important questions about Eric Klinenberg's explanatory theory that many of the deaths were due to "broken spaces, broken families."[1] Likewise, Christopher Jencks was able to use government statistics to revise some of the numbers in Edin and Shaefer's *$2 a Day*, most importantly by reducing their estimate of "extreme poverty" in the United States by more than half. Jencks also questioned Edin and Shaefer's definition of extreme poverty, proposing a more realistic alternative in which "the prevalence of extreme poverty among households with children fell . . . from 4.3 to 1.6 percent in 2011."[2] None of this affects the impact of severe poverty on Edin and Shaefer's research subjects, or the poignancy of their stories, but it does show the usefulness of further research into ethnographers' claims.

Even in the absence of available documentation, it may be possible to engage what one noted ethnographer calls "external verification," meaning checking stories for consistency with the "experiences of others," seeking confirmation from "members of the community," and otherwise exploring the "available evidence base."[3]

The transportation blogger Joseph Brennan did just that with regard to the "available evidence base" for Jennifer Toth's *The Mole People*, in which the author—a journalist, not an ethnographer—claims to have made repeated visits to a colony of homeless people who had established a well-organized society in the abandoned subway tunnels of New York City. Brennan, who is an expert on the New York City transit system, reviewed the details in Toth's book and determined that "every fact in this book that I can verify independently is wrong." He identified dozens of instances in which Toth either described a nonexistent or physically impossible location or made claims inconsistent with the actual layout of the subways. Although Brennan did not question the plight of homeless people who shelter in subway tunnels, and he conceded that Toth had no doubt interviewed many of them, he concluded from his own research and knowledge that "the book is full of myth" amounting to "something worse than a little sloppiness." "Is she just making some of it up?" he asked.[4]

Such circumstantial evidence, as lawyers would call it, can be extremely valuable when it comes to testing assertions that seem exaggerated, implausible, or rumor-based. The best ethnographers use similar methods to confirm their own work, and the profession would benefit if they would more often apply the same standards when reviewing the work of others.

REVISITS AND RE-INTERVIEWS

Replication is the gold standard for validity in both the physical and social sciences, and most results are considered at best provisional until they have been independently reproduced. In September 2011, for example, a team of physicists in Italy announced that they had measured a neutrino that traveled between their Gran Sasso National Laboratory and the CERN particle accelerator at a rate 0.002 percent faster than the speed of light, contrary to Einstein's theory of special relativity. This result would have been paradigm-shifting if true, and other scientists therefore set about trying to confirm or falsify it through replication. Eventually, five separate teams of physicists determined that the subatomic particles travel only at the speed of light, thereby putting "the nail in the coffin of faster-than-light neutrinos." Another group at the Gran Sasso Laboratory itself discovered that the mismeasurement had been due to a loose fiber-optic cable and the original result was withdrawn.[5] This outcome is far from unique; many studies in the hard sciences turn out to have reached mistaken conclusions for one reason or another.

Richard Horton, editor-in-chief of the United Kingdom's leading medical journal, has cautioned that "much of the scientific literature, perhaps half, may simply be untrue." The problem, said Horton, is that research is frequently "afflicted by studies with small sample sizes, tiny effects, invalid exploratory analyses, and flagrant conflicts of interest, together with an obsession for pursuing fashionable trends of dubious importance." Thus, the "quest for telling a compelling story" too often leads researchers to "sculpt data to fit their preferred theory of the world."[6] Although Horton was addressing biomedical science, the lesson for ethnography is unmissable, especially regarding his call for greater emphasis on "replicability."

Similar problems have dogged the social sciences. A recent study of 100 published psychology experiments concluded that "more than half of the findings did not hold up when retested."[7] As the authors of the study explained,

> We conducted replications of 100 experimental and correlational studies published in three psychology journals using high-powered designs and original materials when available . . . . [C]ollectively these results offer a clear conclusion: A large portion of replications produced weaker evidence for the original findings despite using materials provided by the original authors, review in advance for methodological fidelity, and high statistical power to detect the original effect sizes.[8]

No one knows how ethnographies would fare under similar scrutiny, because so few rigorous attempts at re-investigation have been made. People and neighborhoods change over time, of course, and they are not comparable to particles that move according to physical laws. Nonetheless, repeated studies in the same locale would allow us to test propositions against a developed knowledge base. Thus, ethnographers would do well to heed the authors of the reproduction study in psychology, who express concern that "the incentives for individual scientists prioritize novelty over replication."[9] John Ioannidis, of the Stanford Medical School, goes further, criticizing "the convenient, yet ill-founded strategy of claiming conclusive research findings solely on the basis of a single study" and observing that "claimed research findings may often be simply accurate measures of the prevailing bias."[10] Whatever the extent of the problem, an obvious remedy lies in replication and fact-testing, which, in the case of ethnography, would consist of revisits or re-interviews.

As Jerolmack and Murphy note, ethnographic revisits are often made difficult or impossible by the convention of site and subject masking.

Tellingly, those ethnographers who later revisited their own research locales have sometimes come away with mixed feelings about the accuracy or fairness of their original studies.[11]

There is vigorous scholarly debate within ethnography, as there is in every academic discipline, but it centers for the most part on issues of theory and methodology.[12] Only occasionally has one ethnographer reinvestigated another's field work, as Duneier did when he tracked down the some of the victims of Chicago's 1995 heat wave in order to test the hypothesis of Klinenberg's *Heat Wave*. Using "names and addresses supplied by the Cook County Medical Examiner," Duneier managed to interview the relatives and neighbors of many of the deceased, who informed him that most of the victims had not, as Klinenberg believed, "died alone because they lived in social environments that discouraged departure" from their homes.[13]

Efforts such as Duneier's, however, are quite rare and not always well received. In one instance, Marianne Boelen visited "Cornerville" over a number of years, beginning in 1970. She succeeded in locating some of Whyte's original informants, who sharply disagreed with some of Whyte's descriptions of the neighborhood.[14] Whyte deeply resented Boelen's re-investigation, calling it "a sloppy hatchet job," and he mounted a defense at a meeting of the American Sociological Association, where statements of support were presented by other prominent ethnographers and the attendees responded with a standing ovation.[15] Following an initial flurry of controversy, Boelen's work "barely rippled the disciplinary waters" because, as Michael Burawoy observed, the "sociological establishment mobilized to defend its archetypical ethnography." "It is always an uphill task," Burawoy added, "to refute an entrenched study that has become a pillar of the discipline."[16]

It is unfortunate that ethnographers have so seldom essayed revisits to others' research sites. Despite the obvious difficulties, there are cases in which the impediments can be readily overcome. It would not take long for an ethnographer to interview personnel at the hospitals in West Philadelphia where Alice Goffman claims to have seen police cordons at the entrances. Moreover, there are only six hospitals in Philadelphia with maternity services, so it would be possible, even now, to fact-check Goffman's story of having observed the arrests of three new fathers on the same ward in a single evening.[17]

Such an investigation would be routine in many disciplines—the hard sciences, journalism, law—but it is little seen in ethnography.[18] In the absence of on-the-ground scrutiny, however, the best a reader can do is to search for "falsifying passages by comparing different segments" of the text and notes.[19]

FIELD NOTES

Data sharing, which is now considered almost obligatory in the physical and quantitative sciences, presents unique problems in ethnography, where field notes typically include confidences that cannot easily be anonymized. Consequently, the Code of Ethics of the American Sociological Association provides an exception to the usual expectation:

> Sociologists make their data available after completion of the project or its major publications, except . . . when it is impossible to share data and protect the confidentiality of the data or the anonymity of research participants (e.g., raw field notes or detailed information from ethnographic interviews).[20]

This inevitably impedes verification, as field notes may often be the only existing evidence that certain events occurred as reported. As we saw with police reports and government memorandums, contemporaneous notes can be uniquely useful and reliable, and they are therefore afforded favorable status in the law of evidence.[21] When facts come into question—in ethnography, journalism, or other disciplines—answers can often be provided by reviewing field notes or their equivalent.

In both "Jimmy's World" and "A Rape on Campus," for example, serious incidents of fraud were eventually uncovered when the reporter was required to produce her original notes for her editors. It turned out that Janet Cooke had fabricated her entire story of a young drug addict for the *Washington Post*. Such wholesale deceit is obviously unlikely to occur in ethnography, but the problems with "A Rape on Campus" hit closer to home. In that case, *Rolling Stone*'s Sabrina Erdely had placed far too much faith in a single informant, whose account had never been confirmed by anyone else at the magazine. The events were related solely through the use of pseudonyms, and even editors at *Rolling Stone* were unaware of the real names and identities of the key participants. All of this came to light when Erdely's notes were reviewed for the Coll report, which emphasized the dangers of blanket anonymization, especially in the absence of "data sharing" with other journalists.

It also works the other way around. The journalist Janet Malcolm was eventually able to defeat a libel suit brought by Jeffrey Masson, a psychoanalyst and a former director of the Sigmund Freud Archives, in part by producing interview notes for an article in *The New Yorker* that formed the basis of her book *In the Freud Archives*.[22] In *Patient H.M.*, the journalist Luke Dittrich recounts an interview with MIT neuropsychologist Suzanne Corkin, in which she seemed to admit having shredded the original notes of her research on Henry Molaison, whose surgically induced amnesia made him "the most studied individual in the history of neuroscience." The intentional destruction of such irreplaceable notes, covering over forty years of research and experiments, would have been professionally irresponsible, but it appears that Prof. Corkin had been trying only to discourage Dittrich's inquiry for reasons of her own. The head of the Department of Brain and Cognitive Sciences at MIT subsequently issued a statement affirming that all of the Molaison files were intact:

> We believe that no records were destroyed and, to the contrary, that Professor Corkin worked in her final days to organize and preserve all records. Even as her health failed (she had advanced cancer and was receiving chemotherapy), she instructed her assistant to continue to organize, label, and maintain all records related to Henry Molaison. The records currently remain within our department.

An open letter signed by over two hundred members of the International Community of Scientists also supported Prof. Corkin's integrity regarding the "proper disposition of confidential data."[23]

The actual absence of notes can be revealing. In 1990, a Chicago man named Madison Hobley was convicted of seven counts of murder and sentenced to death, in part on the basis of a confession that he had allegedly given to two police detectives. Hobley denied ever making a confession, but the detectives testified at trial, claiming that Hobley had admitted setting a fire that killed his wife and child, and five others. The notes of the confession had been thrown away, according to the police, because they had gotten wet, but that did not prevent the conviction. Hobley spent thirteen years on death row before his guilt was effectively challenged by lawyers who re-investigated the case and discredited the alleged confession, leading to his pardon on the ground of innocence.[24] In the same vein, the Brooklyn District Attorney was compelled to re-investigate scores of convictions that had been obtained through the work of Detective Louis Scarcella, including many in which he had testified to confessions for which there turned out to be no documentation.[25]

In the most famous academic case of missing notes, the historian Michael Bellesiles was found by an independent "Investigative Committee," empaneled by Emory University, to have engaged in "serious deviations from accepted practices" and guilty of "unprofessional and misleading work" with regard to his Bancroft Prize–winning book, *Arming America*. Among other serious problems, Bellesiles had failed to produce his underlying research notes, which he claimed had been destroyed when his office was flooded.[26] The Bancroft Prize was rescinded and Bellesiles lost his position as a tenured history professor at Emory.

It is now common for quantitative scientists to post their data sets on the internet for public examination. It would be impractical to expect ethnographers to make their field notes equally available—given the complications of confidentiality—but it should also be unacceptable for field notes to be held in absolute secrecy, or even to be destroyed.[27] Someone—whether it is an editor, advisor, or colleague—should be able to review ethnography field notes, both before and after publication.

As in other regards, Matthew Desmond set a standard by retaining an independent fact-checker (named Gillian Brassil) who made sure that his manuscript was supported by his notes:

> I provided Gillian with all of my field notes after she signed a non-disclosure agreement . . . . Besides asking for documentation for several details recorded in this book, Gillian also randomly selected 10 percent of the book's manuscript pages and asked me to show her where she could find corresponding scenes or observations in the field notes.[28]

Many ethnographers will be working with smaller budgets than Desmond's, but they can still follow his example. As Desmond explained to *New York Magazine*'s Jesse Singal,

> I think there are ways that we can do this that don't require massive amounts of resources. So let's say you and I were in grad school together and I was doing an ethnography — I could give you my fieldnotes and you could do the same for me, and we could fact-check [each other's] claims, and we could write that in our publication so that we hold each other accountable for that.[29]

Finally, ethnographers could enhance their credibility by citing the dates and locations of interviews or observations—which should be readily determinable in their own notes—even while maintaining the anonymity of their subjects. Although that might result in too many endnotes for a trade publisher, it could be adopted as a standard practice in scholarly books and dissertations.[30]

TRUTH IN ETHNOGRAPHY

Urban ethnography has many important virtues that have led to greatly increased understanding and considerable public good. Ethnographic stories can deliver messages that are far more compelling than surveys or empirical studies, even when they are describing the same phenomena.[31] The dedication of ethnographers, who spend countless hours, and sometimes years, in painstaking observation, deserves much admiration. On the other hand, I am aware of no other discipline in the physical or social sciences—or in related fields, including law and journalism—that relies so heavily on anonymous sources, often as reported by a single investigator whose underlying data remain unseen. Although such practices may be widely accepted, and perhaps necessary to some degree, they will always risk generating "false-positive findings," even among "perfectly well-intentioned researchers."[32]

My research led me to many ethnographic assertions that were well-founded and even revelatory, but I also found too many others that were dubious, exaggerated, tendentious, or just plain wrong. Because my investigations were limited to accounts that appeared facially questionable, it is impossible to determine how many of the more mundane statements—of which I read many thousands—were also unreliable. Even if the proportion is relatively small, it is fair to say that there is an accuracy problem in the practice of ethnography, and that it has been largely overlooked by professionals in the field. Reforms are needed to bring ethnography into line with other evidence-based disciplines, in the following three regards:

- **Accuracy**. Ethnographies should rely less on unsourced generalities; when used, they should be related, whenever possible, to specific incidents of observed behavior. Descriptions of "typical" behavior should be accompanied by explanations of frequency while noting the likelihood of exceptions. Composites should be avoided; if used, they should be clearly identified in the text—not simply mentioned in the preface or appendix—and should not be presented with personality traits and physical descriptions as though they are actual people. Field sites should be identified with precision, pseudonyms should be used only when there is no alternative, and other personal descriptors should be unaltered. Assurances that only "minor" details have been changed should, at a minimum, be accompanied by examples (although it would be best not to change them at all).
- **Candor**. Clear distinctions must be made between direct observations and information from other sources. Second-hand accounts from informants should not be reported as statements of fact. Care must be taken to identify rumors and folklore. Statements included for the purpose of giving voice to informants, or representing their views and perceptions, should be identified as such in the text. Skepticism of potentially unreliable informants should be expressly noted. The "argument" of the book should be openly acknowledged, while contrary facts and inconvenient witnesses should be prominently featured.
- **Documentation**. Sources and informants should be clearly identified, including the dates and nature of communications with anonymous research subjects. Informants' statements should verified and documented whenever possible. Field notes should be provided to a third party and checked against the text for accuracy. Dates and locations should be stated accurately, to facilitate verification.

Ethnographers should routinely fact-check one another's work, including revisits and attempts at replication when feasible.

More attention must be paid to the quality of evidence in qualitative social science, and the ways in which it may be enhanced through rigorous questioning and testing. And while I do not recommend that ethnographers adopt a purely adversary system, with its requisite dedication to advancing opposing points of view, I do think they would benefit from greater formal skepticism of one another's work. An ethnographer's observations and conclusions should not go unchallenged simply because they are the product of extensive field work and consonant with a widely accepted world view (even when that world view has much to recommend it). Using trials as a template, I have attempted in the preceding pages to outline some of the ways in which such challenges can be respectfully and meaningfully advanced. In an era when public discourse has been increasingly dominated by fake news and alternative facts, the accuracy of social science is more important than ever.

ACKNOWLEDGMENTS

Many people helped me at various stages of the conception, development, and completion of this project. I have especially benefitted from thoughts, comments, input, and assistance of Jesse Bowman, Gary Alan Fine, Eric Posner, Melissa Montemayor, David Tuller, Andrew Koppelman, Gabriel Snyder, Sasha Belenky, Gwyneth Kelly, Terry Williams, Ryan Kearney, César Ayala, John Conroy, Jeanne Herrick, Victor Rios, Shamus Khan, Colin Jerolmack, Steven Drizin, Shericka Pringle, Zachary Schrag, Yvonna Lincoln, Tobias Barrington Wolf, Shari Diamond, César Rosado, Ronald Allen, Robert Burns, Rachel Maines, Garrel Pottinger, Christel Bridges, Richard Leo, Philip Cohen, Oscar Arroyo, Bob Yovovich, Paul Campos, Rob Baker, Meredith Martin Rountree, Michele Goodwin, Lucy Shackelford, Craig LaMay, Deborah Tuerkheimer, James Forman, Julie Coplon, Whitman Soule, Jonathan Koehler, JC Lore, Hank Greenspan, Ann Miller, Enrique Guerra-Pujol, Dan Filler, Al Brophy, David Shapiro, Sheila Bedi, David Lurie, Dana Amato, David Dana, Cristina Messerschmidt, Michael Carrithers, Anthony Burrows, Juliet Sorenson, David Dana, Janice Nadler, Anita Bernstein, Laura Nirider, Dwayne Betts, Alex Lubet, Jeff Rice, Amy Wax, participants at a Northwestern University Pritzker Law School faculty workshop, and colleagues at the Unicorn Roundtable.

I am also grateful to the many people who answered questions and provided me with information in either interviews or correspondence, including Gary Austin, Todd Berger, John Boston, Joseph

Byham, Jeffrey Carter, Margaret Claw, Randol Contreras, Karen
Daniel, Matthew Desmond, Mitchell Duneier, Kathryn Edin, Phil
Ellingsworth, Anna Foster, Everett Gillison, Summer Graves, Bernice
Ho, Lisa Hull, Cliff Johnson, Caitlin Kelly, Gail Wright Lowery, Ari
Maas, Rebecca Madison, Akillie Malone-Oliver, Heather McTeer
Toney, Michael Morrissey, Francis Mullen, Nandan Nelivigi, Jed
Oppenheim, Carlos Palmer, Tiffany Palmer, Ted Palys, Samuel Popkin,
Ashish Prasad, Laurence Ralph, Dewayne Richardson, Kyle Rozema,
Luke Shaefer, Jeffrey Urdangan, Noah Veltman, Sudhir Venkatesh,
John Verrecchio, Deja Vishny, Jeremy Walter, and several anonymous
court sources, city officials, police officers, community members, and
prosecutors in Philadelphia.

This project would not have been possible without the generous
support of Dean Daniel Rodriguez and the Robert Childres Memorial
Fund and the Faculty Research Fund of the Northwestern Pritzker Law
School. I also benefitted immeasurably from the outstanding editorial
input of David McBride, Niko Pfund, Claire Sibley, Paul Tompsett,
and Wendy Walker.

Most important, of course, has been the love and encouragement of
my family: Linda, Natan, Sarah, Willard, Frankie, and Doris.

NOTES

Preface

1. Kotlowitz, "Deep Cover"; Newburn, "Book Review."
2. Jencks, "America's Front Lines."
3. It was reassuring to discover that there had also been some critical reviews of *On the Run.* James Foreman, in *The Atlantic*, Dwayne Betts, in *Slate*, and Christina Sharpe, in *The New Inquiry*, had all raised questions about Goffman's methods and ethics. Perhaps it was a coincidence, but all three are African Americans, and they had seen serious flaws in the book that others had missed. Foreman is a former public defender and Betts, who expressed the deepest concern about Goffman's criminality, had himself spent eight years in prison in his youth. Foreman, "Society of Fugitives"; Betts, "The Stoop"; Sharpe, "Black Life, Annotated."
4. Some readers will be aware of my earlier critical reviews of *On the Run* in which I questioned Goffman's "accuracy and reliability" while also calling her "brilliant and dedicated," both of which continue to be my view. See Lubet, "Ethics on the Run"; Lubet, "Getaway Car."
5. Denzin, "Politics of Evidence." See also Peregrine, "Seeking Truth"; Wade, "Anthropology a Science?"
6. Desmond, *Evicted*, pages 326–27.
7. Desmond, *Evicted*, page 404.

Introduction

1. Duneier, "How Not to Lie," page 2.
2. Duneier, "How Not to Lie," pages 2, 8.
3. Bosk notes with pride that most readers and reviewers have believed "Pacific" to be a regional designation rather than an ironic reference to the non-peaceful nature of the hospital setting. Bosk, *What Would You Do?*, pages 212, 216.

4. According to Duneier, the sociologist William Foote Whyte believed "that not all impoverished and congested areas with substandard housing were alike." Duneier, *Ghetto*, page 46.

5. Gawande, "Cost Conundrum." Dittrich, *Patient H.M.*, page 260. Bosk's theory of presumed typicality cannot account for such stark differences between two surgical programs with a shared history, located at hospitals only an hour's drive apart.

6. Bosk, *Forgive and Remember*, pages 8–11. The question of representativeness or generalizability presents a complex issue in ethnography, with some scholars arguing that it "should never be statistical, only logical." Harvard's Mario Small argues that the selection of either an ostensibly typical or apparently atypical case "would be *immaterial*" in certain situations. Small, "How Many Cases?," pages 22, 23 (italics original).

7. Bosk, *What Would You Do?*, page 216. The second passage is Bosk's approving quotation of Hughes, *The Sociological Eye*, page xix.

8. The burden of proof at trial is divided into the "burden of production" and the "burden of persuasion." The former governs the need to present sufficient evidence on a particular issue, while the latter defines the more familiar requirement of convincing the factfinder by either a preponderance of evidence or beyond reasonable doubt. Allen, "Burdens of Proof."

9. Jerolmack and Murphy, "Ethical Dilemmas"; Murphy and Jerolmack, "Ethnographic Masking."

10. Duneier, *Sidewalk*, pp. 342–46. The "ethnological fallacy" quotation is from Steinberg, "The Urban Villagers."

11. Duneier, *Sidewalk*, p. 345. Regarding the difference between malpractice and negligence in social science, see Guerra-Pujol, "Liability for Research Fraud."

12. Forrest Stuart also searched out an "inconvenience sample" for his book about policing on Los Angeles's skid row, but its publication in August 2016 came too late for inclusion in my project. Stuart, *Down, Out & Under Arrest*, pages 282–84.

13. Van Cleve, *Crook County*, p. 94 (italics original). The ethnographic trial did not change her mind.

14. Wigmore, *Evidence*, section 1367, p. 32.

Chapter 1

1. Wacquant, *Body & Soul*, pages 249–54; Grazian, *Blue Chicago*; Anderson, *Streetwise*; Rios, *Punished*, page 127.

2. Hoang, *Dealing in Desire*, page 41.

3. Small, *Villa Victoria*, pages 98–99.

4. Nippert-End, *Watching Closely*, page 9.

5. Weinstein and Berger, *Weinstein's Evidence*, section 1402 (1).

6. Mueller and Kirkpatrick, *Evidence*, pp. 721–22.

7. Hattem, "FBI Head Doubles Down."

8. Jerolmack and Khan, "Talk Is Cheap," page 189. Carolyn Ellis put it this way: "I don't know if the stories they told me happened or not . . . or if I took what they said too literally, limited by my own sense of the 'truth' and storytelling." Ellis, "Returning to the Field," page 93.
9. Stack, *All Our Kin*, page 20.
10. Anderson, *Streetwise*, pages 107, 131–32.
11. Duneier, *Slim's Table*, page 110.
12. Hoang, *Dealing in Desire*, pages 42, 78, 175.
13. Ralph, *Renegade Dreams*, pages 16–17.

Chapter 2

1. Jack Webb played Detective Sergeant Joe Friday, of the Los Angeles Police Department, on the radio and television show *Dragnet*, in the years 1949–59 and 1967–70. Of particular interest to ethnographers would be the opening lines of each episode: "The story you are about to see is true. The names have been changed to protect the innocent." The stories, however, were fiction. The use of pseudonyms in ethnography is addressed in Chapter Seven.
2. See Rules 701 and 702, Federal Rules of Evidence. *United States v. Smith* (7th Cir. 2016).
3. Williams, *Crackhouse*, pages 88–89.
4. Anderson, *Streetwise*, page 107, and *Code of the Street*, page 30; Rios, *Punished*, page xiii; Venkatesh, *American Project*, passim.
5. Jones, *Between Good and Ghetto*, page 97; Van Cleve, *Crook County*, pages 75–76; Edin and Shaefer, *$2 a Day*, page 159.
6. Duneier, *Slim's Table*, page 138.
7. Grazian, *Blue Chicago*, page 146.
8. Edin and Shaefer, *$2 a Day*, pages 157–74. Contreras, *Stickup Kids*, page 237. Ralph, *Renegade Dreams*, pages 167–80.
9. Whyte, *Street Corner Society* (second edition, 1955), page 327–28 (italics original). Whyte also opined that neighborhood status could be used to predict bowling scores, and that "group structure" has a pronounced impact on individual performance. He believed that bowling scores would correspond to "the structure of the gang," even though the gang leaders were not "better natural athletes than the rest." In his own case, he thought that his temporary position "close to the top of the gang" had endowed him with preternatural bowling skills that he never experienced "before—or since." It was "as if something larger than myself was controlling the ball." Following the most important tournament of the year, Whyte was "excited to discover that the men had actually finished in the predicted order with only two exceptions that could readily be explained in terms of the group structure." Indeed, he suspected "that a systematic study of the social structure of a baseball team" would reveal the same results. Whyte, *Street Corner Society*, pages 318–19. It is understandable that athletic prowess would affect social

standing, but it is highly unlikely that elevated status would consistently lead to better bowling. Whyte's conclusions therefore seem far-fetched—as does his offhand dismissal of the two nonconforming outcomes—but at least they are sociological.

10. Federal Rules of Evidence, Rule 702.
11. Desmond, *Evicted*, page 308 (italics original).
12. Desmond, *Evicted*, page 312. For a description of a group unlikely to be affected by housing vouchers, see *Righteous Dopefiend*, by Philippe Bourgois and Jeff Schonberg, in which the authors report on, and present photographs of, an outdoor encampment of homeless "heroin injectors" in San Francisco.
13. Housing economists estimate that elimination of the mortgage tax deduction would result in depression of housing prices by as much as 20 percent, and an immediate change might cause them to "tumble." Email from Kenneth Rosen, July 14, 2016; email from Kyle Rozema, July 15, 2016. See also Bourassa and Yin, "Tax Deductions." Elimination of the capital gains exclusion would have an additional effect on the housing market. Regarding the possibility for other unintended economic consequences from Desmond's proposal, see Dana, "Invisible Crisis."
14. Desmond, *Evicted*, page 262.
15. Desmond's previous book is about wildland firefighting. Desmond, *Fireline*. In an article published while this book was in press, Desmond expanded greatly on his critique of the home mortgage tax deduction, with many additional details. Desmond, "Homeownership."
16. Desmond, *Evicted*, pages 304–05. As of this writing, the New York City Council is considering a bill that would provide lawyers at city expense to those facing eviction or foreclosure whose income is below $44,000 (twice the federal poverty level). According to the *New York Times*, which editorialized in favor of the bill, about 80 percent of eviction defendants would qualify, amounting to about 128,000 cases annually. "A Right to a Lawyer to Save Your Home."
17. Desmond, *Evicted*, page 305.
18. Email from Nandan Nelivigi, June 21, 2016. Regarding the difficulty and expense of obtaining effective counsel in the Indian legal system, including evictions, see Boo, *Behind the Beautiful Forevers*, pages 200–12, 224.
19. The quoted passages are from Desmond, *Evicted*, pages 218–19. For critique, see, e.g., Sykes, "Let Them Eat Lobster."
20. Charles Bosk, *What Would You Do?*, page 144.
21. Van Cleve, *Crook County*, page xii. There are 46 references to "the workgroup" in *Crook County*.
22. Contreras, *The Stickup Kids*, pages 113, 197–98.
23. Rules 803 and 803(7), Federal Rules of Evidence. There is also a special rule that excludes the observations of police officers—if offered by the prosecution, though admissible for the defense—from otherwise admissible reports. Rule 803(8), Federal Rules of Evidence.

24. Edin and Shaefer, *$2 a Day*, pages 3–4.
25. Email from Kathryn Edin, June 2, 2016.
26. Kelly, *Malled*, pages 1, 6, 60–61, 147. See also Mitchell, *Hug Your People*.
27. Gill, *Starbucks Saved My Life*, pages 211, 218.
28. Email from Caitlin Kelly, March 7, 2016. Kelly is the author of *Malled*.
29. Email from Luke Shaefer, June 2, 2016.
30. Edin and Shaefer, *$2 a Day*, pages 3, 168.
31. Lewis-Kraus, "The Trials of Alice Goffman." When pressed for confirmation of some of her claims, Goffman objected to "getting officials who are white men in power to corroborate them." "Finding 'legitimate' people to validate the claims—it feels wrong to me on just about every level," she said. According to the "czar and editor" of Ethnography.com, only a "police advocate" would rely on police sources to fact-check ethnography. Waters, "Alice Goffman's On the Run."
32. Moskos, *Cop in the Hood*, p. 78 (italics omitted). For a description of the circumstances in which police use contrived "cover stories," see Hunt and Manning, "Police Lying," pages 60–62. For the drawbacks of using police and crime statistics as sources of data in social science, see Becker, *Evidence*, pages 113–25.
33. *People v. Oduwole*, Appellate Court of Illinois, March 6, 2013.
34. http://www.law.northwestern.edu/legalclinic/wrongfulconvictions/exonerations/il/maurice-patterson.html.
    The ethnographer Jennifer Hunt notes that "problems often arise in the wake of police shootings because officers lie about what happened even in situations in which the truth would not undermine their case." Nonetheless, she used "internal police reports" in her book on the arrest and near-fatal shooting of two "terrorists who were in possession of bombs that they planned to detonate in New York." Hunt, *Seven Shots*, pages 1, 327. Likewise, in her remarkable account of life in the Mumbai slums, the journalist Katherine Boo demonstrated that it was possible to make good use of police reports and court records even while recognizing that the appallingly corrupt "Indian criminal justice system was a market like garbage." Boo, *Beautiful Forevers*, pages 107, 250–52.

Chapter 3

1. Thomas, "Impeaching One's Own Witness"; Notes of Advisory Committee on Proposed Rules, Federal Rules of Evidence.
2. Duneier, *Sidewalk*, page 338.
3. Fine, "Ten Lies," pages 277–78, 287.
4. "There are always two sides to a story and a third one to tell it." Williams and Milton, *Con Men*, pages 25–26.
5. Williams, *Crackhouse*, pages 130–31.
6. Interestingly, Gavilan did fight a man named Ralph "Tiger" Jones three times, losing to him once in 1958. Tiger Jones was born in Brooklyn, however, and Williams's subject was born in South Carolina, so they could

not have been the same man. Perhaps Williams's Tiger borrowed both his nickname and achievements from the more accomplished Jones.

7. Rios, *Punished*, page 15.
8. Rios, *Punished*, pages 46–51.
9. Emails from Jeffrey Carter, June 20 and 21, 2016. The OHA is the Oakland Housing Authority, located in Alameda County. The agency does have a special re-entry program for single mothers coming out of jail—called the MOMS program—which is the only gender-restricted program I have found.
10. Desmond, *Evicted*, page 244.
11. According to one veteran Chicago defense lawyer, between 80 and 90 percent of his clients have spun, shaded, fibbed, or lied to him about the facts in order to make themselves appear less culpable. Email from Jeffrey Urdangen, November 8, 2016. Many others have recognized that criminal defendants often "fail to provide complete and accurate versions of events to attorneys, especially at the early stages of representation when the attorney-client relationship has just been formed." Eldred, "Psychology of Conflicts."
12. Desmond, *Evicted*, page 265. Desmond told me that "I attended Vanetta's sentencing hearing and reviewed court records from that hearing and previous ones. The victims did not testify at the hearing, and I didn't speak to them." Email from Matthew Desmond, June 20, 2016.
13. Desmond, *Evicted*, page 267.
14. Email from Deja Vishny, March 22, 2016. For statistics on probation in Milwaukee, see Court Tracker: Criminal Case Research for Wisconsin Attorneys: http://www.courttracker.com/.
15. Edin and Schaefer, *$2 a Day*, pages 149–51.
16. The authors mention a subject commuting to Greenville, which is in Washington County, and Tabitha is from the hamlet of "Percy" in "Sunshine County," which appears to be a pseudonym for the adjacent Sunflower County. There are 18 unincorporated communities in Sunflower County, though none are called Percy.
17. Interview with Dewayne Richardson, April 28, 2016. For good measure, I also contacted the attorneys for the adjoining Holmes, Humphreys, and Yazoo Counties, who all denied having received such a complaint. Email from Akillie Malone-Oliver (district attorney for Holmes, Humphreys, and Yazoo Counties), January 28, 2016; email from Gary Austin (prosecuting attorney for Sunflower County), January 28, 2016; email from Cliff Johnson (following his interview with Eric Hawkins, prosecuting attorney for Washington County, March 22, 2016). Heather McTeer Toney, who was the mayor of Greenville at the time, also said that she had never heard of such a report. Email from Heather McTeer Toney, April 29, 2016.
18. Email and letter from Carlos Palmer, May 6, 2016.
19. Letter from Carlos Palmer, June 2, 2016. The Mississippi child abuse reporting requirement is in Miss. Code Ann. § 43-21-353. The Public Records Act is Miss. Code Ann. § 25-61-9(2).

20. Interview with H. Luke Shaefer, June 3, 2016.
21. Small, *Villa Victoria*, page 195.
22. Email from JC Lore, August 3, 2015.
23. Email from Todd Berger, August 3, 2015.
24. The bail story makes no sense even on its own terms. The Philadelphia police make between 60,000 and 70,000 arrests annually, but only a fraction of the arrestees would ever be the subject of a warrant. It is implausible that the police would have the time or resources to compile or update over 1,000 dossiers each week, just in case they might someday need the information to locate a fugitive. Fazlollah and Purcell, "Phila. Police Report."
25. Email from Todd Berger, August 3, 2015.
26. Contreras, *Stickup Kids*, pages 173–75.
27. Van Cleve, *Crook County*, pages 93, 96–97.
28. Van Cleve, *Crook County*, pages 99–103.
29. I shared Van Cleve's passages with a senior public defender in Chicago who was offended by her charge of complicity. Interview with Michael Morrissey, June 2, 2016.
30. Jerolmack and Khan, "Talk Is Cheap," page 179. Of course, it is sometimes the case that the informant's subjective viewpoint is the very purpose of the research.
31. Fahri, "Talese Disavows." Talese later disavowed his disavowal. Alter, "Talese Defends."
32. Fahri, "New Yorker Never Mentioned." The article was based on an excerpt from *The Voyeur's Motel* that was published in *The New Yorker* in advance of the book itself.

Chapter 4

1. Ogbu, *Black American Students*, page xx.
2. Williams and Milton, *Con Men*, pages 23, 25.
3. Kerr, *Scream*, pages 87, 102.
4. Whyte, *Street Corner Society*, pages 144–45.
5. Ralph, *Renegade Dreams*, page 68.
6. Hoang, *Dealing with Desire*, pages 60, 72–73.
7. Anderson, *Streetwise*, page 121.
8. Edin and Shaefer, *$2 a Day*, page 131.
9. Edin and Shaefer, *$2 a Day*, pages 148–49.
10. Email from Heather McTeer Toney, June 8, 2016; interview with Rebecca Madison, July 20, 2016; interview with Summer Graves, July 22, 2016; email from Cliff Johnson, July 17, 2016.
11. *TV IV*, "Nielsen Ratings/Historic/Network Television by Season/2000s," http://tviv.org/Nielsen_Ratings/Historic/Network_Television_by_Season/2000s, accessed June 9, 2016.
12. *Target Market News; The Black Consumer Market Authority*, "Story Archives," http://targetmarketnews.com/storyarchive.htm, accessed June 10, 2016.

13. In the years 2005–09, the popular program *Everybody Hates Chris* (created and narrated by the African-American comedian Chris Rock) told the story of a black middle-school student in Brooklyn, a borough with over 10,000 active elevators. The elevator numbers were compiled by Noah Veltman of the WNYC Data News Team and posted on GitHub. Email from Noah Veltman, June 13, 2016. See https://github.com/datanews/elevators, accessed June 13, 2016.

14. See http://whatculture.com/tv/8-sitcoms-that-did-the-baby-born-on-the-elevator-thing?page=9 and https://www.quora.com/What-are-some-of-the-best-elevator-scenes-in-film-and-television, both accessed June 9, 2016.

15. http://teacher.scholastic.com/activities/bhistory/inventors/miles.htm, accessed July 19, 2016.

16. http://www.oxfordsd.org/page/280, accessed July 19, 2016.

17. Jones, *Between Good and Ghetto*, page 179.

18. Goffman, *On the Run*, page 12.

19. Email from anonymous Philadelphia prosecutor, who was not authorized to speak on the record, May 21, 2015.

20. Interview with JC Lore, May 18, 2015; email from JC Lore, May 21, 2015; email from Todd Berger, May 21, 2015.

21. Singal, "Goffman's Dissertation." According to Philadelphia police records, Tim was arrested when he was caught in the act of hot-wiring a car in March 2006.

22. Goffman states that the brothers were arrested when Chuck was driving Tim to school, but Chuck's arrest was at 2:00 a.m., and the police report makes no mention of a passenger, much less the arrest of a juvenile. Tim, however, had been arrested separately two months earlier, when he was caught in the act of hot-wiring a car in a parking lot that was under police surveillance. Chuck and Tim were arrested many times on various charges, but these are the only records I could locate regarding auto theft. Philadelphia Police Department Arrest Report, May 11, 2006; email from anonymous Philadelphia official, November 14, 2016.

    Other details in Chuck's lengthy arrest record also contradict representations in *On the Run*. Police reports are not invariably accurate, but there was obviously no reason for an officer to falsely state information such as the time of an arrest or the nature of an auto theft when the reports were first filed.

    Goffman's TED talk is titled "How We're Priming Some Kids for College—and Others for Prison."

23. E. Goffman, *Presentation of Self*, page 141. "It is well known that persons protect themselves with all kinds of rationalizations when they have a buried image of themselves which the facts of their status do not support." E. Goffman, "Cooling the Mark," page 452.

24. In reply to my earlier critique of this story, Goffman posted a response on her webpage insisting that her account of Tim's arrest was accurate. Goffman's response quoted the website of a Pittsburgh defense attorney and

a case in which she said "the courts have upheld these types of charges." Neither citation, however, supports her claim. Although omitted from Goffman's quote, the Pittsburgh lawyer's website noted that the charge against his client—who was an adult, not an eleven-year-old—had actually been dismissed. In the cited case, *Sanders v. City of Philadelphia*, the charges were likewise dismissed, as stated in the first paragraph of the opinion, which again contradicts Goffman's description. Goffman, "Reply to Professor Lubet's Critique." There is no known instance where a Pennsylvania child was arrested, much less convicted, for riding in a stolen car.

25. Goffman, "Reply to Professor Lubet's Critique."
26. Shafer, "Checking In."
27. Du Bois, *Philadelphia Negro*, page 348.
28. Two other African Americans served as ambassadors to Haiti in the nineteenth century—John E.W. Thompson and Frederick Douglass—but neither they nor Langston lived in Philadelphia.
29. Teal, *Hero of Hispaniola*, pages 164–65. See also http://diplomacy.state. gov/discoverdiplomacy/explorer/peoplehistorical/169797.htm and http:// explorepahistory.com/hmarker.php?markerId=1-A-3C1, accessed June 11, 2016. Bassett had also lived in Philadelphia in the 1850s, when he served as principal of the Institute for Colored Youth. Unusually for the time, he and his wife had a house "in an integrated neighborhood in the city's 7th Ward on Lombard Street, alongside European immigrants as well as white native-born families." He was active in the abolitionist movement, even meeting with John Brown in 1859, shortly before the Harpers Ferry raid. When Brown's papers were revealed following the raid, Bassett was among the "names of men to call for assistance." In fact, Bassett had declined to join Brown, but the adverse publicity may have accounted for the hostility of his neighbors. Teal, *Hero of Hispaniola*, pages 42, 43.
30. Anderson, *Code of the Street*, page 242.
31. Email from Todd Berger, June 22, 2015; email from JC Lore, June 22, 2015.
32. Contreras, *Stickup Kids*, pages 70, 78, 84.
33. Email from long-time New York criminal defense lawyer John Boston, June 4, 2016; Ravo, "It's Near Canada."
34. Grazian, *Blue Chicago*, page 90.
35. Grazian, *Blue Chicago*, pages 90, 108.
36. Fornek, "Blues Guitarist Slain"; Fornek, "Deadly Feud." Tail Dragger and Boston Blackie were not pseudonyms invented by Grazian, but were the musicians' own stage names. Jones was sentenced on July 19, 1994. *People v. James Jones*, 93 CR 17924 (Circuit Court of Cook County). The conviction was affirmed by the Illinois Appellate Court, First District, No. 1-94-2939, on September 13, 1996.
37. Small, *Villa Victoria*, pages 199–201; Valentine, *Hustling*, page 153; Jackall, *Wild Cowboys*, passim.

38. Adler, *Wheeling and Dealing*, pages 20–21.
39. Williams and Milton, *Con Men*, pages 24–25, 118.
40. Desmond, *Evicted*, pages 217, 377.
41. Desmond, *Evicted*, pages 63, 327, 351. Not every ethnographer is equally concerned about documentation. Robert Weiss writes, "Occasionally, there are records we can look to for documentation. But for the most part we must rely on the quality of our interviewing for the validity of our material." Weiss, *Learning from Strangers*, page 150.
42. Desmond, *Evicted*, pages 242, 383.
43. Desmond, *Evicted*, page 327. I have seen relatively few other accounts of non-verification. Charles Bosk reports a similar decision, in which he chose not to include "a series of unexpected deaths and complications" at the hospital he was studying, because he did not see any other similar "rash of failures" and was thus unwilling to draw any inferences from the events. Bosk, *What Would You Do?*, page 179. Tamara Hareven tells of textile workers who said they had stopped working at a factory under study due to a strike. Upon checking the factory ledger, however, Hareven discovered that the employees had continued working after the strike. Hareven, *Family Time and Industrial Time*, page 376.
44. The quotes in this paragraph are taken from Bosk, *What Would You Do?*, pages 192–96. Bosk's admission was first made in a section titled "An Amended Appendix—An Ethnographer's Apology, a Bioethicist's Lament: The Surgeon and the Sociologist Revisited," in the 2003 edition of *Forgive and Remember*, which was reprinted as a chapter in *What Would You Do?*
45. A few pages later, Bosk concludes that the omission was "trivial" because "it was so startling, so beyond the ordinary, and so offensive that the real danger existed that this behavioral outlier would skew the interpretation of the data." *What Would You Do?*, page 198. This is hard to square with his earlier statement about avoiding inconsistency with his "central thesis," and even harder to square with his insistence, discussed in the Introduction, that "If one quite clearly sees something happen once, it is almost certain to have happened again and again." Had there been an ethnographic trial, I believe the ruling would have been to include the vignette and allow readers to decide for themselves. *What Would You Do?*, page ix.

Chapter 5

1. A lawyer must sometimes present or disclose evidence contrary or damaging to his or her case. Most important is the constitutional duty of the prosecution to provide a criminal defendant with any exculpatory or mitigating evidence. In civil cases, both sides are subject to pretrial discovery and, in the federal system, mandatory disclosures. Also in civil cases, lawyers are required to inform the court if a witness has committed perjury or produced fraudulent evidence; prosecutors have the same obligation in criminal cases, but the extent of a defense lawyer's duty to correct client

perjury is still subject to debate. Lawyers in all cases are required to refrain from knowingly presenting false or fraudulent evidence.

2. Steven Lubet and JC Lore, *Modern Trial Advocacy*, pages 61–62.
3. Lewis-Kraus, "Trials of Alice Goffman"; Bourgois, *In Search of Respect*, page 207.
4. Jackson, *Real Black*, page 23.
5. Jackall, *Wild Cowboy*; Elijah Anderson, *Code of the Street*.
6. Venkatesh, *Gang Leader for a Day* and *American Project*; Ralph, *Renegade Dreams*.
7. Edin and Shaefer, *$2 a Day*, page xxii.
8. Desmond, *Evicted*, page 326.
9. Chapkis, *Live Sex Acts*, page 7. Mary Pattillo similarly refers to the inevitability of "certain but unintended acts of editorial bias." Pattillo, *Black Picket Fences*, page 8.
10. Contreras, *Stickup Kids*; Bourgois, *In Search of Respect*; Moskos, *Cop in the Hood*.
11. Bourgois, *In Search of Respect*, pages 143–54.
12. Bourgois, *In Search of Respect*, pages 4, 170. In a more recent book, Bourgois "fact-checked official records for births, deaths, marriages, military service, employment, and incarceration," and also "consulted newspaper articles and public archives to confirm the veracity of accounts of past events." Bourgois and Schonberg, *Righteous Dopefiend*, page 12.
13. Lubet and Lore, *Modern Trial Advocacy*, page 61.
14. Bourgois, *In Search of Respect*, pages 153, 158, 205.
15. Bourgois, *In Search of Respect*, pages 205–07.
16. Lareau, *Unequal Childhoods*, page 329. Bourgois, *In Search of Respect*, page 207.
17. Robert Rosenthal coined the term "File Drawer Problem" in 1979 to describe the bias introduced in scientific literature by selective publication. Rosenthal, "The File Drawer Problem." It has since been observed in virtually all of the physical and social sciences.
18. Duneier, "How Not to Lie," page 2.
19. Klinenberg, *Heat Wave*, page 87.
20. Klinenberg, *Heat Wave*. Duneier, "Scrutinizing the Heat."
21. Klinenberg, "Overheated."
22. The "snitches get stitches" phenomenon is well known to ethnographers, although it is elided by Goffman. Elijah Anderson explains that it is backed up by "oblique threats" in Philadelphia, as does Nikki Jones, who says that "a fear of retaliation" prevents residents from assisting the police. Sudhir Venkatesh describes the "physical abuse" that is meted out in Chicago public housing to those who cooperate with police investigations, Victor Rios observed a "culture that forbids 'snitching'" in Oakland, and Robert Jackall saw the same thing in New York. Anderson, *Code of the Street*, page 139; Jones, *Between Good and Ghetto*, page 43; Venkatesh, *American Project*,

page 183; Rios, *Punished,* page 60; Jackall, *Wild Cowboys,* page 11. According to the journalist Alex Kotlowitz, the "no-snitch culture" is largely responsible for the cycle of rampant violence in Chicago, where only ten percent of shootings result in arrests—thus, ninety percent of shooters bear no legal consequences. "Most victims and witnesses stay quiet," explains Kotlowitz, "because they're afraid of retaliation by friends of the shooter, not because of some unwritten code of the streets." Kotlowitz, "Solving Chicago's Murders." See also McKinley, Southall, and Baker, "Bronx Killing" (quoting a potential witness to a murder, "The people who did this, you don't want to mess with them").

23. Goffman, *On the Run,* pages 251–61. The information from the police comes from the reports of Officers Palmer and Vizcarrondo, and Detectives Mullen and Verrecchio in Philadelphia Police Department case no. M07-233. I also interviewed and corresponded by email with the two detectives. Additional information about the murder prosecution, including Tim's refusal to cooperate, comes from court records, as well as interviews with lawyers and others familiar with the case who have requested anonymity because they were not authorized to speak on the record. According to the appellate court report, which is available online, Chuck's mother, whom Goffman calls "Miss Linda," did testify at the trial. I confirmed Tim's non-appearance and Miss Linda's testimony with several people who were present throughout the trial, but who requested anonymity for sensitive personal reasons. Interviews with anonymous court sources, June 19, 2015; June 23, 2015; July 15, 2016. There is a longer account of the murder investigation in Lubet, "Ethnography on Trial." Of Mike's involvement, Goffman reports only that the police "grabbed him as he walked into the hospital," implying that he was detained, when in fact he was allowed to proceed to the hospital room. Goffman, *On the Run,* page 255.

24. My research revealed the real names of most of Goffman's main characters, including Chuck, Tim, Mike, Tanesha, and many of their friends and family members. I have also followed the cases of the two men who were convicted of Chuck's murder, although they were not named in *On the Run.* I nonetheless withheld all of the real names in an earlier article in *The New Republic,* as Goffman requested of my editors. Because the accuracy of my identifications was confirmed by *The New Republic*'s fact-checking, and has not been denied by Goffman, I have chosen to continue using the pseudonyms in this book. I confirmed with the lead detective that Goffman never came forward with information about the shooting. Email from John Verrecchio, July 15, 2016.

25. Lubet, "Ethnography on Trial."

26. Jones, *Between Good and Ghetto,* page 161. Anderson, "The White Space," pages 12–13.

27. Goffman's explanation was provided in an email to my editors at *The New Republic.* Lubet, "Ethnography on Trial."

28. Ralph, *Renegade Dreams*, page 208. As it happens, I was a legal services lawyer at the time in the adjacent Garfield Park neighborhood, and I well recall the relocation of Sears and the attendant loss of jobs. Ralph also tells us that Martin Luther King lived in the neighborhood in 1966. *Renegade Dreams*, page 63. That would have been at 1550 S. Hamlin Avenue, as is well known. Another tipoff is the presence of a white pastor who had previously been the football coach at a neighborhood high school. A North Lawndale community leader, he is a widely admired figure in Chicago. The "Divine Knights" are also identifiable as the Vice Lords, given that Ralph uses their quite recognizable gang symbols: cane, top hat, playboy rabbit, and champagne glass. Ralph, *Renegade Dreams*, page 61. Regarding the Vice Lords' symbols, see Dawley, *A Nation of Lords* (cited by Ralph on page 207), and Kirby, *The Chicago Crime Commission Gang Book*. The pseudonymous Divine Knights leader who was "sentenced to fifteen years in prison for killing an Iowa City police officer" is also readily identifiable as an "infamous" (as Ralph puts it) leader of the Vice Lords. Ralph, *Renegade Dreams*, page 69. I have figured out these and other real names, but I have chosen to omit them.

29. Ralph, *Renegade Dreams*, pages 165–66.

30. See, e.g., Conroy, "Killed on Camera"; Zorn, "The Pleasance Shooting"; Sweeney, Gorner, and Hinkel, "Top Cop."

31. Chicago Independent Police Review Authority, *Annual Report* 2008–09. See http://www.iprachicago.org/ipra/homepage/PublicationPress/archived_reports/Quarterly_Report_2009.html, accessed June 28, 2016. The *North Lawndale Community News* issues for July 2008 are not available in the archive.

32. See http://www.iprachicago.org/content/dam/ipra/Documents/Public_Investigation/L1023878U09_05.pdf, accessed June 28, 2016.

33. See http://www.iprachicago.org/wp-content/uploads/2016/07/L1019341U08_30.pdf, and http://www.iprachicago.org/wp-content/uploads/2016/07/L1019180U08_29.pdf, both accessed July 1, 2016.

34. See http://www.iprachicago.org/wp-content/uploads/2016/07/L1017636U08_22.pdf, accessed July 1, 2016. The July 2008 issues of the *North Lawndale Community News* are missing from the archive.

35. For 2008, see http://www.iprachicago.org/wp-content/uploads/2016/07/officer_involved_shootings_2008.pdf; for 2009, see http://www.iprachicago.org/content/dam/ipra/Documents/Officer_Involved_Shooting/officer_involved_shootings_2009.pdf, both accessed June 28, 2016.

36. Email from Laurence Ralph, July 8, 2016.

37. Sweeney, "Police Review Board Clears Cop."

38. Schmadeke, "Slain Teen's Family Gets $8.5M."

39. Venkatesh, *Off the Books*, pages 315, 367. "Murder Victims, City of Chicago, February 2002," "Murder Victims, City of Chicago, November 2003," and "Murder Victims, City of Chicago, December 2003," provided by Chicago

Police Research and Analysis Section in emails May 20, June 15, and July 1, 2016. Venkatesh, *Off the Books*, pages 315, 332, 367. Email inquiries to Sudhir Venkatesh, July 8, 2016, July 25, 2016, and August 28, 2016 (none were answered).

40. I have omitted the name here, as I have done for nearly all of the real names I obtained in my research. I did not initially reach out to Ralph because I assumed that I would be able to confirm the shooting through public records. It was only when that failed—and it briefly appeared that Ralph may have misreported—that I needed to ask him directly.

Chapter 6

1. Fine and Turner, *Whispers on the Color Line*, pages 18–19; Fine and Ellis, *The Global Grapevine*, page 7.
2. Regarding "utterly false" urban legends, see Brunvand, *The Mexican Pet*, page 9.
3. Fine and Turner, *Whispers on the Color Line*, pages 18–19; Fine and Ellis, *The Global Grapevine*, page 7.
4. Regarding half-truths, see Pfeffer and Sutton, *Hard Facts*, page 25.
5. Duneier, *Slim's Table*, pages 74–76.
6. Edin and Shaefer, *$2 a Day*, pages 44, 60, 168.
7. Edin and Shaefer, *$2 a Day*, pages xi–xiii, 48–49.
8. Edin and Shaefer, *$2 a Day*, page 49.
9. American College of Obstetricians and Gynecologists, "Guidelines on Hormonal Contraceptives in Women with Coexisting Medical Conditions"; Planned Parenthood, "Birth Control Q & A," https://www.plannedparenthood.org/learn/birth-control/birth-control-pill/how-effective-is-the-birth-control-pill, accessed March 7, 2017. The only exception is rifampin, which Planned Parenthood describes as "a special medication used to treat tuberculosis." There is no mention of tuberculosis in the many pages devoted to Susan Brown. A slightly contrary opinion can be found on MedicineNet.com, where an unidentified doctor speculates that antibiotics might kill bacteria that "convert the inactive chemicals into active estrogen," thus impeding the effectiveness of the pill, "although it has not been proven that unwanted pregnancies can occur by this means." See http://www.medicinenet.com/script/main/art.asp?articlekey=17192, accessed March 11, 2017.
10. Edin explained as much in a previous book, that an informant's "lackadaisical use of the pill" practically guaranteed her five 'accidents,' " and that many other poor women "drifted into the Russian roulette of unprotected sex." She expressed skepticism of another informant's claim of "taking my pills every day," noting that she had become a mother "before her sixteenth birthday." Edin and Kefalas, *Promises I Can Keep*, pages 39, 168. In a book about unmarried fathers, Edin noted that once a couple "deems themselves 'together,' any serious attempt at contraception usually

fades. Then the inevitable occurs: the woman 'comes up pregnant.'" Edin and Nelson, *Doing the Best I Can*, pages 32–33.

11. In yet a third incident, a nurse's aide was called upon to remove a bullet, while Goffman was again in charge of the scream-muffling music volume. Goffman, *On the Run*, pages x, 152. Police are routinely summoned to investigate gunshot wounds, but not for other injuries.

12. See Washington, *Medical Apartheid*.

13. Duneier, *Slim's Table*, pages 74–75. Many of his informants, however, "would not endorse that view."

14. Turner, *I Heard It Through the Grapevine*, pages 111–12, 144–47. Urban legends tend to spread in times of anxiety, "when there are low levels of trust in official institutions and sources of information." Lovejoy, "What Do the Scary Clowns Want."

15. Fine and Turner, *Whispers on the Color Line*, pages 63, 164.

16. Goffman, *On the Run*, pages vii, ix, x, 34, 55.

17. Email from Bernice Ho (Mercy Philadelphia Hospital), August 27, 2015; email from Jeremy Walter (Temple University Hospital), October 1, 2015; email from Phil Ellingsworth (Hahnemann Hospital), September 11, 2015; interview with Joseph Byham (Jefferson Hospital), September 3, 2015. Regarding Children's Hospital of Philadelphia (CHOP), see Dan McQuade, "Alice Goffman's Book on 'Fugitive Life' in Philly under Attack," *Philadelphia Magazine*, June 11, 2015. It is thus evident that Goffman has at best related a "false positive" by leveraging a rumor into an assertion of fact. Regarding the "institutional incentives [that] are likely to increase the rate of false discoveries," see Smaldino and McElreath, "The Natural Selection of Bad Science."

18. Email from Everett Gillison, January 18, 2016 (capitalization original). Two then-current Philadelphia officials told me the same thing, but neither one was permitted to be quoted on the record. One said there was "absolutely no way" for the police to have access to hospital records. The other said that he had "never, ever heard of police checking IDs at hospitals," and that Philadelphia's "active advocacy community" would have complained to him if such a thing had happened. Interviews with anonymous Philadelphia city officials, January 15, 2016, and January 19, 2016. A New York City police captain told me the same thing: "In all my [twenty] years of working EMS and as a cop, I have never seen police outside poor Black community hospital checking people's ID. And I checked with friends in Philadelphia's Police Department." Email from Ari Maas, March 8, 2017.

19. The sociologist Nikki Jones conducted ethnographic fieldwork in Philadelphia during roughly the same timeframe as Goffman, interviewing young women who had participated in "a city hospital-based violence reduction project (VRP)." She explains that "all program participants were treated in the emergency department following an intentional violent incident, and all had been identified by VRP staff as either moderate or

high risk for injury from similar incidents in the future," but there is no mention of a police gantlet outside the emergency room or anywhere else in the hospitals where she worked. Jones, *Between Good and Ghetto*, pages 13, 97, 168. Other ethnographies set in Philadelphia include Anderson's *Code of the Street* and *Streetwise*, Edin and Kefalas's *Promises I Can Keep*, and Edin and Nelson's *Doing the Best I Can*, none of which report police screenings or routine arrests in hospitals.

Nonetheless, Goffman's claim has been included in at least one well-regarded ethnography textbook: Duneier, Kasinitz, and Murphy (eds.), *The Urban Ethnography Reader*, pages 751, 752. It has also been repeated uncritically in both the social science and legal literature, as well as in the popular press. See, e.g., Jerolmack, "Living within a Web of Entrapment"; Natapoff, "Misdemeanor Decriminalization"; Scott-Hayward, "The Failure of Parole"; Harvard Law Review Association, "Policing and Profit"; Melamed, "Sociologist Chronicles Tenuous Lives."

20. Edin and Kefalas, *Promises I Can Keep*, pages 69–70.
21. Email from Margaret Klaw, June 6, 2016; email from Tiffany Palmer, June 24, 2016.
22. Liebow, *Tally's Corner*, page 95.
23. *King v. Smith*, 392 U.S. 309 (1968).
24. In the film, directed by John Berry, Diahann Carroll plays a single mother on welfare who falls in love with a garbage collector played by James Earl Jones. Her AFDC payments are threatened when her welfare worker discovers that Jones has stayed overnight, and thus may be considered a "man assuming the role of spouse." The film was inaccurate when released, as the MARS rule no longer existed and New York had eliminated home visits years earlier.
25. In an evident reference to the defunct man-in-the-house rule, Stack wrote, "Attempts by those on welfare to formulate nuclear families are effectively discouraged by welfare policy. In fact, welfare policy encourages the maintenance of non-coresidential cooperative domestic networks." Stack, *All Our Kin*, page 127.
26. Venkatesh, *Off the Books*, pages 42–43, and *Gang Leader for a Day*, page 158. In *Off the Books*, he cites Stack for the proposition. He also cites Sharon Hayes's *Flat Broke with Children: Women in the Age of Welfare Reform*, although the latter refers to the rule as historical.
27. Venkatesh, *Floating City*, pages 105–09. Venkatesh notes in a parenthetical that the rule had been held "unconstitutional by the Supreme Court in 1968," but Silvia's complaint is stated in the present tense, which makes it seem as though the provision is nonetheless being enforced. (The Supreme Court ruling in *King v. Smith* was actually based on the language of the statute, not the Constitution.)
28. *James v. Goldberg*, 302 F.Supp. 478 (1969). The U.S. Supreme Court later dissolved the injunction, but home visits never resumed afterward. Email from Toby Golick, April 25, 2016.
29. Edin and Shaefer, *$2 a Day*, pages 1–33.

30. Duneier, *Slim's Table*, page 73.
31. Contreras, *Stickup Kids*, pages 143–45.
32. Contreras, *Stickup Kids*, page 166 (brackets and italics original).
33. Salvatore "Sammy the Bull" Gravano, however, is definitely a real person. A former underboss in the Gambino crime family, he became a government informer and provided crucial testimony against John Gotti. By his own account, Gravano was responsible for "eighteen or nineteen murders." Maas, *Underboss*, page 289.
34. Contreras, *Stickup Kids*, page 167 (brackets and spelling original).
35. Williams and Milton, *Con Men*, pages 116–17.
36. A single bill of any denomination is 0.0043 inches thick. $350,000 would thus require 3,500 one-hundred dollar bills, which would reach 15.05 inches if new bills were fully compressed. An actual stack, especially of used bills, would be much higher. A stack of twenties would measure over six feet.
37. Williams and Milton, *Con Men*, pages 123–24.
38. Van Cleve, *Crook County*, page 103.
39. I have omitted his name at my informant's request. Interview with Michael Morrissey, June 2, 2016.
40. Van Cleve, page 103.
41. Interview with Michael Morrissey, June 2, 2016.

Chapter 7

1. Exceptions can be made on a case-by-case basis for witnesses who may be risking their lives or safety by testifying, such as undercover officers, confidential informants, or witnesses who have defied threats of retaliation. See, e.g., *United States v. Abu Marzook*, 412 F. Supp. 4ᵗʰ 913 (2006). Rule 10(a) of the Federal Rules of Civil Procedure requires all plaintiffs to identify themselves by name, but that too can be waived in exceptional circumstances, as when prosecution of the case would subject the party to extreme danger or expose information of "the utmost intimacy." The most famous such case was *Roe v. Wade*, 410 U.S. 113 (1973), which was brought under the pseudonym "Jane Roe" by a woman who later came forward as Norma McCorvey. More recent examples include *Doe v. Porter*, 370 F.3d 558 (6ᵗʰ Cir. 2004), and *Doe v. Dordoni*, No. 16-00074 (E.D. Mich. 2016). The general principle, however, is that "privacy in one's identity in a public forum—such as a federal court—is the exception, not the rule." *Doe v. Shalushi*, No. 10-11837 (E.D. Mich. 2010).
2. For the history of IRB oversight of social science research, see Schrag, *Ethical Imperialism*. Beginning in January 2018, federal regulation of social science research, including ethnography, will be substantially reduced, although it remains to be seen how university IRBs will interpret the new regulations. Shweder and Nisbett, "Research Deregulation."
3. Contreras, *Stickup Kids*, page 14.
4. Shamus Khan, *Privilege*, page 203.

5. Van Cleve, *Crook County*, pages xiii–xiv, 52. In a footnote, Van Cleve refers to the judge as a "yeller," that being a well-known type in the Cook County criminal court. *Crook County*, page 222.

6. Moskos, *Cop in the Hood*, page 12. In her study of female visitors at San Quentin prison, for example, Megan Comfort says only that her subjects "chose their own pseudonyms," with no explanation of necessity. Comfort, *Doing Time Together*, page 206.

7. Undated statement of Prof. Alice Goffman, produced by the University of Wisconsin pursuant to the Wisconsin Open Records Act via email from Lisa Hull, August 21, 2015.

8. Jerolmack and Murphy, "Ethical Dilemmas" (italics original). Others take an even less forgiving view.

9. Jerolmack and Murphy, "Ethical Dilemmas" (italics original).

10. Mitchell Duneier used the real names of his research participants (with their permission) in *Sidewalk*, as did Colin Jerolmack in *The Global Pigeon*. In both cases, subjects believed that they benefited from the exposure. Jerolmack and Murphy provide other examples of subjects who want to see their real names in print.

11. Duneier, "Ecological Fallacy," page 687.

12. See Neyfakh, "Ethics of Ethnography."

13. Anderson, *Code of the Street*, pages 149–50.

14. Goffman, *On the Run*; Jones, *Between Good and Ghetto*; Edin and Kefalas, *Promises I Can Keep*. In a co-authored article about unmarried fathers in Philadelphia, Edin questioned Anderson's characterization of young men's single-minded "quest for sex" as "not consistent with a growing body of qualitative evidence." Augustine, Nelson, and Edin, "Why Do Poor Men Have Children?," page 102.

15. Ralph, *Renegade Dreams*, pages 165–66.

16. Ralph, *Renegade Dreams*, pages 29, 38, 41, 103, 148, 151, 155.

17. Ralph, *Renegade Dreams*, pages xix, 97. I was able to identify the main character behind Pastor Tim, as the only minister in the neighborhood who was previously a high-school football coach (and I know the high school, too), but there is no way to determine which of the actions attributed to him in the book were his and which were performed by one of the other three who make up the composite. Kemo remains a mystery, perhaps because he is more of a true composite. I was able to identify the real names of other notorious leaders of the "Divine Knights," including "Erving Beamer," who died a year after the publication of *Renegade Dreams*, having survived a prison term in Iowa for killing a police officer, as well as an assassination attempt that left him paralyzed.

18. "Fabrication of any type is unacceptable. We do not create composite characters." *Los Angeles Times* Ethics Guidelines. See also The Center for Investigative Reporting, "Ethics Guide." According to the nonfiction author Philip Gerard, "Most writers agree that making up a 'composite'—a character

invented out of parts of several real people but not himself a real person—crosses the line" between fiction and nonfiction. Gerard, *Creative Nonfiction*, page 201. The Poynter Institute's Roy Peter Clark is even more adamant, declaring that composites have "no place in journalism or other works that purport to be nonfiction" and proposing an "absolute prohibition against composites." Clark, "The Line Between Fact and Fiction," in Kramer and Call, *Telling True Stories*, page 168. Composites are sometimes used in the less rigorous genre of memoir, as in David Dow's *Autobiography of an Execution*. This practice has been criticized as privileging "emotion over detail, and narrative over precision." Lithwick, "Death Penalty Lawyer." In contrast, J.D. Vance's memoir about his own difficult childhood uses "no composite characters and no narrative shortcuts." Vance, *Hillbilly Elegy*, page 9.

19. Likewise, both Terry Williams, in *Crackhouse*, and John Jackson, in *Real Black*, say without hesitation that their books are set in New York; and Kimberly Hoang's experience as a hostess in several Vietnamese nightclubs, as she recounts in *Dealing in Desire*, obviously took place in Ho Chi Minh City. Philippe Bourgois and Jeff Schonberg even include photographs of the encampment of homeless drug "injectors" they study in *Righteous Dopefiend*.

20. Katz, "Review: Cracks in the Pavement," pages 1950–52.

21. Bosk, *What Would You Do?*, page 215.

22. Jerolmack and Murphy, "Ethical Dilemmas."

23. Bosk, *What Would You Do?*, page 212.

24. Duneier, *Sidewalk*, page 348.

25. Jackson, *Harlemworld*, pages 1–2.

26. The journalist Gideon Lewis-Kraus claims to have found newspaper stories with "corroborating examples in Dallas, New Orleans and Brockton, Mass.," although evidently none in Philadelphia. Lewis-Kraus, "The Trials of Alice Goffman." I tracked down his three stories, only to discover that none of them involved either a doorway checkpoint or routine access to visitors' lists. Two of the cases involved teenaged mothers who had been statutorily raped. The police did arrest the much older fathers on the maternity floor, but not as the result of routine screening or checking a visitors' list. The third case was the result of a twenty-three-defendant drug sweep conducted by the state police and the FBI, and again not a routine check of hospital records. If there is any lesson in these diverse reports, it is that maternity floor arrests are so rare as to be reported in the newspapers—the New Orleans story made it all the way to New York—although Goffman claims to have witnessed three in one night. Selk, "Expectant Father Arrested" (Dallas); Nolan, "40-year-old Man Arrested" (New Orleans); Boyle, "Feds, State and Brockton Police Arrest 23" (Brockton, Mass.).

27. Campos, "Alice Goffman's Implausible Ethnography."

28. Edin and Kefalas, *Promises I Can Keep*, pages 11–19; Khan, *Privilege*; Contreras, *Stickup Kids*; Bourgois, *In Search of Respect*. Other examples are legion, and the variations are too many for the following list to be at all

comprehensive: Carol Stack completely anonymized both "Jackson Harbor" and "The Flats" in *All Our Kin*; Peter Moskos identified both Baltimore and its Eastern District in *Cop in the Hood*; Kimberly Hoang identified Ho Chi Minh City in *Dealing in Desire*, but changed the names of the nightclubs where she worked as a hostess; Matthew Desmond named Milwaukee as his research site in *Evicted*, while masking the mobile home park where he sometimes lived during the study (though it is easy to identify via Google); Elijah Anderson referred to his research site as "Eastern City" in *Streetwise*, but he later identified it as Philadelphia in *Code of the Street* (1999); Sudhir Venkatesh named Chicago's Robert Taylor Homes in both *American Project* and *Gang Leader for a Day*, but he inexplicably changed the names of the streets where the various buildings are located. In *Sidewalk*, Mitchell Duneier followed the "practice of the journalists" by using the real names of people and places, although he later resorted to pseudonyms for the deceased "alcoholics and drug addicts" whose deaths he investigated in "The Ecological Fallacy." Likewise, Nancy Scheper-Hughes called her Irish village "Ballybran" in *Saints, Scholars, and Schizophrenics*, but she revealed it to be An Clochan when she chronicled her disastrous return visit in "Ire in Ireland." Laurence Ralph anonymized both the Chicago neighborhood ("Eastwood") and street gang ("Divine Knights") that he studied in *Renegade Dreams*, although both are readily identifiable (North Lawndale; the Vice Lords) by anyone familiar with Chicago. In *Black Picket Fences*, Mary Pattillo likewise used the pseudonym "Groveland" for a neighborhood on Chicago's South Side, while including enough details for it to be recognized as Avalon Park. Robert Vargas, on the other hand, accurately named both the setting ("Little Village") and the gang ("Latin Kings") in *Wounded City*. The historian William Sheridan Allen called his field site "Thalberg" in the initial edition of *The Nazi Seizure of Power*, but he disclosed it as Northeim in the second edition (although the "secret" had already been revealed by *Der Spiegel*). And so on.

29. Undated statement of Prof. Alice Goffman, produced by the University of Wisconsin pursuant to the Wisconsin Open Records Act via email from Lisa Hull on August 21, 2015.

30. Some ethnographers have referred generally to the rearrangement of dates and events. Following an interview with Alice Goffman, *Slate*'s Leon Neyfakh wrote:

[T]he majority of what I'm calling "inaccuracies" were introduced into *On the Run* because the conventions of sociological ethnography required them. In keeping with the methodological protocols of her chosen discipline, which typically demands that researchers grant their subjects total anonymity, Goffman changed details and scrambled facts in order to prevent readers from deducing the identities of the people she was writing about. In the process, she made her book all but impossible to fact-check.

Neyfakh, "Ethics of Ethnography." As we have seen, however, it is not correct that the ethics of ethnography require such extreme measures.

31. The spelling and possessive of Lévi-Strauss are per the original. The passages in the following discussion first appeared in "An Amended Appendix," in the second edition of *Forgive and Remember* (2002), which was reprinted under the same title as a chapter in *What Would You Do?*, pages 187–92.

32. For a more extensive discussion of foundations and authenticity, see Steven Lubet and JC Lore, *Modern Trial Advocacy: Law School*, pages 224, 228–46.

33. Neyfakh, "Ethics of Ethnography."

34. Edwards and Weller, "Ethical Dilemmas around Anonymity," in Tolich (ed.), *Qualitative Ethics in Practice*, pages 97–108; Gerard, *Creative Nonfiction*, page 200. Some alterations are more likely to be innocuous than others. Mary Pattillo, for example, refers to making "small factual substitutions," such changing the Chicago community college that one of her subjects attended. Pattillo, *Black Picket Fences*, page 264.

35. "Ethnography Meets Journalism," Institute for Public Knowledge, New York University, September 21, 2015, http://livestream.com/ipk-nyu/events/4355261, accessed September 26, 2016.

36. Ralph, *Renegade Dreams*, page xx.

37. Bosk, *What Would You Do?*, page 204.

38. Bosk, *What Would You Do?*, page 213. Katherine Boo used only real names in *Behind the Beautiful Forevers*. Veteran investigative journalist Maurice Possley gave me this account of investigating Medicaid fraud in Chicago: "We managed to do our series—it involved the Illinois Medicaid program—and as part of it, we persuaded a physician in a storefront Medicaid clinic at 64th and Cottage Grove to allow us to more or less have free roaming privileges for a month during which we spent 13 days from the moment they opened until the doors closed for the day. I remember sitting in the examining room when patients would come in to see the doctor. He introduced me and asked if the patients minded if I was there. They always consented. This was about getting their RX filled. There were no examinations, no one got their blood pressure taken, let alone have to remove any clothing for an examination. We never changed a single name or detail." Email from Maurice Possley, July 27, 2016. Journalism professor Craig LaMay confirmed the same phenomenon, noting that many sources, though perhaps unsophisticated, are actually "eager to be identified." Email from Craig LaMay, November 2, 2016.

39. Society of Professional Journalists, "Code of Ethics," http://www.spj.org/pdf/spj-code-of-ethics.pdf, accessed September 2, 2016.

40. Sullivan, "Tightening the Screws on Anonymous Sources." Regarding the description of anonymous sources, see Spayd, "Unnamed Sources, Unhappy Readers."

41. The following account is taken from Green, "Janet's World."

42. It is worth noting that the ultimate key to the fraud was the preservation of Cooke's original notes, in which the editors found no mention of "Jimmy"

or anyone like him. Lawyers spend tremendous amounts of time on discovery, searching for the proverbial "smoking gun," but sometimes it is the absence of evidence that makes all the difference.

43. Coronel, Coll, and Kravitz, "Rolling Stone and UVA." On November 7, 2016, a jury ordered Erdely and *Rolling Stone* to pay $3 million in damages to Nicole Eramo, a University of Virginia rape counselor who had sued for defamation. Spencer and Sisario, "Rolling Stone Defamation Case." A lawsuit on behalf of the subject fraternity is still pending as of this writing.

44. "Ethnography Meets Journalism," Institute for Public Knowledge, New York University, September 21, 2015, http://livestream.com/ipk-nyu/events/4355261, accessed September 26, 2016.

Chapter 8

1. Whyte, *Street Corner Society*, pages 291–92.
2. Whyte, *Street Corner Society*, pages 314–15.
3. Whyte, *Street Corner Society*, pages 316–17.
4. Geertz, "Balinese Cockfight," page 4.
5. Becker, *Becoming a Marihuana User* (italics original), pages 39, 58.
6. Humphreys, *Tearoom Trade*, pages 26–28 and passim.
7. Horowitz and Rainwater, "Sociological Snoopers," in *Tearoom Trade* (enlarged edition, 1975), page 185. "From the beginning, my decision was to continue the practice of the field study in passing as a deviant." Humphreys, *The Tearoom Trade*, page 25.
8. Humphreys, "Research Retrospect," in *Tearoom Trade* (enlarged edition, 1975), pages 228–30.
9. Miller, "A Scholarly Taxi to the Toilets," pages 39–40.
10. Galliher, Brekhus, and Keys, *Laud Humphreys*, page 47. My own research, though admittedly non-extensive, has failed to locate any evidence of "watchqueens" other than from Humphreys. In a 1972 study of gay cruising at truck stops, roughly contemporaneous with Humphreys's work and probably also in or near St. Louis, the authors noted that "There is no role in the sexual marketplace we studied similar to that of 'watch queen' . . . which would have permitted us to observe the exchange of sexual services." In their observation, "available roles would have required participation in the sexual activity or covert 'spying.'" Corzine and Kirby, "Cruising the Truckers," page 184. In a study of Canadian police records in the late 1980s, Frederick Desroches documented behavior quite similar to Humphreys's data, while noting that "the voyeur-lookout role Humphreys assumed as participant observer appeared to be absent." Desroches, "Tearoom Trade: A Research Update," page 42.

The general literature emphasizes the importance of privacy to gay men in that era, even in public bathrooms. See, e.g., Berube, "The History of Gay Bathhouses," in Colter et al. (eds.), *Policing Public Sex*, page 187; Alexander, "Bathhouses and Brothels," in Colter et al. (eds.), *Policing Public Sex*, page 221; Jones, *Alfred C. Kinsey*, page 385. The legal historian William Eskridge, for example, refers to the struggle "to assure *private gay spaces*—the home, the car, the toilet booth" and the importance of "the enclosed toilet stall" during the years 1961–81. Eskridge, *Gaylaw*, pages 15, 99 (italics original).

11. Humphreys, *The Tearoom Trade*, page 42. To my knowledge, Humphreys never named his collaborator and no one has ever come forward.

12. *Lawrence v. Texas*, 539 U.S. 558 (2003).

13. Before Humphreys, "no one had systematically analyzed the participants of public sexual acts." Nardi, "Breastplate of Righteousness," pages 2–3. Humphreys's biographers make repeated references to his contribution to "normalizing" homosexuality. Galliher, Brekhus, and Keys, *Laud Humphreys*, pages 46, 96, 98.

14. Becker, *Outsiders*, p. 171. Perhaps as a concession to his editors or department chair, Becker added that a participant-observer need not commit "the deviant acts under study."

15. Venkatesh, *Gang Leader for a Day*, pages 185–86 (italics original). In another book, Venkatesh explains that he participated in mediating neighborhood disputes, while avoiding "anything that I determined 'serious'—which tended to be cases involving drugs, prostitution, and stolen goods." Venkatesh, *Off the Books*, page xvii.

16. Contreras, *Stickup Kids*, page 16.

17. Contreras, *Stickup Kids*, page 143.

18. Venkatesh, *Gang Leader for a Day*, pages 135, 170.

19. Contreras, *Stickup Kids*, page 11.

20. In a longer description of what seems to have been the same incident, Contreras explains that he intended to act only as a sounding board, giving responses "in the form of, *Yeah, you're right, bro*, no matter what was said" (italics original). Still, readers of the extended exchange may read Contreras's replies to Gus as affirmation of his plan, or at least agreement that it was doable:

> "Yo, tell me, if we send Melissa to the apartment, aren't those niggas gonna open that door?"
> "Yeah, they probably will," I answered.

Someone else proposed pulling their guns in the hallway, rather than using Melissa as bait, but Gus thought that would be too noisy. He turned again to Contreras:

> "Bro, that shit's just gonna attract mad attention. Tell me, bro, that shit's just gonna make a lot of noise, right??"
> "Yeah, that shit's gonna make a lot of noise," I agreed. "You right."

Contreras, *Stickup Kids*, page 15. In a later interview, Contreras described himself "chuckling, smiling and 'high-fiving' as Gus, Pablo, Neno and others told him about their violent robberies." Grove, "From Selling Crack to Sociology." Contreras characterizes his responses as neutral, but there is no way to know whether Gus and the others interpreted his comments as support for their plans. For a more recent example of the same sort of drug-related plot, including mutilation of victims and the use of a female decoy, see Hawkins, "Four Sentenced in 'Almost Indescribable' Kidnapping."

21. Goffman, *On the Run*, pages 260–63.

22. Email from anonymous prosecutor whose current position would not allow him to speak on the record, May 16, 2015. I also showed these passages to three other current or former prosecutors in New York and Chicago, all of whom agreed that the stated facts amounted to conspiracy to commit murder. It is not unknown for prosecutors to bring charges in thwarted or ineffective conspiracies in which the targeted victim was not harmed. See, e.g., Nathan-Kazis, "Murder Plot Sheds Light."

23. Goffman, "A Reply to Professor Lubet's Critique." For my reaction, see Lubet, "Alice Goffman's Denial of Murder Conspiracy."

    In fact, Goffman's posted response was her third shifting version of the events. In a radio interview conducted a few days earlier, she made no mention of play-acting or an innocuous mourning ritual, but instead admitted that she had "gone too far" by acting as Mike's driver:

    > So I think the appendix, the part that comes up in this most recent critique that I was acting in a criminal way, I mean the person I think is using a part of the appendix where I was trying to illustrate a moment where I had really messed up and gone too far and made the wrong choice . . . . I wanted to be honest about a moment where I had made the wrong choice and I think I certainly wasn't trying to say "here's what you should be doing fellow fieldworkers." I was trying to say "here was the worst day I ever had."

    A Public Affair ("On the Run"), WORT Radio, Madison, WI.

24. The rhetorical questions would be asked of the jury during final argument. Capable cross-examiners know better than to put "Why?" questions to witnesses.

25. Lewis-Kraus, "The Trials of Alice Goffman." Other rationalizations for Goffman's changed narrative are even more strained. Van Maanen and de Rond speculate that *On the Run* omitted the revised story—of mourning rather than revenge—because "perhaps Alice felt that to do so in the book would have distanced herself and therefore misrepresented her deep penetration into the lives of those researched and the emotional intensity, the blood lust, she felt at the moment." But how could telling the truth have been a misrepresentation? If everyone really believed they were only play acting, describing the situation accurately would not have "distanced" her from the actual reality. In a later passage, Van Maanen and de Rond seem to reject the ritual grieving story, saying that "Alice Goffman, to her credit, didn't hesitate to criminalize" her own life. John Van Maanen and Mark de Rond, "The Making of a Classic Ethnography."

There is an additional inconsistency in Goffman's claimed confidence that no one would be hurt because "I had talked Mike down from violence in the past." First, it would have been impossible for Goffman to talk Mike out of anything as she waited in the car while he was stalking a potential victim in the alley. In any case, if there had been nothing more going on than play acting at revenge, there would have been no need to talk Mike out of shooting someone.

The full story is quite different. As Paul Campos points out in the *Chronicle of Higher Education*, Chuck's murder had been the culmination of an ongoing "war" between the 6th Street Boys and the 4th Street Boys, in which numerous shootings had already occurred. Mike himself had a long history of violence, from which he had not been deterred, in which he had once "shot off a few rounds at the home of a man [Chuck] believed was responsible for blowing up his car." Another time, as related by Goffman, Mike shot at a man preemptively: "Mike told me the man looked at him, he looked at the man, the man tensed, and Mike opened fire. Mike said, 'I ain't know if he was going to start chopping [shooting], you know, thinking I was going to come at him. Better safe than sorry.'" Campos, "Alice Goffman's Implausible Ethnography." As late as 2013, six years after the Glock ride, the 4th Street Boys still apparently raised fears of shooting on 6th Street. Goffman, *On the Run*, page 207.

26. Email from Mitchell Duneier, July 7, 2015; Parry, "Conflict over Sociologist's Narrative." The term "Glock ride" is from Campos, "Alice Goffman's Implausible Ethnography."

27. Goodwin, "Black Lives Matter to Human Research." In the events leading up to the Glock ride, there had already been a series of related shootings in the neighborhood. "In anticipation of his retaliation, Tim received near daily calls and texts from the 4th Street Boys that they were going to kill him, and by the end of July he had been in three shootouts." Goffman, *On the Run*, page 184. Even if the Glock ride had been only a grieving ritual, it would still have been the height of irresponsibility for a sociology graduate student to risk provoking the 4th Street Boys into further gunplay. In contrast, the sociologist Robert Worely had nothing more stern to say than "avenging murders falls a bit outside the boundaries of acceptable social science research." Worely, "Book Review," pages 116–24.

28. Email from César Ayala, July 3, 2015.

29. Parry, "Conflict over Sociologist's Narrative"; Van Maanen and de Rond, "Making of a Classic Ethnography."

30. Ralph, "The Limitations of a 'Dirty' World," pages 441–51.

31. Goffman, *On the Run*, pages 253–60.

32. Email from Gary Alan Fine, July 2, 2015. Fine said:

> In community (urban) ethnography the community is the subject of research. Not any set of individuals. Part of the decision is whether

there is a sense that the community would wish this speculation shared with the police and how that would affect the research. We believe that learning about a community serves a valuable civic purpose that, while it doesn't override everything, overrides a lot if there is no certainty and no legal requirement. Ethnographers have a primary responsibility to their community, but this must be weighed in light of their responsibility as citizens. I would not tell my students what to do, but I would insist that they consider the implications of their choices.

33. Venkatesh, *Gang Leader for a Day*, pages 185–86. Email from Sudhir Venkatesh, July 7, 2015.
34. Email from César Ayala, July 3, 2015 (capitalization original).
35. Desmond, *Evicted*, pages 249, 322.
36. Desmond, *Evicted*, pages 249, 322.
37. Email from Matthew Desmond, June 20, 2016. Desmond did not say anything, in either the book or the email, about obtaining permission from Vanetta or Crystal.
38. "I haven't written about the matter, and writing is how I tend to work things out," he explained. Email from Matthew Desmond, June 20, 2016.
39. According to Marquart, the beatings "certainly went beyond any departmental regulation concerning the proper use of force." He also kept the confidences of prisoners who told him about their much lesser offenses, such as making liquor, stealing food, and selling tattoo patterns. Marquart, "Doing Research in Prison," pages 21–31.
40. In the first homicide, "On a hot afternoon in July, Aisha and I stood on a crowded corner of a major commercial street and watched four officers chase down her older sister's boyfriend and strangle him. He was unarmed and did not fight back. The newspapers reported his death as heart failure." Goffman, *On the Run*, pages 72, 121. In the second homicide, "[A] friend of Chuck's had been shot and killed while exiting my car outside a bar; one of the bullets pierced my windshield, and the man's blood spattered my shoes and pants as we ran away." Goffman, *On the Run*, page 250. She makes no mention of reporting either incident to the police, which is consistent with her silence following Chuck's murder.

    It is impossible to figure out where, when, or how these events occurred, and thus whether they indeed happened as described. I asked a research librarian at Northwestern to search the Philadelphia newspapers for reports of a death in police custody due to heart failure during the years 2002–08. There was only one such case, which occurred in Willingboro, New Jersey, on November 6, 2005. Whatever did or didn't happen to Aisha's sister's boyfriend on a July day in Philadelphia, it was not reported in the press as heart failure. Wood, "Officers Won't Be Charged in Death."
41. "Although the attorney-client privilege shields a client's confidential statements relating to past misconduct, statements seeking the services of an attorney with respect to ongoing or future crimes or frauds are not privileged."

Mueller and Kirkpatrick, *Evidence*, Fourth Edition, section 5.22, page 366. See also Rule 1.6(b)(6), *Model Rules of Professional Conduct*: "A lawyer may reveal information relating to the representation of a client to the extent the lawyer reasonably believes necessary . . . to comply with other law or a court order."

42. The book is Rik Scarce, *Eco-Warriors: Understanding the Radical Environmental Movement*.

43. Scarce, *Contempt of Court*, pages 15–16.

44. *In re Grand Jury Proceedings (James Richard Scarce)*, 5 F.3d 397 (9th Cir. 1993).

45. Scarce, *Contempt of Court*, page 15.

46. Email from Samuel Popkin, March 13, 2017; Schultz and Schultz, *The Price of Dissent*, pages 339–47. In 1984, a sociology graduate student named Mario Brajuha was subpoenaed in the investigation of a suspicious fire at a restaurant where he had been doing field work. The trial judge initially held that Brajuha was entitled to a "scholar's privilege" to withhold the notes of his confidential interviews, but that ruling was reversed by the appellate court. Fried, "Judge Protects Waiter's Notes"; *In re Grand Jury Subpoena (Brajuha)*, 750 F.2d 223 (2d Cir. 1984).

47. Scarce, *Contempt of Court*, pages 4, 6, 20, 207.

48. Marquart, "Doing Research in Prison," page 28.

49. Richard Leo, "Trial and Tribulations," pages 124–28.

50. Emails from Richard Leo, May 17, 2016.

51. "According to [Prof. Rena] Lederman, who sits on the IRB at Princeton, no such demands are placed on researchers at the school." Neyfakh, "The Ethics of Ethnography." In health-related studies, it may be possible to obtain a Certificate of Confidentiality from the National Institute of Health, which protects research data from subpoena or compelled disclosure. Randol Contreras obtained such a certificate for his work leading to *The Stickup Kids*, because it was a specific study of the drug trade. Other studies on urban crime, however, would not generally qualify. Email from Randol Contreras, August 11, 2016.

In Canada, a University of Quebec professor named Marie-Ève Maillé faced subpoena for the notes of her interviews with citizens who were affected by the construction of a wind farm, but only after she had volunteered to testify as an expert witness in a case against the developers of the project. A trial court ordered her to produce the notes, and Maillé's appeal had not been heard as of this writing. Kondro, "Canadian Researcher in Legal Battle." In the United States, expert witnesses are routinely required to produce their relevant research materials to the opposing party, in the interest of fair trials. Lubet and Boals, *Expert Testimony*, pages 50, 174.

52. Regarding the subpoenas for the interviews for Boston College's Belfast Project in oral history, see McMurtrie, "Secrets from Belfast"; Palys and Lowman, "Defending Research Confidentiality"; and Palys and Lowman, "A Belfast Project Autopsy," in Tolich (ed.), *Qualitative Ethics in Practice*,

pages 109–20 (2016). This case is *sui generis*, involving cooperation between the United States and the United Kingdom in the investigation of an abduction and murder committed during "The Troubles" in Northern Ireland. The Belfast Project had compiled oral history tapes and transcripts of interviews with participants in The Troubles, many of them paramilitaries, who had been promised confidentiality during their lifetimes. University officials and the organizers of the project, however, differed over the extent of the commitment and the authorization of the interviewers, and their plans were plagued by "inconsistencies, negligence, and lack of awareness of the legal landscape" from the start. Eventually, the First Circuit Court of Appeals ordered the production of certain transcripts, while holding that others were not relevant to the investigation and thus not reachable by subpoena. *In re Request from United Kingdom Pursuant to Treaty*, 718 F.3d 13 (2013).

Conclusion

1. Klinenberg's book is *Heat Wave: A Social Autopsy of Disaster in Chicago*. Duneier's critique is, "Scrutinizing the Heat." Klinenberg's reply is "Overheated." See also Wacquant, "Scrutinizing the Street."
2. Jencks, "Why the Very Poor Have Become Poorer."
3. Email from Luke Shaefer, June 2, 2016.
4. Toth, *The Mole People*; Brennan, "Fantasy in *The Mole People*."
5. Cho, "Once Again, Physicists Debunk Faster-Than-Light Neutrinos."
6. Horton, "Offline: What Is Medicine's 5 Sigma?" Horton is not alone in his critique. Richard Smith, former editor of the *British Medical Journal*, and Ian Roberts note that some scientists "repeat experiments day after day and publish them only when they become 'right.'" Smith and Roberts, "Time for Sharing Data to Become Routine." John Ioannidis, of the Stanford Medical School, made a similar observation a decade earlier, opining that "most published research findings" may be false, due in part to "data dredging," especially in the "hotter" scientific fields. Ioannidis, "Why Most Published Research Findings Are False."
7. Carey, "Many Psychology Findings Not as Strong as Claimed."
8. Open Science Collaboration (Brian Nosek et al.), "Estimating the Reproducibility of Psychological Science."
9. Open Science Collaboration (Brian Nosek et al.), "Estimating the Reproducibility of Psychological Science."
10. Ioannidis, "Why Most Published Research Findings Are False."
11. See, e.g., Ellis, "Emotional and Ethical Quagmires"; Scheper-Hughes, "Ire in Ireland"; William Foote Whyte, "Revisiting *Street Corner Society* Fifty Years Later" in *Street Corner Society* (4th edition, 1981). In contrast, Mary Pattillo's return to Chicago's "Groveland" neighborhood reinforced most of her original findings. Pattillo, "Epilogue," in *Black Picket Fences* (2nd edition, 2013). See also Burawoy, "Revisits."
12. See, e.g., Wacquant, "Scrutinizing the Street."

13. Duneier, "Ecological Fallacy."
14. Boelen, "Street Corner Society: Cornerville Revisited."
15. Whyte, *Participant Observer*, pages 312, 324.
16. Burawoy, "Revisits." The most famous case of re-investigation involved new interviews of several of Margaret Mead's Samoan informants, conducted decades later. Shankman, *The Trashing of Margaret Mead*.
17. The secondary evidence overwhelmingly indicates that the phenomenon has never existed. In addition to my sources at five hospitals and in city government, noted in Chapter Six, James Forman, Paul Campos, and even Jesse Singal all attempted and failed to locate corroboration for Goffman's claim. James Forman, "The Society of Fugitives"; Campos, "Alice Goffman's Implausible Ethnography"; Singal, "Here's What's in Alice Goffman's Dissertation." The Philadelphia hospitals with maternity services are the Hospital of the University of Pennsylvania, Temple University Hospital, Jefferson Hospital, Hahnemann University Hospital, Pennsylvania Hospital, and Albert Einstein Medical Center.
18. Reinvestigation has led to the exoneration of many wrongfully convicted defendants, including Maurice Patterson and Randy Steidl, who were freed when Northwestern's Center on Wrongful Convictions discovered evidence of their innocence that had been withheld or unavailable at their original trials. Email from Karen Daniel, September 7, 2016. For Patterson, see http://www.law.northwestern.edu/legalclinic/wrongfulconvictions/exonerations/il/maurice-patterson.html; for Steidl, see http://www.law.northwestern.edu/legalclinic/wrongfulconvictions/exonerations/il/randy-steidl.html, both accessed September 11, 2016. In another Chicago case, Madison Hobley was exonerated and freed from over a decade on death row, after his attorneys re-interviewed key witnesses and located other new evidence. Moser, "Madison Hobley Gets His Settlement"; Conroy, "This Is a Magic Can."
19. Katz, "Situational Evidence."
20. American Sociological Association, *Code of Ethics and Policies and Procedures of the ASA Committee on Professional Ethics*, Ethical Standard 13.05(a). According to the editor-in-chief of the *British Medical Journal*, "public access to anonymised data should anyway be the rule, not the exception." Godlee, "Data Transparency Is the Only Way" (British spelling original).
21. In addition to qualifying as "business records," contemporaneous notes may be independently admissible as a "recorded recollection," and they may also be used either to impeach or refresh a witness's recollection. Rules 612, 613, 801, 803(5), 803 (6), and 806, Federal Rules of Evidence.
22. *Masson v. New Yorker Magazine, Inc.*, 501 U.S. 496 (1991). See also Malcolm, *In the Freud Archives*; Janet Malcolm, *The Journalist and the Murderer*, page 151; Stout, "Malcolm's Lost Notes."
23. Dittrich's interview with Corkin was originally published in a book excerpt in the *New York Times Magazine*, as Dittrich, "The Brain That Couldn't Remember." The MIT letter was posted on the university website two days later. DiCarlo, Letter/Statement Submitted to the New York Times, August

9, 2016. See Dittrich, *Patient H.M.*, pages 399–402. See also Begley, "MIT Challenges *The New York Times*"; Dittrich, "Questions and Answers about Patient H.M."; International Community of Scientists, "Letter to the Editor of the New York Times Magazine."

24. Moser, "Madison Hobley Gets His Settlement"; Conroy, "This Is a Magic Can." See also "Madison Hobley," *National Registry of Exonerations*.

25. Robles, "As Doubts over Detective Grew"; Robles and Kleinfield, "Review of 50 Brooklyn Murder Cases."

26. Katz, Gray, and Ulrich, "Report of the Investigative Committee in the Matter of Professor Michael Bellesiles."

27. Alice Goffman told a newspaper reporter that she had destroyed her notes and hard drive to avoid the possibility of subpoena. Melamed, "Sociologist Chronicles Tenuous Lives of Fugitives." See also Neyfakh, "The Ethics of Ethnography." Regarding the virtues of data sharing, and debunking the rationales for data hoarding, see Smith and Roberts, "Time for Sharing Data to Become Routine."

28. Desmond, *Evicted*, page 404.

29. Singal, "What Happens to People Who Get Evicted."

30. As the journalist and historian Adam Hochschild put it, "readers should know that every important detail you use must have a source . . . . I've become more and more a partisan of source notes." Hochschild, "Reconstructing Scenes," in Kramer and Call, *Telling True Stories*, page 135.

31. As David Dana points out, "it took Desmond's book *Evicted* and his exceptional gifts as a narrator" to bring the eviction crisis to public attention. Dana, "An Invisible Crisis in Plain Sight."

32. Smaldino and McElreath, "The Natural Selection of Bad Science."

BIBLIOGRAPHY

Books

Adler, Patricia A. *Wheeling and Dealing: An Ethnography of an Upper-Level Drug Dealing and Smuggling Community*. New York: Columbia University Press, 1993.

Allen, William Sheridan. *The Nazi Seizure of Power: The Experience of a Single German Town, 1922–1945* (revised edition). New York: Franklin Watts, 1984.

Anderson, Elijah. *Code of the Street: Decency, Violence, and the Moral Life of the Inner City*. New York: W. W. Norton & Company, Inc., 1999.

Anderson, Elijah. *Streetwise: Race, Class, and Change in an Urban Community*. Chicago: University of Chicago Press, 1990.

Becker, Howard S. *Becoming a Marihuana User*. Chicago: University of Chicago Press, 2015.

Becker, Howard S. *Evidence*. Chicago: University of Chicago Press, 2017.

Becker, Howard S. *Outsiders: Studies in the Sociology of Deviance*. New York: The Free Press, 1997.

Boo, Katherine. *Behind the Beautiful Forevers: Life, Death, and Hope in a Mumbai Undercity*. New York: Random House, 2012.

Bourgois, Philippe. *In Search of Respect: Selling Crack in El Barrio*. Cambridge, United Kingdom: Cambridge University Press, 1996.

Bourgois, Philippe, and Jeffrey Schonberg. *Righteous Dopefiend*. Berkeley and Los Angeles: University of California Press, 2009.

Bosk, Charles L. *Forgive and Remember: Managing Medical Failure*. Chicago: University of Chicago Press, 1979.

Bosk, Charles L. *Forgive and Remember: Managing Medical Failure* (2nd edition). Chicago: University of Chicago Press, 2013.

Bosk, Charles L. *What Would You Do? Juggling Bioethics & Ethnography*. Chicago: University of Chicago Press, 2008.

Brettell, Caroline, ed. *When They Read What We Write: The Politics of Ethnography*. Westport, CT: Bergin & Garvey, 1993.

Brunvand, Jan Harold. *The Mexican Pet: More "New" Urban Legends and Some Old Favorites.* New York: Norton, 2013.

Chapkis, Wendy. *Live Sex Acts: Women Performing Erotic Labor.* New York: Routledge, 1997.

Charmaz, Kathy. *Constructing Grounded Theory.* (Introducing Qualitative Methods Series.) London: SAGE, 2014.

Comfort, Megan. *Doing Time Together: Love and Family in the Shadow of the Prison.* Chicago: University of Chicago Press, 2008.

Contreras, Randol. *The Stickup Kids: Race, Drugs, Violence, and the American Dream.* Berkeley and Los Angeles: University of California Press, 2013.

Dawley, David. *A Nation of Lords: The Autobiography of the Vice Lords.* Long Grove, IL: Waveland Press, 1992.

Denzin, Norman K., and Yvonna S. Lincoln, eds. *The SAGE Handbook of Qualitative Research* (4th edition). California: SAGE Publications, Inc., 2011.

Desmond, Matthew. *Evicted: Poverty and Profit in the American City.* New York: Crown Publishers, 2016.

Desmond, Matthew. *On the Fireline: Living and Dying with Wildland Firefighters.* Chicago: University of Chicago Press, 2007.

Dittrich, Luke. *Patient H.M.: A Story of Memory, Madness, and Family Secrets.* New York: Random House, 2016.

Dow, David. *The Autobiography of an Execution.* New York: Twelve, 2010.

Drake, St. Clair, and Horace Cayton. *Black Metropolis: A Study of Negro Life in a Northern City.* Chicago: University of Chicago Press, 1945.

Du Bois, W. E. B. *The Philadelphia Negro: A Social Study.* Philadelphia: University of Pennsylvania Press, 1996.

Duneier, Mitchell. *Ghetto: The Invention of a Place, the History of an Idea.* New York: Farrar, Straus, and Giroux, 2016.

Duneier, Mitchell. *Sidewalk.* New York: Farrar, Straus, and Giroux, 1999.

Duneier, Mitchell. *Slim's Table: Race, Respectability, and Masculinity.* Chicago: University of Chicago Press, 1992.

Duneier, Mitchell, Philip Kasinitz, and Alexandra Murphy, eds. *The Urban Ethnography Reader.* New York: Oxford University Press, 2014.

Edin, Kathryn, and Maria J. Kefalas. *Promises I Can Keep: Why Poor Women Put Motherhood Before Marriage.* Berkeley and Los Angeles: University of California Press, 2011.

Edin, Kathryn, and Timothy J. Nelson. *Doing the Best I Can: Fatherhood in the Inner City.* Berkeley and Los Angeles: University of California Press, 2013.

Edin, Kathryn J., and H. Luke Shaefer. *$2 a Day: Living on Almost Nothing in America.* New York: First Mariner Books, 2015.

Emerson, Robert M., Rachel I. Fretz, and Linda L. Shaw. *Writing Ethnographic Fieldnotes.* Chicago: University of Chicago Press, 2011.

Eskridge, William. *Gaylaw: Challenging the Apartheid of the Closet.* Cambridge, MA: Harvard University Press, 1999.

Fine, Gary Alan, and Bill Ellis. *The Global Grapevine: Why Rumors of Terrorism, Immigration, and Trade Matter.* New York: Oxford University Press, 2013.

Fine, Gary Alan, and Patricia A. Turner. *Whispers on the Color Line: Rumor and Race in America*. Berkeley and Los Angeles: University of California Press, 2004.

Galliher, John, Wayne Brekhus, and David Keys. *Laud Humphreys: Prophet of Homosexuality and Sociology*. Madison: University of Wisconsin Press, 2004.

Gill, Michael Gates. *How Starbucks Saved My Life: A Son of Privilege Learns to Live Like Everyone Else*. New York: Gotham Books, 2007.

Goffman, Alice. *On the Run: Fugitive Life in an American City*. New York: Picador, 2015.

Goffman, Erving. *The Presentation of Self in Everyday Life*. New York: Anchor Books, Doubleday, 1959.

Grazian, David. *Blue Chicago: The Search for Authenticity in Urban Blues Clubs*. Chicago: University of Chicago Press, 2003.

Hareven, Tamara K. *Family Time and Industrial Time: The Relationship Between the Family and Work in a New England Industrial Community*. New York: Cambridge University Press, 1982.

Hayes, Sharon. *Flat Broke with Children: Women in the Age of Welfare Reform*. New York: Oxford University Press, Inc., 2003.

Hoang, Kimberly Kay. *Dealing in Desire: Asian Ascendancy, Western Decline, and the Hidden Currencies of Global Sex Work*. Oakland: University of California Press, 2015.

Hughes, Everett. *The Sociological Eye: Selected Papers on Work, Self, and Society*. New Brunswick, NJ: Transaction Books, 1984.

Humphreys, Laud. *Tearoom Trade: Impersonal Sex in Public Places*. Chicago: Adline Pub. Co., 1970.

Hunt, Jennifer C. *Seven Shots: An NYPD Raid on a Terrorist Cell and Its Aftermath*. Chicago: University of Chicago Press, 2010.

Jackall, Robert. *Wild Cowboys: Urban Marauders & the Forces of Order*. Cambridge, MA: Harvard University Press, 1997.

Jackson, John L. Jr. *Harlemworld: Doing Race and Class in Contemporary America*. Chicago: University of Chicago Press, 2001.

Jackson, John L. Jr. *Real Black: Adventures in Racial Sincerity*. Chicago: University of Chicago Press, 2005.

Jerolmack, Colin. *The Global Pigeon*. Chicago: University of Chicago Press, 2013.

Jones, James H. *Alfred C. Kinsey: A Public/Private Life*. New York: W.W. Norton, 1997.

Jones, Nikki. *Between Good and Ghetto: African American Girls and Inner-City Violence*. Rutgers, NJ: Rutgers University Press, 2010.

Kelly, Caitlin. *Malled: My Unintentional Career in Retail*. New York: Penguin Books, 2012.

Kerr, Margee. *Scream: Chilling Adventures in the Science of Fear*. Philadelphia: Public Affairs, 2015.

Khan, Shamus. *Privilege: The Making of an Adolescent Elite at St. Paul's School*. Princeton, NJ: Princeton University Press, 2011.

Kirby, Kate Curran. *The Chicago Crime Commission Gang Book*. Chicago: Chicago Crime Commission, 2006.

Klinenberg, Eric. *Heat Wave: A Social Autopsy of Disaster in Chicago*. Chicago:
University of Chicago Press, 2002, 2015.

Kramer, Mark, and Wendy Call, eds. *Telling True Stories: A Nonfiction Writers'
Guide*. Cambridge, MA: Harvard University Press, 2007.

Lareau, Annette. *Unequal Childhoods: Class, Race, and Family Life*. Berkley and
Los Angeles: University of California Press, 2011.

Liebow, Elliott. *Tally's Corner: A Study of Negro Streetcorner Men*. New York:
Little, Brown, 1967.

Lubet, Steven, and Elizabeth Boals. *Expert Testimony: A Guide for Expert
Witnesses and the Lawyers Who Examine Them*. Boulder, CO: National
Institute for Trial Advocacy, 2014.

Lubet, Steven, and JC Lore. *Modern Trial Advocacy: Law School, Fourth Edition*.
Boulder, CO: National Institute for Trial Advocacy, 2016.

Lubet, Steven, and JC Lore. *Modern Trial Advocacy: Analysis and Practice, Fifth
Edition*. Boulder, CO: National Institute for Trial Advocacy, 2015.

Maas, Peter. *Underboss: Sammy the Bull Gravano's Story of Life in the Mafia*.
New York: HarperCollins, 1999.

Malcolm, Janet. *In the Freud Archives*. New York: The New York Review of
Books, 1997.

Malcolm, Janet. *The Journalist and the Murderer*. New York: Vintage Books,
1990.

Mitchell, Jack. *Hug Your People: The Proven Way to Hire, Inspire, and Recognize
Your Employees and Achieve Remarkable Results*. New York: Hyperion, 2008.

Moskos, Peter. *Cop in the Hood: My Year Policing Baltimore's Eastern District*.
Princeton, NJ: Princeton University Press, 2008.

Mueller, Christopher B., and Laird C. Kirkpatrick. *Evidence*. New York: Wolters
Kluwer Law & Business, 2012.

Nippert-Eng, Christena. *Watching Closely: A Guide to Ethnographic Observation*.
New York: Oxford University Press, 2015.

Ogbu, John U. *Black American Students in an Affluent Suburb*. New York:
Routledge, 2009.

Pattillo, Mary. *Black Picket Fences: Privilege and Peril Among the Black Middle
Class*. Chicago: University of Chicago Press, 2013.

Pfeffer, Jeffrey. *Hard Facts, Dangerous Half-Truths and Total Nonsense: Profiting from
Evidence-Based Management*. Boston: Harvard Business School Press, 2006.

Ralph, Laurence. *Renegade Dreams: Living Through Injury in Gangland Chicago*.
Chicago, London: University of Chicago Press, 2014.

Rios, Victor. *Punished: Policing the Lives of Black and Latino Boys*.
New York: New York University Press, 2011.

Scarce, Rik. *Contempt of Court: A Scholar's Battle for Free Speech from Behind
Bars*. Walnut Creek, CA: AltaMira Press, 2005.

Scarce, Rik. *Eco-Warriors: Understanding the Radical Environmental Movement*.
New York: Left Coast Press, Inc., 2006.

Scheper-Hughes. *Saints, Scholars, and Schizophrenics: Mental Illness in Rural
Ireland*. Berkeley and Los Angeles: University of California Press, 2001.

Schrag, Zachary. *Ethical Imperialism: Institutional Review Boards and Social Sciences*. Baltimore, MD: Johns Hopkins University Press, 2010.

Schultz, Bud, and Ruth Schultz. *The Price of Dissent: Testimonies to Political Repression in America*. Berkeley and Los Angeles: University of California Press, 2001.

Shankman, Paul. *The Trashing of Margaret Mead: Anatomy of an Anthropological Controversy*. Madison: University of Wisconsin Press, 2009.

Small, Mario Luis. *Villa Victoria: The Transformation of Social Capital in a Boston Barrio*. Chicago: University of Chicago Press, 2004.

Stack, Carol B. *All Our Kin: Strategies for Survival in a Black Community*. New York: Basic Books, 1974.

Stuart, Forrest. *Down, Out, and Under Arrest: Policing and Everyday Life in Skid Row*. Chicago: University of Chicago Press, 2016.

Teal, Christopher. *Hero of Hispaniola: America's First Black Diplomat, Ebenezer D. Bassett*. Westport, CT: Praeger Publishers, 2008.

Toth, Jennifer. *The Mole People: Life in the Tunnels Beneath New York City*. Chicago: Chicago Review Press, 1993.

Turner, Patricia. *I Heard It Through the Grapevine: Rumor in African American Culture*. Berkeley and Los Angeles: University of California Press, 1993.

Valentine, Bettylou. *Hustling and Other Hard Work: Life Styles in the Ghetto*. New York: Free Press, 1978.

Van Cleve, Nicole Gonzalez. *Crook County: Racism and Injustice in America's Largest Criminal Court*. Stanford, CA: Stanford University Press, 2016.

Vance, J.D. *Hillbilly Elegy: A Memoir of a Family and Culture in Crisis*. New York: HarperCollins, 2016.

Vargas, Robert. *Wounded City: Violent Turf Wars in a Chicago Barrio*. New York: Oxford University Press, 2016.

Venkatesh, Sudhir. *American Project: The Rise and Fall of a Modern Ghetto*. Cambridge, MA: Harvard University Press, 2002.

Venkatesh, Sudhir. *Floating City: A Rogue Sociologist Lost and Found in New York's Underground Economy*. New York: Penguin Press, 2013.

Venkatesh, Sudhir. *Gang Leader for a Day: A Rogue Sociologist Takes to the Streets*. New York: Penguin Press, 2008.

Venkatesh, Sudhir. *Off the Books: The Underground Economy of the Urban Poor*. Cambridge, MA: Harvard University Press, 2006.

Wacquant, Loic. *Body & Soul: Notebooks of an Apprentice Boxer*. New York: Oxford University Press, 2004.

Washington, Harriet. *Medical Apartheid: The Dark History of Medical Experimentation on Black Americans from Colonial Times to the Present*. New York: Harlem Moon, 2006.

Weinstein, Jack B., and Margaret A. Berger. *Weinstein's Evidence Manual, Student Edition*. Newark, NJ: LexisNexis, 2001.

Weiss, Robert. *Learning from Strangers: The Art and Method of Qualitative Interview Studies*. New York: The Free Press, 1994.

Whyte, William Foote. *Participant Observer: An Autobiography*. Ithaca, NY: ILR Press, 1994.

Whyte, William Foote. *Street Corner Society: The Social Structure of an Italian Slum*. Chicago: University of Chicago Press, 1955.

Whyte, William Foote. *Street Corner Society: The Social Structure of an Italian Slum* (4th edition). Chicago: University of Chicago Press, 1981.

Wigmore, John Henry. *Evidence in Trials at Common Law*, edited by James H. Chadbourn. Boston: Little Brown, 1970.

Williams, Terry. *Crackhouse: Notes from the End of the Line*. New York: Penguin Books, 1992.

Williams, Terry, and Trevor B. Milton. *The Con Men: Hustling in New York City*. New York: Columbia University Press, 2015.

Articles and Chapters

Allen, Ronald. "Burdens of Proof," *Law, Probability, and Risk* 13 (2014): 195–219.

Alexander, Priscilla. "Bathhouses and Brothels: Symbolic Sites in Discourse and Practice." In *Policing Public Sex*, edited by Dangerous Bedfellows, 221–50. Boston: South End Press, 1996.

Alter, Alexandra. "Gay Talese Defends 'The Voyeur's Motel' After Source is Undercut." *New York Times*, July 1, 2016.

Armstrong, Carrie. "ACOG Releases Guidelines on Hormonal Contraceptives in Women with Coexisting Medical Conditions." *American Family Physician* 75, no. 8 (2007): 1252–58.

Anderson, Elijah. "The White Space." *Sociology of Race and Ethnicity* 1, no. 1 (2015): 10–21.

Augustine, Jennifer March, Timothy Nelson, and Kathryn Edin. "Why Do Poor Men Have Children? Fertility Intentions Among Low-Income Unmarried U.S. Fathers." *Annals of the American Academy of Political and Social Science* 624 (2009): 99–117.

Begley, Sharon. "MIT Challenges *The New York Times* over Book on Famous Brain Patient." *Scientific American*, August 10, 2016.

Berube, Allan. "The History of Gay Bathhouses." *Journal of Homosexuality* 44, no. 3-4 (2008): 33–54.

Berube, Allan. "The History of Gay Bathhouses." In *Policing Public Sex*, edited by Dangerous Bedfellows, 187–220. Boston: South End Press, 1996.

Betts, Dwayne. "The Stoop Isn't the Jungle." *Slate*, July 10, 2014. http://www.slate.com/articles/news_and_politics/jurisprudence/2014/07/alice_goffman_s_on_the_run_she_is_wrong_about_black_urban_life.html.

Boelen, W. A. Marianne. "Street Corner Society: Cornerville Revisited." *Journal of Contemporary Ethnography* 12, no. 1 (1992): 11–52.

Bourassa, Steven C., and Ming Yin. "Tax Deductions, Tax Credits, and the Homeownership Rate of Young Urban Adults in the United States." *Urban Studies* 45, no. 5-6 (2008): 1141–61.

Boyle, Maureen. "Feds, state, and Brockton police arrest 23 in drug sweep, including one in maternity ward." *Brockton Enterprise*, July 1, 2009.

Burawoy, Michael. "Revisits: An Outline of a Theory of Reflexive Ethnography." *American Sociological Review* 68, no. 5 (2003): 645–80.

Campos, Paul. "Alice Goffman's Implausible Ethnography." *Chronicle of Higher Education*, August 21, 2015.

Carey, Benedict. "Many Psychology Findings Not as Strong as Claimed, Study Finds." *New York Times*, August 27, 2015.

Cho, Adrian. "Once Again, Physicists Debunk Faster-Than-Light Neutrinos." *Science*, June 8, 2013.

Clark, Roy Peter. "The Line Between Fact and Fiction." In *Telling True Stories: A Nonfiction Writers' Guide*, edited by Mark Kramer and Wendy Call, 164–69. Cambridge, MA: Harvard University Press, 2007.

Conroy, John. "Killed on Camera." *Chicago Reader*, April 19, 2007.

Conroy, John. "This is a Magic Can." *Chicago Reader*, May 25, 2000.

Coronel, Sheila, Steve Coll, and Derek Kravitz. "Rolling Stone and UVA: The Columbia University Graduate School of Journalism Report." *Rolling Stone*, April 5, 2015.

Corzine, John, and Richard Kirby. "Cruising the Truckers." *Urban Life*, July 1977.

Dana, David. "An Invisible Crisis in Plain Sight: The Emergence of the "The Eviction Economy," Its Causes, and the Possibilities for Reform in Legal Regulation and Education." *Michigan Law Review* (forthcoming 2017).

Desmond, "How Homeownership Became the Engine of American Inequality." *New York Times Magazine*, May 9, 2017.

Desroches, Frederick. "Tearoom Trade: A Research Update." *Qualitative Sociology* 13, no. 1 (1990): 39–61.

Dittrich, Luke. "The Brain That Couldn't Remember." *New York Times*, August 7, 2016.

Dittrich, Luke. "Questions and Answers About Patient H.M.: A Response to the Department of Brain and Cognitive Sciences at MIT." *Medium*, August 10, 2016, https://medium.com/@lukedittrich/ questions-answers-about-patient-h-m-ae4ddd33ed9c#.76k2qancq.

Duneier, Mitchell. "Ethnography, the Ecological Fallacy, and the 1995 Chicago Heat Wave." *American Sociological Review* 71, no. 4 (2006): 679–89.

Duneier, Mitchell. "How Not to Lie with Ethnography." *Sociological Methodology* 41 (2011): 1–11.

Duneier, Mitchell. "Scrutinizing the Heat: On Ethnic Myths and the Importance of Shoe Leather." *Contemporary Sociology* 33, no. 2 (2004): 139–50.

Edwards, Rosalind, and Susie Weller. "Ethical Dilemmas Around Anonymity and Confidentiality in Longitudinal Research Data Sharing: The Death of Dan." In *Qualitative Ethics in Practice*, edited by Martin Tolich, 97–108. New York: Routledge, 2016.

Eldred, Tigran W. "The Psychology of Conflicts of Interest in Criminal Cases." *The University of Kansas Law Review* 58 (2009): 43–89.

Ellis, Carolyn. "Emotional and Ethical Quagmires in Returning to the Field." *Journal of Contemporary Ethnography* 24, no. 1 (1995): 68–98.

Fahri, Paul. "Author Gay Talese Disavows his Latest Book amid Credibility Questions." *Washington Post*, June 30, 2016.

Fahri, Paul. "The Murder the New Yorker Never Mentioned." *Washington Post*, April 13, 2016.

Fazlollah, Mark, and Dylan Purcell. "Phila. Police Report: Arrests Down, Crime Up." *Philadelphia Inquirer*, August 8, 2015.

Fine, Gary Alan. "Ten Lies of Ethnography: Moral Dilemmas of Field Research." *Journal of Contemporary Ethnography* 22, no. 3 (1993): 267–94.

Forman, James. "The Society of Fugitives." *The Atlantic*, October 2014.

Fornek, Scott. "Blues Guitarist Slain, Fellow Performer Held." *Chicago Sun-Times*, July 12, 1993.

Fornek, Scott. "Deadly Feud Robs the Blues of Two Voices." *Chicago Sun-Times*, July 18, 1993.

Fried, Joseph. "Judge Protects Waiter's Notes in Fire Inquiry." *New York Times*, April 8, 1984.

Gawande, Atul. "The Cost Conundrum." *New Yorker*, June 1, 2009.

Geertz, Clifford. "Deep Play: Notes on the Balinese Cockfight." *Daedalus* 101:1 (1972): 1–37.

Godlee, Fiona. "Data Transparency Is the Only Way." *British Medical Journal*, March 3, 2016, http://www.bmj.com/content/352/bmj.i1261.

Goffman, Erving. "On Cooling the Mark Out." *Psychiatry*, November 1, 1952.

Green, Bill. "Janet's World: The Story of a Child Who Never Existed—How and Why It Came to Be Published." *Washington Post*, April 19, 1981.

Grove, Jack. "From Selling Crack to Sociology." *Times Higher Education*, October 3, 2013.

Guerro-Pujol, F.E. "Legal Liability for Research Fraud." *Statistical Journal of the IAOS* 33 (2017): 1–7.

Hattem, Julian. "FBI Head Doubles Down on 'Ferguson Effect'." *The Hill*, November 13, 2015.

Harvard Law Review Association. "Policing and Profit." *Harvard Law Review* 128, no. 6 (2015): 1723–46.

Hawkins, Derek. "Four Sentenced in 'Almost Indescribable' Kidnapping, Torture of N.Y. College Students." *Washington Post*, December 23, 2016.

Hochschild, Adam. "Reconstructing Scenes." In *Telling True Stories: A Nonfiction Writers' Guide*, edited by Mark Kramer and Wendy Call, 132–35. Cambridge, MA: Harvard University Press, 2007.

Horowitz, Irving Louis, and Lee Rainwater. "Sociological Snoopers and Journalistic Moralizers, Part II." In *Tearoom Trade: Impersonal Sex in Public Places* (enlarged edition) by Laud Humphreys, 181–90. Chicago: Aldine Pub. Co., 1975.

Horton, Richard. "Offline: What Is Medicine's 5 Sigma?" *The Lancet*, April 11, 2015.

Hunt, Jennifer. "The Logic of Sexism Among Police." *Women & Criminal Justice* 1, no. 2 (1990): 3–30.

Hunt, Jennifer. "Police Accounts of Normal Force." *Journal of Contemporary Ethnography* 13, no. 4 (1985): 315–41.

Hunt, Jennifer, and Peter K. Manning. "The Social Context of Police Lying." *Symbolic Interaction* 14, no. 1 (1991): 51–70.

Ioannidis, John. "Why Most Published Research Findings Are False." *PLOS Medicine*, August 30, 2005.

Jencks, Christopher. "On America's Front Lines." *New York Review of Books*, October 9, 2014, http://www.nybooks.com/articles/2014/10/09/americas-front-lines/.

Jencks, Christopher. "Why the Very Poor Have Become Poorer." *The New York Review of Books*, June 9, 2016.

Jerolmack, Colin. "Living Within a Web of Entrapment." *European Journal of Sociology* 55, no. 3 (2014): 526–30.

Jerolmack, Colin, and Shamus Khan. "Talk Is Cheap: Ethnography and the Attitudinal Fallacy." *Sociological Methods & Research* 43, no. 2 (2014): 178–209.

Jerolmack, Colin, and Alexandra Murphy. "The Ethical Dilemmas and Social Scientific Tradeoffs of Masking Ethnography." *Sociological Methods & Research* (forthcoming; published online, March 30, 2017).

Katz, Jack. "Cracks in the Pavement: Social Change and Resilience in Poor Neighborhoods (Book Review)." *American Journal of Sociology* 115, no. 6 (2010): 1950–52.

Katz, Jack. "Situational Evidence: Strategies for Causal Reasoning from Observational Field Notes." *Sociological Methods and Research*, November 23, 2014, https://www.sscnet.ucla.edu/soc/faculty/katz/pubs/SMR554870_3_my_corrections_11Nov.pdf.

Klinenberg, Eric. "Overheated." *Contemporary Sociology* 33, no. 5 (2004): 521–28.

Kondro, Wayne. "Canadian Researcher in Legal Battle to Keep Her Interviews Confidential." *Science*, November 22, 2016.

Kotlowitz, Alex. "Deep Cover: Alice Goffman's 'On the Run'." *New York Times Book Review*, June 26, 2014.

Kotlowitz, Alex. "Solving Chicago's Murders Could Prevent More." *New Yorker*, September 20, 2016.

Leo, Richard. "Trial and Tribulations: Courts, Ethnography, and the Need for an Evidentiary Privilege for Academic Researchers." *The American Sociologist* 26, no. 1 (1995): 113–34.

Lewis-Kraus, Gideon. "The Trials of Alice Goffman." *New York Times Magazine*, January 12, 2016.

Lithwick, Dahlia. "The Life of a Death Penalty Lawyer." *New York Times Book Review*, February 11, 2010.

Lovejoy, Bess. "What Do Scary Clowns Want." *New York Times*, October 16, 2016.

Lubet, Steven. "Alice Goffman's Denial of Murder Conspiracy Raises Even More Questions." *The New Republic*, June 3, 2015.

Lubet, Steven. "Did This Acclaimed Sociologist Drive the Gateway Car in a Murder Plot." *New Republic*, May 27, 2015.

Lubet, Steven. "Ethics on the Run." *New Rambler Review*, May 26, 2015.

Lubet, Steven. "Ethnography on Trial." *New Republic*, July 15, 2015.

Marquart, James. "Doing Research in Prison: The Strengths and Weaknesses of Full Participation as a Guard." *Justice Quarterly* 3, no. 1 (1986): 15–32.

McKinley, James, Ashley Southall, and Al Baker. "Bronx Killing Leaves Only the Police in the Dark." *New York Times*, December 15, 2016.

McMurtrie, Beth. "Secrets from Belfast." *The Chronicle of Higher Education*, January 26, 2014.

McQuade, Dan. "Alice Goffman's Book on 'Fugitive Life' in Philly Under Attack." *Philadelphia Magazine*, June 11, 2015.

Melamed, Samantha. "Sociologist Chronicles Tenuous Lives of Fugitives." *Philadelphia Inquirer*, May 6, 2014.

Miller, Brian. "A Scholarly Taxi to the Toilets." *The Advocate*, April 15, 1982.

Moser, Whet. "Madison Hobley Gets His Settlement." *Chicago Reader*, January 6, 2009.

Murphy, Alexandra, and Colin Jerolmack. "Ethnographic Masking in an Era of Data Transparency." *Contexts*, March 19, 2016.

Nardi, Peter. "The Breastplate of Righteousness: Twenty-Five Years After Laud Humphreys' 'Tearoom Trade: Impersonal Sex in Public Places'." *Journal of Homosexuality* 30, no. 2 (1996): 1–10.

Natapoffa, Alexandra. "Misdemeanor Decriminalization." *Vanderbilt Law Review* 68, no. 4 (2015): 1055–16.

Nathan-Kazis, Josh. "Murder Plot Sheds Light on Orthodox Divorce Underworld." *The Forward*, September 21, 2016.

Newburn, Tim. "Book Review: 'On the Run: Fugitive Life in an American City,' by Alice Goffman." *London School of Economics Review of Books*, June 10, 2014, http://blogs.lse.ac.uk/lsereviewofbooks/2014/07/10/book-review-on-the-run-fugitive-life-in-an-american-city-by-alice-goffman/.

New York Times Editorial Board. "A Right to a Lawyer to Save Your Home." *New York Times*, September 23, 2016.

Neyfakh, Leon. "The Ethics of Ethnography." *Slate*, June 18, 2015.

Nolan, Heather. "40-Year-Old Man Arrested After Juvenile Girlfriend Gives Birth." *New Orleans Times-Picayune*, March 10, 2015.

Open Science Collaboration. "Estimating the Reproducibility of Psychological Science." *Science*, August 28, 2015.

Palys, Ted, and John Lowman. "A Belfast Project Autopsy." In *Qualitative Ethics and Practice*, edited by Martin Tolich, 109–20. New York: Routledge, 2016.

Palys, Ted, and John Lowman. "Defending Research Confidentiality 'To The Extent that Law Allows': Lessons from the Boston College Subpoenas." *Journal of Academic Ethics* 10, no. 4 (2012): 271–97.

Parry, Marc. "Conflict over Sociologist's Narrative Puts Spotlight on Ethnography." *Chronicle of Higher Education*, June 12, 2015.

Peregrine, Peter Neal. "Seeking Truth Among 'Alternative Facts'." *The Conversation*, February 23, 2017.

Ralph, Laurence. "The Limitations of a 'Dirty' World." *Dubois Review* 12, no. 2 (2015): 441–51.

Ravo, Nick. "It's Near Canada, but It's New York's Jail." *New York Times*, August 31, 1988.

Robles, Frances. "As Doubts over Detective Grew, Prosecutors Also Made Missteps." *New York Times*, September 5, 2013.

Robles, Frances, and N.R. Kleinfeld. "Review of 50 Brooklyn Murder Cases Ordered." *New York Times*, May 11, 2013.

Rosenthal, Ricard. "The File Drawer Problem and Tolerance for Null Results." *Psychological Bulletin* 86, no. 3 (1979): 638–41.

Scheper-Hughes. "Ire in Ireland." *Ethnography* 1, no. 1 (2000): 117–40.

Schmadeke, Steve. "Slain Teen's Family Gets $8.5M." *Chicago Tribune*, August 17, 2013.

Scott-Hayward, Christine. "The Failure of Parole: Rethinking the Role of the State in Reentry." *New Mexico Law Review* 41, no. 2 (2011): 421–65.

Selk, Avi. "Expectant Father Arrested Outside Dallas Maternity Ward; Police Say Mother Is 16." *Dallas News*, October 27, 2011.

Shafer, Jack. "Checking In: Gay Talese's Story of a Motel Owner Who Spied on His Guests Seems to Be Full of Inaccuracies." *New York Times Book Review*, July 17, 2016.

Sharpe, Christina. "Black Life, Annotated." *The New Inquiry*, August 8, 2014, https://thenewinquiry.com/essays/black-life-annotated/.

Shweder, Richard, and Richard Nisbett. "Long-Sought Research Deregulation Is Upon Us. Don't Squander the Moment." *Chronicle of Higher Education*, March 12, 2017.

Singal, Jesse. "Here's What's in Alice Goffman's Dissertation." *The Science of Us* (*New York Magazine*), July 14, 2015.

Singal, Jesse. "What Happens to People Who Get Evicted Over and Over and Over." *Science of Us (New York Magazine)*, March 4, 2016.

Smaldino, Paul, and Richard McElreath. "The Natural Selection of Bad Science." *Royal Society Open Science*, September 21, 2016. http://rsos.royalsocietypublishing.org/content/3/9/160384/.

Small, Mario Luis. "'How Many Cases Do I Need?' On Science and the Logic of Case Selection in Field-Based Research." *Ethnography* 10, no. 1 (2009): 5–38.

Smith, Richard, and Ian Roberts. "Time for Sharing Data to Become Routine: The Seven Excuses for Not Doing So Are All Invalid." *F1000 Research*, April 29, 2016.

Spayd, Liz. "Unnamed Sources, Unhappy Readers." *New York Times*, February 19, 2017.

Spencer, Hawes, and Ben Sisario. "In Rolling Stone Defamation Case, Magazine and Reporter Ordered to Pay $3 Million." *New York Times*, November 8, 2016.

Stout, David. "Malcolm's Lost Notes and a Child at Play." *New York Times*, August 30, 1995.

Sullivan, Margaret. "Tightening the Screws on Anonymous Sources." *Public Editor Blog of The New York Times*, March 15, 2016. http://publiceditor.blogs.nytimes.com/2016/03/15/new-york-times-anonymous-sources-policy-public-editor/?_r=0.

Sweeney, Annie. "Police Review Board Clears Cop in Fatal Shooting of Teen in '07." *Chicago Sun-Times*, March 26, 2009.

Sweeney, Annie, Jeremy Gorner, and Dan Hinkel. "Top Cop Seeks to Fire 7 Officers for Lying about Laquan McDonald Shooting." *Chicago Tribune*, August 18, 2016.

Sykes, Charles J. "Let Them Eat Lobster: Review of 'Evicted' by Matthew Desmond." *Commentary*, April 14, 2016, https://www.commentarymagazine.com/articles/let-eat-lobster/.

Thomas, Ralph C. "The Rule Against Impeaching One's Own Witness: A Reconsideration." *Missouri Law Review* 31, no. 3 (1966): 364–89.

Van Maanen, J., and Mark de Rond. "The Making of a Classic Ethnography: Notes on Alice Goffman's 'On the Run'." *Academy of Management Review*, September 15, 2016.

Wacquant, Loic. "Scrutinizing the Street: Poverty, Morality, and the Pitfalls of Urban Ethnography." *American Journal of Sociology* 107, no. 6 (2002): 1468–532.

Wade, Nicholas. "Anthropology a Science? Statement Deepens a Rift." *New York Times*, December 9, 2010.

Wood, Sam. "Officers Won't Be Charged in Death." *Philadelphia Inquirer*, February 3, 2007.

Worely, Robert. "Book Review: Alice Goffman, 'On the Run: Fugitive Life in an American City'." *Theory in Action*, January 2016: 116–24.

Zorn, Eric. "The Pleasance Shooting, Frame by Frame." *Chicago Tribune*, April 25, 2007.

Cases

Doe v. Dordoni, No. 16-00074 (E.D. Mich. 2016).

Doe v. Porter, 370 F.3d 558 (6th Cir. 2004).

Does 1–114 v. Shalushi, No. 10-11837 (E.D. Mich. 2010).

In re Grand Jury Proceedings (Scarce), 5 F.3d 397 (9th Cir. 1993).

In re Grand Jury Subpoena (Brajuha), 750 F.2d 223 (2d Cir. 1984).

In re Request from United Kingdom Pursuant to Treaty, 718 F.3d 13 (1st Cir. 2013).

James v. Goldberg, 302 F.Supp. 478 (S.D.N.Y. 1969).

King v. Smith, 392 U.S. 309 (1968).

Lawrence v. Texas, 539 U.S. 558 (2003).

Mason v. New Yorker Magazine, Inc., 501 U.S. 496 (1991).

People v. James Jones, 93 CR 17924 (Circuit Court of Cook County).

People v. Oduwole, 985 N.E.2d 316 (Il. Ct. App. 2013).

Roe v. Wade, 410 U.S. 113 (1973).

Sanders v. City of Philadelphia, 209 F.Supp.2d 439 (E.D. Pa. 2002).

United States v. Abu Marzook, 412 F. Supp.2d 913 (N.D. Ill. 2006).

United States v. Smith, 811 F.3d 907 (7th Cir. 2016).

Other

American Bar Association. *Model Rules of Professional Conduct.* Chicago: American Bar Association, Center for Professional Responsibility, 2016.

American Sociological Association. *ASA Code of Ethics and Policies and Procedures of the ASA Committee on Professional Ethics.* http://www.asanet.org/sites/default/files/code_of_ethics.pdf, accessed February 27, 2017.

Brennan, Joseph. "Fantasy in *The Mole People.*" *Columbia University: Abandoned Stations.* https://www.google.com/webhp?sourceid=chrome-instant&ion=1&espv=2&ie=UTF-8#q=columbia.edu&*, accessed September 9, 2016.

Center for Investigative Reporting. *Ethics Guide.* http://cironline.org/ethics-guide, accessed April 2, 2017.

DiCarlo, James J. "Letter/Statement Submitted to the New York Times on August 9, 2016 from Prof. James J. DiCarlo, Head, Department of Brain & Cognitive Sciences at MIT." *Brain & Cognitive Sciences.* http://bcs.mit.edu/news-events/news/letterstatement-submitted-new-york-times-august-9-2016-prof-james-j-dicarlo-head, accessed September 18, 2016.

Dittrich, Luke. "Questions & Answers About 'Patient H.M.': A Response to the Department of Brain and Cognitive Sciences at MIT." *Medium.* https://medium.com/@lukedittrich/questions-answers-about-patient-h-m-ae4ddd33ed9c#.477epru98, accessed September 18, 2016.

Goffman, Alice. "How We're Priming Some Kids for College—and Others for Prison." *TED: Ideas Worth Spreading.* https://www.ted.com/talks/alice_goffman_college_or_prison_two_destinies_one_blatant_injustice?language=en, accessed November 11, 2016.

Goffman, Alice. "A Reply to Professor Lubet's Critique." University of Wisconsin. http://www.ssc.wisc.edu/soc/faculty/docs/goffman/A%20Reply%20to%20Professor%20Lubet.pdf, posted May 2015; accessed March 1, 2017.

Goffman, Alice. Undated Statement of Prof. Alice Goffman, produced by the University of Wisconsin Pursuant to the Wisconsin Open Records Act on August 21, 2015.

Goodwin, Michele. "Black Lives Matter to Human Research—Lessons from 'On the Run'." Harvard Law: Petrie-Flom Center. http://blogs.harvard.edu/billofhealth/2015/06/13/black-lives-matter-to-human-research-lessons-from-on-the-run/, accessed August 3, 2016.

International Community of Scientists. "Letter to the Editor of the New York Times Magazine." *Brain & Cognitive Sciences.* http://bcs.mit.edu/news-events/news/letter-editor-new-york-times-magazine, accessed September 18, 2016.

Katz, Stanley N., Hanna H. Gray, and Laurel Thatcher. "Report of the Investigative Committee in the matter of Professor Michael Bellesiles." Emory University, July 10, 2002. https://www.emory.edu/news/Releases/Final_Report.pdf.

Los Angeles Times Ethics Guidelines. http://www.latimes.com/la-times-ethics-guidelines-story.html, accessed April 2, 2017.

Mississippi Code Annotated § 25-61-9(2).

Mississippi Code Annotated § 43-21-353.

Society of Professional Journalists. *Code of Ethics.* http://www.spj.org/pdf/spj-code-of-ethics.pdf, accessed September 2, 2016.

Steinberg, Stephen. "The Urban Villagers: A Critique." Paper presented at the Eastern Sociological Society Meeting, Boston, April 19, 1993.

United States. *The Federal Rules of Evidence.* Grand Rapids, MI: Michigan Legal Publishing Ltd., 2017.

United States. *Federal Rules of Evidence: With Advisory Committee Notes and Legislative History.* New York: Wolters Kluwer, 2016.

Waters, Tony. "Alice Goffman's 'On the Run': Ethnography in Action!" *Ethnography.com.* http://www.ethnography.com/2015/09/alice-goffmans-on-the-run-ethnography-in-action/comment-page-1/, posted September 9, 2015; accessed March 8, 2017.

Web Sources

"8 Sitcoms That Did The "Baby Born On The Elevator" Thing." *WhatCulture.* http://whatculture.com/tv/8-sitcoms-that-did-the-baby-born-on-the-elevator-thing?page=9, accessed June 9, 2016.

"Birth Control Q&A." *Planned Parenthood.* https://www.plannedparenthood.org/learn/birth-control, accessed February 27, 2017.

"Court Tracker: Criminal Case Research for Wisconsin Attorneys." *Court Tracker.* http://courttracker.com/, accessed March 5, 2016.

"Ebenezer Don Carlos Bassett: Diplomat and Educator." *Discover Diplomacy.* https://diplomacy.state.gov/discoverdiplomacy/explorer/peoplehistorical/169797.htm, accessed June 11, 2016.

"Ebenezer Don Carlos Bassett (1833–1908) Historical Marker." *ExplorePAhistory.com.* http://explorepahistory.com/hmarker.php?markerId=1-A-3C1, accessed June 11, 2016.

"Ethnography Meets Journalism." *Institute for Public Knowledge, New York University.* https://livestream.com/ipk-nyu/events/4355261, accessed September 26, 2016.

"Famous African American Inventors." *Scholastic: Teacher's Activity Guide.* http://teacher.scholastic.com/activities/bhistory/inventors/, accessed July 19, 2016.

"Gordon (Randy) Steidl." *Bluhm Legal Clinic: Center on Wrongful Convictions.* http://www.law.northwestern.edu/legalclinic/wrongfulconvictions/exonerations/il/randy-steidl.html, accessed September 11, 2016.

Independent Police Review Authority, Chicago. http://www.iprachicago.org/, accessed March 7, 2017.

"Inventions and Discoveries." *Oxford (Mississippi) School District.* https://www.oxfordsd.org/page/280, accessed July 19, 2016.

"Madison Hobley." *University of Michigan: The National Registry of Exonerations.* https://www.law.umich.edu/special/exoneration/Pages/casedetail. aspx?caseid=2977, accessed September 15, 2016.

"Maurice Patterson." *Bluhm Legal Clinic: Center on Wrongful Convictions.* http:// www.law.northwestern.edu/legalclinic/wrongfulconvictions/exonerations/il/ maurice-patterson.html, accessed February 27, 2017.

"New York City Elevators." *Git Hub, Inc.* https://github.com/datanews/elevators, accessed June 13, 2016.

"Nielsen Ratings / Historic / Network Television by Season / 2000s." *TV IV.* http://tviv.org/Nielsen_Ratings/Historic/Network_Television_by_Season/ 2000s, accessed June 9, 2016.

"On the Run." *WORT Radio: Madison, WI.* http://www.wortfm.org/on-the-run/, accessed October 3, 2016.

"Story Archives." *Target Market News: The Black Consumer Market Authority.* http://targetmarketnews.com/storyarchive.htm, accessed June 10, 2016.

"What Are Some of the Best Elevator Scenes in Film and Television?" *Quora.* https://www.quora.com/What-are-some-of-the-best-elevator-scenes-in-film-and-television, accessed June 9, 2016.

"What Are the Effects of Antibiotics on Birth Control Pills?" *MedicineNet.com.* http://www.medicinenet.com/script/main/art.asp?articlekey=17192, accessed March 11, 2017.

INDEX

accuracy in ethnography, 1, 6,
  136. *See also* reliability
Adler, Patricia, 55–56
advocacy vs. objectivity, 62, 73
African Americans
  Bassett as first black U.S.
    ambassador
    to Haiti, 52, 149n28
  community traditions and
    folklore among, 85–86
  death rates during
    Chicago's killer heat
    wave of 1995 and,
    66–67
  fact-checking W.E.B. Du
    Bois's *The Philadelphia
    Negro*, 52
  fatal police shootings in
    Chicago, 70–72
  housing discrimination
    against, ethnographer
    reporting, 120
  rumors showing
    community attitudes,
    75–81
  television shows popular
    with, 48
Agnew, Spiro, 3
Aid to Families with
  Dependent Children
  (AFDC), 82–83,
  156nn24–28
AIDS virus rumors, 79

Alameda County, alleged
  housing discrimination
  against men, 32
*All Our Kin: Strategies for
  Survival in a Black
  Community* (Stack), xiii
  hearsay used for
    demonstrating states of
    mind in, 13
  on MARS rule, 84, 156n25
  masking of location in,
    160n28
Allen, William Sheridan,
  160n20
amateur psychoanalysis,
  17–18
American College of
  Obstetricians and
  Gynecologists, 77
*American Project: The Rise and
  Fall of a Modern Ghetto*
  (Venkatesh)
  fear of retaliation for
    snitching, 151n22
  location revealed in, 96,
    160n20
American Sociological
  Association, xii, 131, 132
  Ethical Standard 13.05(a),
    169n20
American Sociological Review
  (journal), xii
anchoring, 62

Anderson, Elijah, 10, 69,
  151n22. *See also Code of
  the Street; Streetwise*
Angola Penitentiary and
  Correctional Academy, 56
Animal Liberation Front, 122
anonymity and
  pseudonymization,
  91–108
  authenticity and, 101–103
  composites, use of, 94–96,
    136, 158nn17–18
  credibility and, 40, 93
  details, masking, 99–101
  ethnography's argument
    for, 107–108, 160n30
  ethnography's reliance on,
    135–136
  generalizability and, 97
  informant cooperation and,
    103–104
  in journalism, 103–108
  locations, masking, 96–99,
    159–160n28
  reasons for and against,
    92–99
  risks involved in, 100, 102,
    104
*Arming America: The Origins of
  a National Gun Culture*
  (Bellesiles), 134
attorney-client privilege,
  166–167n41

authenticity, 54, 101–103,
    161n32
Ayala, César, 118, 120

Balinese Cockfight (Geertz),
    110–111, 113
Bancroft Prize, 134
Bassett, Ebenezer Don Carlos,
    52, 149n29
Becker, Howard, 111–112,
    113–114, 163n14
Becoming a Marihuana User
    (Becker), 111–112
Belfast Project, 167–168n52
belief perseverance, 62
Bellesiles, Michael, 134
Betances Festival (*Villa
    Victoria*), 10–11
Betts, Dwayne, xii
*Between Good and Ghetto:
    African American Girls
    and Inner-City Violence*
    (Jones), xiii
    fear of retaliation for
        snitching, 151n22
    on police actions in inner-
        city, 69
    questioning assumptions
        of ethnographers as
        prerequisite, 49
bias of witness, 22, 29, 39–40
birth control, rumors and
    folklore about, 77–78,
    154nn9–10
*Black Metropolis: A Study of
    Negro Life in a Northern
    City* (Drake & Cayton),
    xiii, 92
*Blue Chicago: The Search for
    Authenticity in Urban
    Blues Clubs* (Grazian)
    confirmation of stories in,
        54–55
    expert opinions in, 17
*Body and Soul: Notebooks of
    an Apprentice Boxer*
    (Wacquant), 10
Boelen, Marianne, 131
Boo, Katherine, 145n34, 161n38
Bosk, Charles. *See also Forgive
    and Remember*
    on anonymity, 103

compared with Duneier's
    approach, 2
cross-site typicality of
    locations for, 3–4, 141n3,
    142nn5–6
"An Ethnographer's
    Apology," 58–59, 100–101,
    150nn44–45
    intentional omissions by,
        150n43
Boston Blackie, murder of, 55,
    149n36
Boston College's Belfast
    Project, 167–168n52
Bourgois, Philippe. *See In
    Search of Respect;
    Righteous Dopefiend*
boxing and boxers, 10, 30–31
Brajuha, Mario, 167n46
Brassil, Gillian, 134
Brennan, Joseph, 128–129
Bronx, 20, 38, 92
Brooklyn District Attorney, 134
Brown, John, 52
Burawoy, Michael, 131
burden of proof, 3–4, 81, 142n8
business records, 169n21

Campos, Paul, 165n25, 169n17
Cayton, Horace, 92
Centers for Disease Control, 79
CERN particle accelerator, 129
Chapkis, Wendy, 63
Chicago, xi. *See also
    American Project*
    (Venkatesh); *Blue
    Chicago* (Grazian);
    Cook County; *Crook
    County* (Van Cleve);
    Gang Leader for a Day
    (Venkatesh); *Renegade
    Dreams* (Ralph); *Slim's
    Table* (Duneier); *$2 a
    Day* (Edin & Shaefer)
Chicago Police Department,
    71–73
Chicago Sun-Times on police
    shooting of black teen, 72
Child Abuse Reporting Act
    (Mississippi), 35, 146n19
Children's Hospital of
    Philadelphia (CHOP), 80

Chronicle of Higher Education,
    Katz interview
    regarding *On the Run*
    (Goffman), 118
circumstantial evidence, use of,
    25, 45–49
Clark, Roy Peter, 159n18
Claudine (film), 83–84,
    156n24
Clinton, Bill, 85
Code of Ethics of the
    Society of Professional
    Journalists, 104
*Code of the Street: Decency,
    Violence, and the Moral
    Life of the Inner City*
    (Anderson)
    anonymization and
        pseudonymization in,
        93–94, 160n20
    confirmation of stories in,
        52–53
    fear of retaliation for
        snitching, 151n22
    multiple perspectives used
        in, 62
Coll, Steve, 106–107
Comey, James, 12
Comfort, Megan, 158n6
composites, use of, 94–96, 136,
    158–159nn17–18
*The Con Men: Hustling in New
    York City* (Williams &
    Milton), 43, 56, 87–88
confirmation
    bias, 107
    of observations and
        ethnographic trials, 2
    of stories, 51–55
Contreras, Randol. *See The
    Stickup Kids*
Cook County (Illinois), 86
    Criminal Courts, 21
    criminal courts, persecution
        of public defenders in, 89
    Medical Examiner, 131
    Public Defender, 26, 39
    suicide of public defender,
        myth of, 88–89
Cooke, Janet, 104–106, 132
Corkin, Suzanne, 133, 169n23
Coronado, Rod, 122, 124

counsel, right to, for eviction
    defendants, 20, 144n16,
    144n18
counter-evidence, 1–5, 55–59
Crackhouse (Williams)
    exercising caution with
        informants in, 30–31
    fact-checking in, 145n6
    location revealed in, 159n19
    credibility enhanced by
        personalization of
        witnesses, 93
credulity of the researcher,
    43–59
    acceptance of unimportant
        details, 44–45
    circumstantial evidence, use
        of, 45–49
    confirmation of questionable
        stories, 51–55
    disconfirming evidence, 55–59
    suspension of disbelief,
        40–41, 49–51
criminality, 109–126
    ethnographers participating
        in criminal activity,
        109–119
    ethnographers reporting
        crimes, 119–122, 166n32
    subpoenaed testimony,
        122–126, 167nn51–52
*Crook County: Racism and
    Injustice in America's
    Largest Criminal Court*
    (Van Cleve), xiii
    anonymity of subjects in, 92
    criticism of criminal defense
        system in, 39–40, 147n29
    folklore and story of public
        defender's suicide, 88–90
    "inconvenience sample,"
        creation of, 5
    opinions implied within
        other observations in,
        21–22
cross-examination, usefulness
    of, 6, 164n24
Cruz, Irene, 41

Dana, David, 170n31
de Rond, Mark, 118–119,
    164n25

*Dealing in Desire: Asian
    Ascendancy, Western
    Decline, and the Hidden
    Currencies of Global Sex
    Work* (Hoang)
    hearsay used in, 14
    location revealed in, 159n19,
        160n20
    motivations of subjects in,
        43–44
defamation, 162n43
Desmond, Matthew. *See Evicted*
Desroches, Frederick, 162n10
details, masking of, 99–101, 136
disconfirming evidence, 1–5,
    55–59
Dittrich, Luke, 3, 133, 169n23
documentary evidence, 15,
    22–27, 150n41
    circumstantial evidence used
        as, 25
    defined, 15
    disconfirming evidence
        through use of, 55–56
    field notes, 125–126, 132–35,
        170n27
    police reports used for
        fact-checking, 25–27,
        55, 145nn31–32, 145n34,
        148nn21–22
    public records, 23, 151n12
    secondary sources, 25
Doing the Best I Can (Edin &
    Nelson)
    on birth control beliefs,
        154–155n10
Dow, David, 159n18
Dragnet (television show) and
    Joe Friday detective, 15,
    143n1
Drake, St. Clair, 92
Du Bois, W.E.B., 52
Duneier, Mitchell. *See also
    Sidewalk; Slim's Table*
    counter-evidence and
        skepticism of, 4–5
    critique of sociologists, 17
    on ethical implications
        of Goffman's "Glock
        ride," 118
    ethnographic trial proposed
        by, 1–2, 70

fact-checking *Heat Wave*
    (Klinenberg), 66–67,
    128, 131
    on masking location, 97
    on rumors, 76

Edin, Kathryn. *See Doing
    the Best I Can;
    Promises I Can Keep;
    $2 a Day*
Edwards, Rosalind, 102
elevators, children in
    Mississippi reaction to,
    47–48, 148n13
Ellis, Carolyn, 143n8
Emory University, investigative
    committee into
    Bellesiles and *Arming
    America,* 134
Erdely, Sabrina Rubin,
    106–107, 132
Eskridge, William,
    162–163n10
ethnographers
    alerting readers to
        undependability of
        subjects, 30. *See also*
        reliability
    credentials of, 16
    credulity of, 43–59. *See
        also* credulity of the
        researcher
    expert opinions offered by,
        17–19
    fact-checking and, 5. *See
        also* fact-checking
    focus on lived experiences,
        ix–x
    masking identities
        and locations. *See*
        anonymity and
        pseudonymization
    participating in criminal
        activity, 109–119. *See also*
        criminality
    primary responsibility
        to community being
        studied, 166n32
    reporting crimes, 119–122,
        166n32
    revisiting own research
        locales, 131

ethnographic trials
    benefits of, ix, 4
    cross-examining expert
        opinion in, 19
    disproving unsourced
        hearsay in, 45
    Duneier's proposal of, 1–2
    objective of, 2
*Evicted: Poverty and Profit
    in the American City*
    (Desmond)
    ethnographer giving
        opinion beyond
        expertise in, 18–21,
        144nn12–16
    ethnographer reporting
        crimes in, 120–121
    fact-checking approach in,
        56–58, 134–135, 146n12
    housing voucher policy
        recommendation, 18–20
    location revealed in,
        160n20
    methodology for evidence
        in, xiii–xv
    omission of unreliable
        stories in, 58
    public records and
        documentation used
        in, 23
    selection bias in, 62–63
    transparency by providing
        names in, 7
    vouching for informants
        in, 32–34
evidence-based ethnography,
    127–137
    fact-checking, 128–129
    field notes, 132–135
    revisits and re-interviews,
        129–132
evidence law, 10–11, 15.
    See also Federal Rules of
        Evidence
    admissibility rules, 10
    fraudulent evidence,
        150–151n1
    plea bargains and, 29
    pretrial discovery, 150n1
    vouching for witnesses, 29
exclusionary rule, 14
expert opinions, 15, 17–22,
    167n51

eyewitness testimony, 9–10, 22
    documentation vs., 22–23

Facebook, 34
fact-checking, xv, 5, 7, 25, 55,
    128–129, 134–135, 145n31.
    See also verification
    police reports used for,
        145nn31–32, 145n34,
        148nn21–22
fathers
    characterization of
        unmarried fathers, 158n14
    reluctance of unmarried
        women to name, 44–45
Federal Rules of Civil Procedure,
    Rule 10(a), 157n1
Federal Rules of Evidence
    Rule 612, 169n21
    Rule 613, 169n21
    Rule 701, 143n1
    Rule 702, 143n1, 144n10
    Rule 801, 169n21
    Rule 803, 144n23
    Rule 803(5), 169n21
    Rule 803(6), 169n21
    Rule 803(7), 144n23
    Rule 803(8), 144n23
    Rule 806, 169n21
Ferguson effect, 12
fictitious names, use of.
    See anonymity and
        pseudonymization
field notes, 125–126, 132–135,
    161–162n42, 170n27
"File-Drawer Problem," 66–
    67, 151n17
Fine, Gary Alan, 30, 75–76,
    79, 119, 120–121,
    165–166n32
First Amendment, 123
first-order evidence, 10–11
*Floating City: A Rogue
    Sociologist Lost and
    Found in New York's
    Underground Economy*
    (Venkatesh), welfare
    rumors and MARS rule
    in, 84–85, 156n27
folklore, 85–90
    in *The Con Men* (Williams
        & Milton), 87–88
    need to identify, 29, 136

in *Slim's Table* (Duneier),
    85–86
in *The Stickup Kids*
    (Contreras), 86–87
Foreman, James, xii
*Forgive and Remember:
    Managing Medical
    Failure* (Bosk)
    "An Ethnographer's
        Apology" (revised
        appendix), 58–59, 100–
        101, 150nn44–45
    masking details in, 2–4, 97,
        100–101, 141n3
foundation, 101, 161n32
framing, 12, 62

*Gang Leader for a Day: A
    Rogue Sociologist Takes to
    the Streets* (Venkatesh)
    ethnographer participating
        in crimes in, 114, 115,
        116, 163n15
    ethnographer reporting
        crimes in, 119
    location revealed in, 160n20
    welfare rumors and MARS
        rule in, 84–85
Gawande, Atul, 3
Geertz, Clifford, 110–111, 113
gender discrimination in
    housing, 31–32
generalizability, 3–4, 97, 136,
    142nn4–6
Gerard, Philip, 102
Gillison, Everett, 81
Goffman, Alice. *See On the Run*
Goodwin, Michele, 118
Gran Sasso National
    Laboratory, 129
Gravano, Salvatore (Sammy
    the Bull), 157n33
Graves, Summer, 47
Grazian, David. *See Blue Chicago*

Hahnemann University Hospital
    (Philadelphia), 80
Hareven, Tamara, 150n43
Harlem, 63–64, 84, 97–98
*Harlemworld: Doing Race and
    Class in Contemporary
    Black America* (Jackson),
    97–98

Hayes, Sharon, 156n26
hearsay, 11–14
    defined, 11
    to demonstrate state of
        mind, 12–13, 31, 143n8
    difficulty of disproving
        unsourced, 45
    exceptions, when
        admissible, 12
Heat Wave (Klinenberg),
    Duneier's fact-checking
    of, 66–67, 128, 131
Hoang, Kimberly. *See Dealing
    in Desire*
Hobley, Madison, 133–134,
    169n18
Hochschild, Adam, 170n30
Horton, Richard, 129–130,
    168n6
housing
    eviction and right to
        counsel, 20, 144n16,
        144n18
    tax effects on housing
        market, 19, 144n13,
        144n15
Human Subjects Committees,
    92
Humphreys, Laud, 112–113
Hunt, Jennifer, 145n34
*Hustling and Other Hard Work:
    Life Styles in the Ghetto*
    (Valentine), 55

identification of witnesses,
    157n1
impeachment, 70, 169n21
*In Search of Respect: Selling Crack
    in El Barrio* (Bourgois)
    fact-checking in, 63–66,
        151n12
    working in an office, 63–66
In the Freud Archives
    (Malcolm), 133
"inconvenience sample,"
    creation of, 5, 142n12
Independent Police Review
    Authority (Chicago), 72
India, right to counsel in, 20,
    144n18
Indonesia, 110–111
informants, 23, 27, 30–32. *See
    also* witnesses

challenging the credibility
    of, 51
fact-checking stories of, 55–58
giving voice to, 136
masking for protection and
    cooperation of, 99, 103
recollection vs. observation,
    31–32
statements to show state of
    mind, 12–13
suspension of disbelief and
    reliance on, 49–51
unattributed statements of,
    36–41
unreliability of, 29–41, 43.
    See also reliability
vouching for, 32–36, 146n11
institutional review boards
    (IRBs), anonymization of
    subjects and, 91–92, 157n2
International Community of
    Scientists, 133
invasion of privacy, 112–113,
    162n10
Ioannidis, John, 130

Jackall, Robert, 55, 62, 151n22
Jackson, John, 62, 97, 159n19
James v. Goldberg (1969),
    156n28
Jefferson Hospital
    (Philadelphia), 80
Jencks, Christopher, x, xii, 128
Jerolmack, Colin
    giving real identity of
        research participants in
        The Global Pigeon, 158n10
    on masking and integrity
        of ethnographies, 92–93,
        96–97, 99–100, 103
    on revisiting an
        ethnographic study, 130
    on states of mind of
        declarants, 12
    on unreliable informants, 40
"Jimmy's World" (Cooke),
    104–106, 132
Joe Friday (television
    detective), 15, 143n1
Jones, James Yancey (Tail
    Dragger), 54–55, 149n36
Jones, Nikki. *See Between Good
    and Ghetto*

journalism, anonymity and
    pseudonymization in,
    103–108, 160n20

Katz, Jack, 96, 103, 118
Kefalas, Maria, 82, 94, 99. *See
    also Promises I Can Keep*
Kelly, Caitlin, 24
Kerr, Margee, 43
Khan, Shamus. *See Privilege*
King, Martin Luther, Jr., 76
King v. Smith (1968), 156n27
Klinenberg, Eric, 66–67,
    128, 131
Kotlowitz, Alex, xi, 152n22
Ku Klux Klan, rumors about,
    75, 79

Langston, John Mercer, 52
Lareau, Annette, 66
lay witnesses, 15
Lederman, Rena, 167n51
Leo, Richard, 124–125
Lewis-Kraus, Gideon, 118,
    159n26
Liebow, Elliot, 82
locations
    Bosk's cross-site typicality
        of, 3–4, 142nn5–6
    masking of, 2, 96–99, 136,
        159–160n28
    revealed by authors,
        159–160nn19–20
    revisits not possible due to
        masking, 130–131

Madison, Rebecca, 47
Maillé, Marie-Ève, 167n51
Malcolm, Janet, 133
malpractice model, 5, 6, 142n11
Marquart, James, 121, 124,
    166n39
MARS (man assuming the role
    of spouse) rule, 83–85,
    156nn24–28
masking. *See* anonymity and
    pseudonymization
Masson, Jeffrey, 133
Mead, Margaret, 169n16
Medicaid fraud investigation,
    161n38
memory, unreliability of,
    22–23, 27

Mercy Philadelphia Hospital, 80
Miles, Alexander, 48
Milofsky, Carl, 96
Milton, Trevor, 30, 43, 56, 87
Mississippi
  Child Abuse Reporting Act, 35, 146n19
  Department of Child Protection Services, 47
  Department of Human Services, 35
  Public Records Act, 35, 146n19
  school children's trip to Washington D.C., 45–49
  Sunflower County Consolidated School District, 35, 48, 146n16
Model Rules of Professional Conduct, Rule 1.6(b)(6), 167n41
Molaison, Henry, 133
The Mole People: Life in the Tunnels Beneath New York City (Toth), 128–129
Moskos, Peter, 26, 160n20
murder, confirming evidence in stories of, 67–73
Murphy, Alexandra
  on masking and integrity of ethnographies, 92–93, 96–97, 99–100, 103
  on revisiting ethnographic studies, 130

names, masking of, 92–96, 103–104, 161n38
National Institute of Health, Certificate of Confidentiality, 167n51
negligence, 5, 142n11, 168n52
Nelson, Timothy J. *See Doing the Best I Can*
New York City, 53–54, 99. *See also Floating City* (Venkatesh); *Harlemworld* (Jackson); *The Mole People* (Toth); *Sidewalk* (Duneier)
  Department of Corrections, 54
New York state prison system, 53–54

The New York Times
  policy on anonymity of sources, 104
  on providing counsel for eviction defendants, 144n16
New Yorker
  on Freud archives, 133
Newburn, Tim, xi
Neyfakh, Leon, 100–101
Nippert-Eng, Christena, 11
Northwestern University
  Bluhm Legal Clinic, 26
  Center on Wrongful Convictions, 26, 169n18
  MacArthur Justice Center, 26
Nutter, Michael, 81

Oakland Housing Authority (OHA), 32, 146n9
observation
  distinguishing between informant recollection and, 31–32, 136
  as first-order evidence, 10–11
  opinion based on, 16–17
Off the Books: The Underground Economy of the Urban Poor (Venkatesh)
  confirming accounts of murder in, 72–73
  mediation of neighborhood disputes, author participating in, 163n15
  obscuring facts to support observations in, 73
  welfare rumors and MARS rule in, 84–85, 156n26
OHA (Oakland Housing Authority), 32
omissions, 5, 6, 62
  intentional omissions, 150n43
  unfavorable evidence, 66–70
  unreliable stories, 58–59, 150n43, 150n45
On the Run: Fugitive Life in an American City (Goffman)
  author's (Lubet) critique of, x–xiii, xv, 141n4, 148–149n24

bias in, xii
changing narrative after publication, 164–165n25, 164n23
critical reviews of, 141n4
defense of inaccuracies in, 160n30
destruction of notes and hard drive to avoid subpoena, 170n27
ethnographer and crimes in, 67, 70, 116—122, 164, 141n3, 164nn22–25, 165nn 25-27, 166n40
fact-checking and police records, 145n31, 148nn21–22, 152n23, 166n40
hospitals and alleged police collusion in, 78–81, 131, 152n23, 155–156nn17–19, 169n17
identifying location in, 96-99
omission of unfavorable evidence in, 67–70, 73
Philadelphia bail system in, 36–38, 147n24
response to Lubet critique of, 148–149n24, 164n23
reviews of, x–xi, 141n3
revisting sites, possibility of, 131, 160n30, 169n17
suspension of disbelief and reliance on informants in, 49–51, 148nn22–24
opinion testimony, 15–22
  beyond ethnographer's expertise, 17–21
  defined, 15
  expert, 17–18
  implicit value judgments in, 21–22
  lay vs. expert, 15–16
  observation-based, 16–17

Pacific Hospital. *See Forgive and Remember: Managing Medical Failure* (Bosk)
Patient H.M. (Dittrich), 133
Patterson, Maurice, 169n18
Pattillo, Mary, 160n20, 161n34, 168n11
Pennsylvania. *See also* Philadelphia
  child-support orders in, 82

Criminal Code in, 50, 117
juvenile policing in, 50
unlawful firearm possession
penalties in, 53
perjury by witness, 150–151n1
Personal Responsibility and
Work Opportunity
Reconciliation Act of
1996, 85
Pfeffer, Jeffrey, 76
Philadelphia, x, xi, 10, 117. *See
also Code of the Street*
(Anderson); *On the Run*
(Goffman); *Promises
I Can Keep* (Edin &
Kefalas)
Philadelphia Magazine on law
enforcement access to
patient database, 80–81
*The Philadelphia Negro: A
Social Study* (Du Bois),
xiii, 52
Philadelphia Police
Department, 38, 69
Planned Parenthood, 77, 154n9
plea bargains, 29
police
author's (Lubet) experiences
with, 25–26
contrived stories by, 145n32,
145n34
hospitals and alleged police
collusion in, 78–81,
131, 152n23, 155n11, 155–
156nn17–19, 169n17
misconduct and brutality,
25–26, 67–70, 78–81,
121, 166n37
observations of police
officers, admissibility of,
144n23
risks of cooperating with,
67–70, 151n22, 165n32
statistics, use as drawback
in social science,
145n32
use of police reports, 25–27,
145nn31–32, 145n34,
148nn21–22
policy recommendations as
expert opinions, 17
Popkin, Samuel, 123
Possley, Maurice, 161n38
Press, Eyal, 106–107

*Privilege: The Making of an
Adolescent Elite at St.
Paul's School* (Khan)
location revealed in, 99
pseudonym use in, 92
*Promises I Can Keep: Why Poor
Women Put Motherhood
Before Marriage* (Edin &
Kefalas)
skepticism toward
informants in,
154–155n10
welfare, 82
pseudonymization. *See*
anonymity and
pseudonymization
psychology experiments found
not replicable, 130
public assistance. *See* welfare
public defenders viewed
as evasive and biased,
39–40
Public Records Act
(Mississippi), 35, 146n19
public records as evidence,
23, 151n12. *See also*
documentary evidence
Pulitzer Prize awarded to
Cooke and returned,
104–106
*Punished: Policing the Lives of
Black and Latino Boys*
(Rios)
exercising caution with
informants in, 31–32
identifying location in, 96
observations of Rios in,
10, 16

Ralph, Laurence, 14, 103–104,
119. *See also Renegade
Dreams*
"A Rape on Campus" (Erdely),
106–107, 132
rapport, 30
Real Black (Jackson), 159n19
relevance, 1, 2, 27, 29
reliability
caution with informants,
30–32
criminal clients, likelihood
to spin story, 146n11
determination of, 1, 6, 23,
30, 38, 40

ethnographers as unreliable
narrators, 30
informants' unreliability,
22–23, 27, 29–41, 43
unattributed statements,
use of, 36–41
vouching for informants,
32–36, 146n11
*Renegade Dreams: Living Through
Injury in Gangland
Chicago* (Ralph)
creating character
composites in, 94–96
masking location , 70–72,
94, 96, 153n28, 160n20
multiple perspectives used
in, 62
police shooting teenager,
70–72, 73
policy recommendation as
expert opinion in, 17
understanding motivations
of subjects, 44
replicability, 129–130
*Request from United Kingdom
Pursuant to Treaty, In re*
(2013), 168n52
revisits and re-interviews,
129–132
Richardson, Dewayne, 35–36
right to counsel for eviction
defendants, 20, 144n16,
144n18
Righteous Dopefiend (Bourgois
& Schonberg)
homelessness in, 144n12
location revealed in, 159n19
Riker's Island (jail), 53–54
Rios, Victor, 10, 16, 31–32, 96,
151n22
Robert Taylor Homes
(Chicago), 62, 96, 115
Roberts, Ian, 168n6
Roe v. Wade (1973), 157n1
Rolling Stone, "A Rape on
Campus" (Erdely),
106–107, 132–133
rumors. *See also* folklore
about welfare, 81–85
benign, 76–78
harmful, 78–81
as illustration of attitudes
and beliefs, 75–76
need to identify, 27, 29, 136

St. Paul's School (Concord), 92, 99
Scarce, Rik, 122–124, 125
Scarcella, Louis, 134
Scheper-Hughes, Nancy, 160n20
Schonberg, Jeff. *See Righteous Dopefiend*
Scream: Chilling Adventures in the Science of Fear (Kerr), 43
secondary sources, 25, 29
selectivity, 61–73
  bias in, 62–63
  error of details, 70–72
  limits of communities under study and, 63
  obscuring facts to support observations, 72–73
  omissions, 58–59, 66–67
  transparency and, 65
  unreliable witnesses and, 29
self-interest of hearsay declarants, 12
self-reports, 30, 43
sensory perceptions, 15–16
Shaefer, Luke, 16, 19. *See also $2 a Day*
Sidewalk (Duneier)
  disconfirming evidence in, 4–5
  giving real identity of research participants in, 158n10, 160n20
  location revealed in, 96, 160n20
  revisiting, possibility of, 127
Singal, Jesse, 50, 134, 169n17
skepticism, 4–5, 31, 39–40, 43
Slate
  Neyfakh article in, 102
  Winship interview in, 93
Slim's Table: Race, Respectability, and Masculinity (Duneier), xiii
  folklore and story of Cook County judge, 85–86
  hearsay to demonstrate state of mind in, 13
Small, Mario Luis, 10–11, 55, 142n6

Smallville: Institutionalizing Community in Twenty-First (Milofsky), 96
Smith, Richard, 168n6
snitches, 68, 86, 151–152n22
social constructions, 43
sources. *See* informants
Stack, Carol. *See All Our Kin*
states of mind, 11–13, 31, 51, 136, 143n8, 148n23. *See also* folklore; rumors
Steidl, Randy, 169n18
stereotypes created by use of pseudonyms, 93
The Stickup Kids: Race, Drugs, Violence, and the American Dream (Contreras)
  Certificate of Confidentiality from National Institute of Health, author obtaining, 167n51
  confirmation of stories in, 53–54
  ethnographer participating in crimes in, 114–116, 163n20
  field site revealed in, 92, 99
  limitations on research for, 63
  opinions implied within other observations in, 22
  policy recommendation as expert opinion in, 17
  pseudonym use in, 91–92
  unreliable informants in, 38–39
Street Corner Society: The Social Structure of an Italian Slum (Whyte), xiii
  ethnographer giving opinion beyond expertise in, 17–18, 143–144n9
  ethnographer participating in crimes in, 109–110
  masking locations in, 96
  masking names in, 92
  re-investigation of Cornerville by Boelen, 131

Streetwise: Race, Class, and Change in an Urban Community (Anderson), xiii
  credulity of researcher and acceptance of details in, 44–45
  hearsay used to demonstrate states of mind in, 13
  observation as first-order evidence in, 10
Stuart, Forrest, 142n12
subpoenaed testimony of ethnographers, 122–126, 167n51, 167nn51–52
suspension of disbelief, 40–41, 49–51
Sutton, Robert, 76

Talese, Gay, 40–41
Tally's Corner: A Study of Negro Streetcorner Men (Liebow), xiii
Teach for America, 34
Tearoom Trade: Impersonal Sex in Public Places (Humphreys), xiii
  fact-checking and, 162n10, 163n11
  invasion of privacy of subjects in, 112
  normalizing homosexuality and, 163n13
  reporting criminal behavior in, 112–113, 162n7
Temple University Hospital (Philadelphia), 80
testimony, 9–14. *See also* observation; witnesses
  hearsay, 11–14. *See also* hearsay
  opinion testimony, 15–22. *See also* opinion testimony
  of subpoenaed ethnographers, 122–126, 167nn51–52
Texas Department of Corrections in prison brutality suit, 124
Tolstoy, Leo, 3
Toney, Heather McTeer, 47
Toth, Jennifer, 128–129

trial techniques, use in
    ethnography, 1–7.
    See also ethnographic
    trials; evidence law
trust
    foklore and trust issues
        with emergency room
        doctors, 79
    importance in ethnography, 1
    minority communities' trust
        issues with police, 26
    poor people's trust issues
        with public agencies,
        81–82
    reliance on informants
        and, 30
    reporters and, 105–107
Turner, Patricia, 75–76, 79
Tuskegee Experiment, 79
*$2 a Day: Living on Almost
    Nothing in America*
    (Edin & Shaefer),
    xiii
    benign rumors in, 76–78
    circumstantial evidence in,
        45–49, 148n13
    expert opinion in, 17
    fact-checking by Jencks, 128
    identifying locations in, 99
    selectivity in, 62–63
    vouching for informants
        in, 34–36
    welfare discussion in, 85

unattributed or undocumented
    statements, use of,
    36–41
University of Chicago, 76, 114
University of Connecticut
    medical school, 3
University of Pennsylvania
    Hospitals, 80
University of Virginia, 106,
    162n43
unmarried fathers,
    characterization of, 44
unreliability of informants,
    29–41. *See also*
    reliability
urban legends, 78–81, 131,
    152n23, 155n14, 155nn17–
    19, 155n26, 169n17

Valentine, Bettylou, 55
Van Cleve, Nicole Gonzalez.
    See Crook County
Van Maanen, John, 118–119,
    164n25
Vance, J.D., 159n18
Vargas, Robert, 160n20
Venkatesh, Sudhir. *See American
    Project; Floating City;
    Gang Leader for a Day;
    Off the Books*
verification, 93–94, 99, 137.
    See also omissions;
    fact-checking
    re-investigation of Margaret
        Mead's Samoan
        informants, 169n16
    revisits and re-interviews,
        129–132
*Villa Victoria: The
    Transformation of Social
    Capital in a Boston Barrio*
    (Small)
    ethnographer observations
        in, 10–11
    fact-checking in, 55
The Voyeur's Motel (Talese),
    40–41, 147n32

Wacquant, Loic, 10
Warren, Earl, 83
Washington D.C., Mississippi
    school children's trip to,
    45–49
The Washington Post
    on credibility of *The
        Voyeur's Motel*, 40
    "Jimmy's World" (Cooke),
        104–106, 132
Watertown Correctional
    Facility (New York),
    53–54
Weiss, Robert, 150n41
welfare
    fact-checking details about,
        57
    MARS rule and, 83–85,
        156nn25–28
    Medicaid fraud
        investigation, 161n38
    naming of fathers and,
        44–45

Personal Responsibility
    and Work Opportunity
    Reconciliation Act of
    1996, 85
    rumors about, 81–85,
        156n26
Weller, Susie, 102
*Wheeling and Dealing: An
    Ethnography of an
    Upper-Level Drug
    Dealing and Smuggling
    Community* (Adler),
    55–56
*Whispers on the Color Line:
    Rumor and Race in
    America* (Fine &
    Turner), 75–76
Whyte, William Foote. *See also
    Street Corner Society*
Wigmore, John Henry, 6
*Wild Cowboys: Urban
    Marauders & the Forces
    of Order* (Jackall)
    fact-checking in, 55
    fear of retaliation for
        snitching, 151–152n22
    multiple perspectives in, 62
Williams, Terry. *See The Con
    Men; Crackhouse*
Winship, Christopher, 93, 102
witnesses. *See also* evidence
    law; informants
    direct observation vs.
        hearsay, 9–14
    ethnographic trial and,
        1, 5
    expert. *See* expert opinions
    eyewitness testimony,
        9–10, 22
    identification of, 157n1
    opinion testimony,
        15–22. *See also* opinion
        testimony
    perjury or fraud committed
        by, 150–151n1
    personalization enhancing
        credibility of, 93
    unreliability of, 29. *See also*
        reliability
wrongful convictions, 169n18

Yale medical school, 3